Jacqueline O'Brien is married to Vincent O'Brien and lived in Ireland at Ballydoyle for over fifty years. She is an honours graduate of the University of Western Australia and the Open University, co-author and photographer of *Great Irish Houses and Castles* and *Dublin, a Grand Tour*, and photographer of *Ancient Ireland*. She is co-author of *Vincent O'Brien's Great Horses*. All her four books were number one bestsellers. *Vincent O'Brien The Official Biography* was shortlisted for the National Sporting Club Illustrated Book of the Year.

Ivor Herbert has written twenty-three books, of which fourteen have been about horses and racing, including the continuing bestsellers *Red Rum* and *Arkle*. He trained racehorses himself, with some success, winning the Gold Cup in 1957, the youngest Englishman to do so since the Second World War (though Vincent was younger by a year when Cottage Rake won in 1948). Ivor has been a friend of the O'Brien family for over thirty years.

Acclaim for *Vincent O'Brien The Official Biography*:

'It is not easy to do justice to a career as brilliant as that of Vincent O'Brien, but this latest biography succeeds triumphantly . . . Perceptive, exhaustive, authoritative, rigorously researched and lavishly illustrated with many rare photographs, this is the racing book of the year . . . The length and variety of Vincent O'Brien's achievements testify to his status as the master horseman of his age, and this definitive work is the biography he deserves'
Racing Post

'Sometimes in this game you get lucky. Arriving home late on Sunday night from Aintree, I found a package waiting for me from Bantam Press, the publishers. "Not another racing book" was my first reaction. As I was leaving for New York the next morning, I put the book in my hand luggage, for perusal on the long flight. I never gave it another thought. I was not to know I had just packed a volume that would entertain and fascinate me for the entire seven-hour journey. The book, *Vincent O'Brien, The Official Biography*, written by Jacqueline O'Brien, Vincent's wife, and Ivor Herbert, is the story of the greatest racehorse trainer of all time. It gives a detailed account of the various twists in his progression from humble beginnings in Co. Cork to establishing the world-famous Ballydoyle stables. This is a major contender for the best racing book I have read, beautifully laid out with cuttings and photographs from family albums'
Daily Telegraph

VINCENT O'BRIEN

THE OFFICIAL BIOGRAPHY

JACQUELINE O'BRIEN

& IVOR HERBERT

BANTAM BOOKS

LONDON • TORONTO • SYDNEY • AUCKLAND • JOHANNESBURG

VINCENT O'BRIEN
THE OFFICIAL BIOGRAPHY
A BANTAM BOOK: 0553817396
9780553817393

Originally published in Great Britain by Bantam Press,
a division of Transworld Publishers

PRINTING HISTORY
Bantam Press edition published 2005
Bantam edition published 2006

1 3 5 7 9 10 8 6 4 2

Set in 10.5/14.5pt Scala by
Falcon Oast Graphic Art Ltd.

Bantam Books are published by Transworld Publishers,
61–63 Uxbridge Road, London W5 5SA,
a division of The Random House Group Ltd,
in Australia by Random House Australia (Pty) Ltd,
20 Alfred Street, Milsons Point, Sydney, NSW 2061, Australia,
in New Zealand by Random House New Zealand Ltd,
18 Poland Road, Glenfield, Auckland 10, New Zealand
and in South Africa by Random House (Pty) Ltd,
Isle of Houghton, Corner of Boundary Road & Carse O'Gowrie,
Houghton 2198, South Africa.

Printed and bound in Great Britain by
Cox & Wyman Ltd, Reading, Berkshire.

Papers used by Transworld Publishers are natural, recyclable products
made from wood grown in sustainable forests. The manufacturing
processes conform to the environmental regulations of the
country of origin.

ACKNOWLEDGEMENTS

The authors wish to acknowledge the help they have been given by so many people who worked with Vincent O'Brien, especially his family. Noel O'Brien, his nephew, provided valuable information about Clashganiff and the early days.

Vincent's assistant trainers Brian Molony, Dhruba Selvaratnam, Michael Kauntze and John Gosden have passed on their impressions of the original Master of Ballydoyle. Jockeys who have helped us with their memories include the late Aubrey Brabazon, T.P. Burns, Liam Ward, Lester Piggott, Scobie Breasley, Pat Eddery, Vincent Rossiter, Tommy Murphy and Tommy Stack.

From Vincent's loyal staff have come many lively contributions: Peter McCarthy, Johnny Brabston, Gerry Gallagher and Denis Hickey. Our special thanks to John Brabston Jnr and Eleanor O'Neill, who have been totally involved over many months in the preparation of this book.

Those who have helped with the typing and research of the text include Molly Scott, Kelvin Oxwell, Katie Brown, Peter Beck, John Derby, Richard Henry of Primus, Geoff Greatham of Timeform, Denis Egan, Keeper of the Match Book, Sean Magee, and Tony and Annie Sweeney, who provided the racing statistics.

Ray Johnson from Perth, Australia, has been responsible for the reconstruction and enhancement of most of the old black and white and coloured photographs used in this book. We are deeply grateful to him for his invaluable work, which has given new life to photographs that would otherwise have been lost forever.

The O'Brien scrapbooks and photographs collected over sixty years have been a great source of information, but in many cases it has not been possible to identify the copyright holders. This will be rectified in future editions if the publishers are notified.

Jacqueline and Ivor wish to thank Ray Johnson and Miriam Rosenbloom for their excellent design of the paperback edition and Katrina Whone and Judith Welsh, managing editors at Transworld Publishers, for their immense editorial input.

We are so grateful to all those not mentioned here who gave us such valuable help. And finally to Vincent himself, who coped most patiently with persistent questioning.

October 2006

CONTENTS

INTRODUCTION

During January and February 2003 the *Racing Post*, Britain's last remaining racing daily, loosed off an intriguing challenge. It asked its readers around the world and a panel of forty-five experts to select the top 100 racing greats, having taken its cue from the BBC's popular programmes on the top 100 Great Britons. That public vote had chosen Sir Winston Churchill as the greatest of an army of notables. Would racing pick someone of similar stature in its own field?

The *Racing Post* cast its net wide and deep, going right back to Charles II, 'Old Rowley', who had launched British thoroughbred racing on Newmarket Heath nearly 350 years earlier (the king, in the end, came fiftieth). Thousands of votes flooded in over the twenty-four days of selection. Although there is always a tendency to think first of personalities currently in or making the news, only forty-five of the final 100 were still alive on voting day. Seventy-seven of them were naturally Britons, but the galaxy of those long dead and still living brightly also included seventeen Irish, three Americans, and three famous men from other lands. The list featured five women too.

The *Racing Post*'s distinguished panel then had to pick a top twelve, out of whom the public would choose their champion. Many famous names failed to reach the final dozen. Aidan O'Brien was just edged out at thirteenth, Henry Cecil was fourteenth, and Sir Peter O'Sullevan sixteenth, just behind Sir Noel Murless. John Francome at nineteenth headed Pat Eddery at twentieth. Lower down the list came the American Steve Cauthen, who just beat John Magnier, who was in turn ahead of Steve Donoghue, Sir Michael Stoute, the bookmaker William Hill, Jenny Pitman (just behind Queen Elizabeth II), Ginger McCain, Charlie Smirke and the Irish owner J. P. McManus. Peter Savill, former head of the British Horseracing Board, the great artist George Stubbs and Grand National winner Bob Champion all had their supporters, but not enough of them.

The top twelve was published on Friday, 24 January 2003, in alphabetical order with some notes on each of the personalities. They were Fred Archer, Phil Bull, Frankie Dettori, Tony McCoy, Sheikh Mohammed, Vincent O'Brien, Lester Piggott, Martin Pipe, Queen Elizabeth the Queen Mother, Sir Gordon Richards, Admiral Henry Rous and Fred Winter.

The consummate victor, with 28 per cent of the total vote, was Irishman Vincent O'Brien, well ahead of the runner-up Lester Piggott, his one-time jockey.

The *Racing Post* was delighted, but not surprised. Three years earlier they had selected the greatest flat race trainers of the twentieth century. Vincent O'Brien came top. They did the same for jump trainers. Vincent came top. It is this extraordinary superiority in both fields that has made Michael Vincent O'Brien, born in Churchtown, Co. Cork in 1917, racing's number one, the greatest of the greats.

THE BOSS, BALLYDOYLE

The Boss is a neat man. Every morning, his row of gleaming boots and shoes is drawn up correct as guardsmen inside the side door opening on to the stable yard. They are polished with zeal by Noel – Noel of small stature, the envy of jockeys, who, when the need arises, acts as butler at grand luncheon parties in the dining room at Ballydoyle. Noel serves the guests excellent food and wines around the long mahogany table when the Boss is entertaining his American, English, Scottish and French owners, and his Irish friends and neighbours.

The Boss works regimentally. He strides out into the yard, briskly, body leant forward, head inclined too. You can see why those sixty or so staff of his fear the fierce looks he can give them whenever he spots an imperfection. He never fails publicly to thank his loyal and devoted staff and to give them credit for his successes, but in the yard, they say, he rarely says 'well done'. They say that nothing but perfection is good enough. He doesn't shout, but if he's angry, looks can kill. Some shudder even years later, reflecting on some rocket they received.

The Boss dresses nattily, as well as neatly. His tweed jacket, twill trousers and trilby hat (though sometimes he wears a cap) look newly brushed and pressed, as if from a fashion shoot in a gentleman's magazine. Carrying, as always, his stick, he strides into one of his barns, big enough to be an aircraft hangar for a 747. By the entrance is a pan of water, so that on leaving he can keep his boots spotless. Inside the barn, lit up by shafts of pale Irish sunlight and split by long rows of straw bales high as a horse's belly, a score of millionaire, sometimes multi-millionaire racehorses follow one another behind the bales in a long snake. Their footfalls are almost silent on the peat.

Each horse is scrutinized by the Boss. As they trot on, the loudest sounds are the snuffles coming from their soft nostrils. The lads, all boys and men – no girls – are silent too. They, like their horses, are like cavalry under precise inspection from the brisk little general standing just inside the doors. His eyes dart about, his chin very firm. You can see what a handsome young man he was, dashing enough to pursue Jacqueline to England to persuade her to postpone her return to Perth, Western Australia, the furthest side of the world, and to marry him.

From trotting, the horses canter on in a winding line behind the walls of straw. Then out into the light, and down onto the famous Ballydoyle gallops. These were all created by the Boss and his brother Dermot. The hedges and the banks were removed, the old drains moved or restored. Beyond the gallops the Galtee mountains soar behind the other stables on the far side, where the Boss's son David O'Brien trained so successfully for just ten years, winning three Derbys. Two far earlier Derby winners were named after the two highest peaks

– Galtee More (1897) and Ard Patrick (1902). The mountain facing the house is Slievenamon, the Hill of the Woman. Up here on the summit in the old days sat the local king, awaiting the race of potential brides. Up the slope would storm the country maidens, and the one with the best stamina and speed – like the horses now in training here – would win the crown as his queen. To the left of the gallops stands a stern sentinel, a Norman watchtower more than 800 years old. The Boss glances meaningfully at the Englishman standing with him and staring at the tower. 'That was when the Normans were occupying us,' says the Boss. 'They could signal to each other, tower to tower.'

The Boss returns to his home. As he passes through the door to his office he ceases to be the Boss and becomes instead Vincent O'Brien, husband and father. Quiet, preoccupied, but more approachable. Inside the comfortable Georgian home, once a working farm, now beautifully decorated, some guests gather. If Vincent doesn't want to see them, he makes his excuses and escapes. He's been busy all his adult life. Work takes up most of the day, but he always has time for the family, for reading to his young children, perhaps sitting through one of their concerts – Liz played the viola, Jane the piano and Sue the violin. Concerned that his offspring never learn to gamble, he cuts out the betting instructions printed by bookmakers in the diaries sent to him at Christmas before passing them to the children.

Too diffident to need an audience, and shy of visitors unless they are old friends or potential customers of very expensive horses, Vincent has a magical knack of appearing among a group of people and attending acutely, head cocked to catch phrases of interest to him, and then, just as magically, disappearing again. What is of interest to him is anything that could affect his horses, or his plans. Are so-and-so's horses in form or coughing? Has there been rain at Ascot? Gossip is of little interest. Vincent smiles politely, nods and vanishes again.

Relaxing has never been an easy thing with so much to be done. On the land there are always trees to plant and walls to build. His passion for constructing things means that at Ballydoyle no wall was ever safe in its isolation but would soon find something extended from it or leaning onto it. There are so many calls upon his time, but he loves to fish, especially at Careysville, the beautiful stretch of the Blackwater belonging to the Duke of Devonshire. 'I remember coming here one Sunday morning and I hooked six fish before lunch and beached them myself on a shallow, gravelly part of the bank,' he recalls. 'Usually you need a net or a ghillie. When fishing I forget all about the horses and business. You are always waiting for the magic moment when you hook a fish, and then you wonder, could you be doing it a little better?'

The relentless pursuit of total perfection made Vincent O'Brien supreme.

CHAPTER 1

BEGINNINGS

'This lad is something different'

On Good Friday, 9 April 1917, as the snow drifted almost hedgerow high, Mr Daniel O'Brien, a tall, popular and sporting gentleman-farmer and horseman in the north of Co. Cork, greeted the birth of his fifth son, Michael Vincent, the first child of his second marriage. Vincent was the latest addition to the white farmhouse and his christening was celebrated in the parish church of St Nicholas in Churchtown, a mile across the fields from their farm, Clashganiff.

Dan's first wife, Helena, had sadly died at the age of thirty-six, in childbirth. The Duhallow hounds were hunting across their land that day and the cry of hounds disturbed the sorrow in the farmhouse. Dan O'Brien went out to tell the Master that his wife had died, and the hounds were immediately taken home. Within eighteen months, at the age of forty-seven, he had married again, this time to Helena's young cousin and good friend Kathleen Toomey. A year later Vincent appeared. With four boys ahead of him from the first marriage, he would have no expectations whatsoever of inheriting any part of the 162-acre farm. That would go by an earlier marriage settlement to the two older sons, Donal and John.

Vincent's future, however, seemed certain to lie in rural Ireland, a poor country then, still part of the British Empire and impatiently awaiting the Home Rule promised it by Gladstone in the nineteenth century but not yet granted as the Great War began in 1914. Vincent's birth came just a year after the flawed Easter Rising in Dublin, when the Irish leaders of the revolt were shot by firing squad. In 1920 'the Troubles' darkened; brutal suppression of the nationalists by the infamous Black and Tans was followed by the feared RIC Auxiliaries putting Cork City to the torch. Both preceded Ireland's own civil war of 1922, fought between supporters of Michael Collins (who were prepared to live temporarily with the separation of Northern Ireland from the South), and those led by Eamon de Valera, who demanded a United Ireland. In that war 3,000 lives were lost in eleven months, including that of Michael Collins, who was ambushed and shot in Co. Cork. The O'Brien family supported the Collins cause, and Vincent remembers sheltering behind hedges on the way to and from school, terrified of being fired at. The Irish Free State was created by British government decree in 1920, but it was not until 1949 that the South of Ireland finally became a republic.

By the start of the nineteenth century the O'Brien family had moved from Co. Limerick to Ballinagrath, a farm near Charleville in Co. Cork, just to the north of Clashganiff. Vincent's great-grandfather Daniel, born in 1807, married and moved to Clashganiff House, Churchtown in 1852 with his nine children. His first son, John, became a priest and went to

America. His second son, Daniel, born in 1839, married Johanna Culhane of Corrough, Shandrum, Co. Cork in 1858. The couple first lived with Johanna's family in Corrough. Johanna was an only child; she and Daniel eventually inherited her father's large farm. They had thirteen children, nine of whom were girls; the first son, James, also became a priest.

Great-grandfather Daniel died and was buried in Mount Melleray Abbey in 1877. The Cistercian monk Father O'Keeffe wrote to the family, saying, 'Mr Daniel O'Brien was a highly respectable farmer from near Churchtown . . . he was a benefactor to this Monastery and a pious Catholic. He came here every year to make a week's retreat in our guest house and at length entered the guest house as a permanent boarder and there spent the rest of his life . . . when he came here he had his temporal affairs settled and his children reared and properly provided for.' Quite why Daniel lived with the monks became clear from Father O'Keeffe's additional words: 'He was a very large man and generally enjoyed good health. Nothing could induce him to leave here even for a single day or to keep any money in his hand. He feared the temptations of the world and fled from them.'

Upon great-grandfather Daniel's death, Clashganiff House went to grandfather Daniel's younger brother James. When he was gored to death by a bull on 6 May 1879 the place passed to his maiden sister. She, however, decided to become a nun, Sister Mary of St Patrick, and entered the Reparation Convent in Merrion Square, Dublin. She gave the farm to Vincent's grandfather, Daniel, in 1893. He sold his own farm at Corrough and moved back to Clashganiff with Johanna and the children.

Vincent's mother used to relate a story that one of the O'Brien aunts had gone to a convent in Belgium to become a nun. She set off on her long journey from Ireland but found no-one at the station to meet her. A child appeared and led her to the convent, vanishing mysteriously at the iron entrance gate. Mrs O'Brien said the family held that it must have been divine guidance.

Vincent remembers his grandfather in bed a couple of days before he died, when he and brother Dermot went to see him; they were only seven and four years old then. He caught Vincent by the hand and wouldn't let him go, terrifying both of them.

Vincent's father, Dan, was born on 7 June 1870, and when his family moved to Clashganiff he was twenty-three. Clashganiff, sheltered by the Ballyhoura mountains to the east, has changed little since Vincent's childhood. The farm of 162 acres is today the same acreage as it was in 1917. Clashganiff is predominantly grassland. 'Dairying, beef cattle and some National Hunt mares,' says Vincent's step-nephew Noel, who now owns the farm. 'Some cows for the house,' recalls Vincent's youngest brother, Phonsie, 'and some arable land providing corn to feed the cattle.' Behind the farmhouse the River Awbeg, a mere brook in the summer of 2004, meanders through flat meadows. Edmund Spenser, the Elizabethan poet who lived nearby, described it in his poem *The Faerie Queene* as the 'Gentle Mulla, full of white troutes'. Awbeg is Irish for 'little river', and its width varies between twenty and forty feet before it joins the Blackwater flowing into the sea near Youghal. Beyond it, across a wooden bridge, lay some extra land rented by Dan O'Brien which his family vainly hoped he might buy one day. On the Blackwater is the Duke of Devonshire's famous fishing stretch Careysville. The late Andrew Devonshire, charming, modest and a lover of racing, was a fishing friend of Vincent's. It was on this stretch that Vincent, when suspended for alleged doping, was fishing the day his colt Chamour won the Irish Derby.

Churchtown village lies in the fertile, rolling countryside of the Golden Vale, and it has some charming Georgian and Victorian houses. The school, the market house and the church were rebuilt in cut stone just before the famine and subsequent decline in population. In 1920 Churchtown numbered about 200 people, with a church and, of course, a school, four pubs, a police station, a post office, two bakeries and one of the most important creameries in the south of Ireland – some 3,000 gallons of milk per day were processed. The pony, horse and donkey carts delivering milk in churns in the mornings stretched for a quarter of a mile. Clashganiff House lies one and a half miles away by road, but fewer across the fields to the school which all the O'Brien children attended. It was built in 1846 to accommodate 200 children but held only eighty when Vincent was a pupil – boys with two masters on the ground floor, girls upstairs with two mistresses. Opposite was a pump with a large iron cup chained to the railing, providing crystal-clear drinking water to countless generations of boys and girls.

There is a life-sized bronze horse with jockey at the intersection of Churchtown's four streets. A stone plaque on the base, under the horse's head, carries the words DR M. V. O'BRIEN, HORSE TRAINER. On the left-hand side another reads DR BARRY EDMUND O'MEARA, NAPOLEON'S SURGEON, and opposite that is a plaque inscribed to the GAELIC POET AND

SCHOLAR SEAN CLARACH MAC DONHNAILL, 1691 TO 1754. The village is very proud of its equine tradition. Jack Moylan, a leading jockey and Pat Eddery's grandfather, was a Churchtown man. He won the Irish Derby in consecutive years, and in 1924 was second in the Aintree Grand National on Fly Mask.

Vincent's father was an astute dealer in horses, and this innate ability was inherited to an outstanding degree by Vincent. It was Dan's habit to ride or go by pony and trap to the nearby Cahirmee Fair at Buttevant, five miles away, to buy and sell horses of all sorts. Cahirmee Fair is said to originate from the time of Brian Boru, last King of Ireland, famous for driving out the Danes in 1014. It had been one of the most important horse fairs in Europe and was described as the 'Fair Field of Cahirmee' in documents of the reign of Charles II in the seventeenth century. The Duke of Wellington's charger Copenhagen, ridden by him at the Battle of Waterloo, was bought here around 1810. Napoleon's white horse Marengo was also reputed to have been bought at Cahirmee Fair, in 1799. In 1921 the fair was moved from its twenty-acre fields to the town of Buttevant where it continues as a one-day fair held annually on 12 July. Now the horses stand along the main street, heads to the pavement, hindquarters to the road.

English dealers were always buying young store horses for racing, point-to-pointers, ponies and hunters, and any one dealer might purchase as many as a hundred horses. The English army were big buyers of remounts for their cavalry regiments. It was said that Dan would buy on the first day of the fair a dozen unkempt, bedraggled, rough horses, ride or lead them home, get his stablemen to clean them up, pull and plait their manes, trim their tails and fetlocks, and polish their hooves, and have them ridden back the next day for resale at snug profits. Dermot, Vincent's brother, remembers, 'My father took great pride in getting horses to look smart, but he was difficult to buy from, putting a high value on his own stock. A famous horse dealer in Buttevant, Tom O'Donnell, once picked up the tail of a horse for which my father had asked what Tom thought was an excessively high price, and peering under the tail asked, "Dan, where are the diamonds concealed?" '

This area of north Cork was famous for raising horses. Brood mares, hunters, ponies, young horses and horses in training were all around during Vincent's growing years. One of the first stud farms in all Ireland, Churchtown Stud Farm, owned by the Flannery family, was based close to Churchtown. As a boy of three Vincent sat on his father's knee reciting not his ABC but, as he recalls eighty-four years later, 'singing out the breeding of the horses we had at the time'. He proudly declares, 'Whatever knowledge I may have of horses, I owe a great deal of it to my father. He would have been considered one of the best judges of a young horse in the country. I went literally everywhere with him – to races, to sales and to various farms all over – looking for young stock to make hunters, point-to-pointers and racehorses. I learnt so much in those years and I have no doubt that my father realized my great interest in, and love for, horses and that he fostered it.'

Vincent and his father travelled by horse and pony until 1926, when the death of Dan's brother, James, the priest from Bar Harbour, Maine in the USA, brought about a miraculous change in the family's fortunes, for he left them the very substantial legacy of £30,000. Part of this fortune was used to buy a maroon Dodge motorcar, and Dan, who never drove it himself, despatched eldest son Donal to Limerick to learn how to drive and maintain it.

Vincent's earliest recollection of a racecourse came from the day his father took him, at the age of seven, to the opening day of the new racecourse at Mallow. The famous jockey Steve Donoghue was due to fly in from England, and Vincent remembers gazing vainly up at the grey clouds which cruelly prevented his hero from landing. Years on, Vincent became the life chairman of this course, renamed Cork Racecourse in 1997. The track has been improved under his guidance as part of a £7 million refurbishment.

Dan O'Brien used to tell a story about a horse he had in the 1920s called Holy Foulks. The original Holy Foulks was a character who lived back in the nineteenth century around Kanturk. On one occasion he was fighting a duel on horseback, and when he came face to face with his adversary he rattled a seasoned pig's bladder stuffed with lead shot. This made such a terrifying sound that the opponent's horse turned tail and ran away, with Foulks chasing him and shouting, 'Come back, you coward!' Vincent says, 'My father later sold Holy Foulks to Florrie Burke, who went on to win many top hurdle races with him, including the Galway Hurdle.' Burke, a shrewd man with figures, set up the Tote in Ireland for the Turf Club.

Dan O'Brien was not himself a public trainer, but he had a number of young horses which he was training to race and then sell on to others. His only weakness with these was a lack of patience: he wanted to find out quickly how good they were. Dan's interest in them was on the racecourse, not working at home. 'My father loved the horses and everything to do with them except the actual training,' Vincent says. 'The working of the horses fell to the head man in the yard. I somehow automatically took over, and at an early age I was working the horses. Of course it was great experience for me.' Dan had laid out a gallop round the farm, cutting through fences, ringing the boundary lanes and circling the farm buildings in the centre. Vincent, whose aim would always be for speed, added a short (three-and-a-half-furlong) straight gallop running up a rise, down a slope and then up a final rise towards the lane to Churchtown.

The large yard behind the house remains almost the same as it was during Vincent's childhood, with stabling and farm buildings on three sides and large barns behind. The extensive kitchen that stood at the back of the farmhouse has now been removed, but the place where the three Cheltenham Festival winners of 1949 were stabled is still pointed out with glee: 'Box 1 – Hatton's Grace; Box 2 – Cottage Rake; Box 3 – Castledermot.' The Gold Cup, Champion Hurdle and the National Hunt Chase were all garnered in Vincent's sixth year of training.

In the black days of 1931 following the Wall Street crash, Dan O'Brien asked his stud-owning friend and neighbour Frank Flannery to find him a mare at Newmarket Sales. During the Depression horses were of little value; he selected Golden Emblem and bought her for thirty-five guineas, then the knackers' price. Her daughter, Golden Meter, the Tetrameter filly she was carrying, was later covered by Vesington Star three times and produced three good full-brother handicappers – Astrometer, Astrologer and Astronomic – all of them trained by

Dan O'Brien at home. Astrometer won the Irish Cesarewitch and then the Naas November Handicap in 1941. These three horses won fourteen races on the flat between them, the distances varying between five furlongs and two miles. Any young trainer nowadays who complains about 'lack of decent facilities' should ask to walk around Clashganiff for a few minutes and see the site of the miracles a wizard of a trainer could produce on ordinary pastured farmland.

* * *

Vincent's birth had been followed by three more additions to the second family at Clashganiff – Dermot, Pauline and Phonsie. Dermot joined the Irish Army in 1938, and from 1944 became one of Vincent's most trusted and longest-serving assistant trainers; without him, Vincent maintains, he could never have achieved what he did. He was popularly known as 'Unk', and dearly loved by all members of the family. Pauline, the only daughter, was sent as a small girl of eight to the Ursuline Convent at Blackrock in Co. Cork where her aunt was the Reverend Mother; her parents feared she would become too much of a tomboy if left at home with so many brothers. Phonsie, the seventh male child of the family, was aptly christened Alphonsus Septimus in the church of St Alphonsus in Limerick.

Kathleen O'Brien now had seven boys and a daughter under her care. Phonsie remembers her with sadness: 'She was always tired, poor thing, and never in real stout health. She slaved away, looking after the others too. She was frequently in bed when we walked back from school, and often we found her in tears.' Kathleen was frail, certainly suffering from overwork and fatigue. She had, however, a lively mind and the courage to battle on when setbacks occurred. It may well have been from her that Vincent inherited his exceptional drive and ambition. After Vincent had moved to Ballydoyle he found her a pleasant house in Clonmel, Co. Tipperary, close to the family, and in her autumnal years she grew stronger and blossomed. She was deeply religious and stormed heaven for the success of Vincent's horses, calling on every individual saint in the calendar for support.

As in so many Irish Catholic households at that time, the rosary, in addition to long litanies to the saints, was said every evening by family and staff in the dining room. Dan was a fervent Catholic, and Mass was held in the house each year to give thanks for a good harvest. Having Mass in the house is an old Irish privilege carried on from the days when practice of the Catholic religion was forbidden by the Penal Laws of the eighteenth century. Hidden priests held services in private houses. In Ballydoyle, as at Churchtown and later at Coolmore, Mass is held each year. The family, stable staff, the farm men, the domestic and office staff gather together and pray for God's blessing in the coming season. The priest, after a good lunch, goes round the stables giving each horse his individual blessing.

The kindness and companionship of Vincent's genial father Dan made up for his mother's physical frailty. As well as introducing young Vincent to the exciting world of dealing and punting, Dan was a shrewd card player and enjoyed playing cards with the priests and neighbours. Vincent was to become even shrewder; it was said he earned his pocket money playing poker. Dan was hugely popular, and loved to race his horses, gambling on them in a small way and chatting with friends on racecourses. 'He loved buying drinks for his friends, although he did not drink himself except for the occasional glass of whisky in milk if he felt tired after a long day,' Dermot remembers. 'He also loved playing cards, poker or nap, with his friends. He generally won.'

The younger O'Briens, like the older family before them, went first to the National school, a mile across the fields in Churchtown. Then, as now, in rural Ireland, children started school very young. Vincent was only three years and five months old in his first September at school. He was led across the fields by a member of Dan O'Brien's stable staff, many of whom stayed with Vincent when he moved to Ballydoyle. One of these was Danny O'Sullivan, who with his two brothers had been taken in as orphans by kindly Dan and Kathleen O'Brien. When Mrs O'Sullivan, a widow and neighbour, lay dying in her cottage, she sent one of the boys up the road with a message for the O'Briens asking if they would look after her three boys when she was gone. So they did. Another early-days member of staff was Maurice O'Callaghan, also from Churchtown, who became Vincent's famous head man. Vincent said that 'though Maurice knew every horse's foibles exactly, he had never learned to read and write. He had wonderful powers of observation and memory, maybe as a result.'

Vincent liked his school lessons but it diminished the time he could spend with his pony and his father's horses. His schoolmaster, Tom Tierney, reported, 'This lad is something different.' In Vincent's case it proved resoundingly true. Few are the Irish boys who turned out to be so far from the run of the mill as M. V. O'Brien. He appears, smaller than most, in the back row of the school photograph – a group of 31 serious school boys under the stern regard of Mr Tierney. All wear jackets, some have ties. Many wear broad white 'Eton' collars and fixed stares. The front row wear little farmers' ankle boots, although often the boys went bare-footed. Phonsie cried when he started his second day at school because 'I'm the only one wearing shoes'. In the photograph one tiny boy in the centre of the front row clutches a blackboard with an inscription in Irish and the date. Vincent's expression is one of frowning resolution. He doesn't talk about his lessons, nor about the games of hurling, at which he excelled, in the grass meadow between the white farmhouse and the road which Phonsie recalls so cheerfully.

When he was only ten Vincent left home to stay with his god-father in Bruff, Dan O'Leary, the local bank manager and a great friend of his father. O'Leary's wife had died and his family had left home. In Bruff, Vincent was able to attend the De La Salle Brothers' school. The town has a very famous trout river, the Morning Star, running through it, and Vincent spent his entire leisure time fly-fishing. He remembers his father coming to see him in a pony and trap just once. Three years later he went in tears to the strict and 'clever' Jesuit College at Mungret. Although he enjoyed his schooldays in Churchtown, when he was sent away to board he found it unbearable. His brother Dermot, three years younger, went with him – Vincent had pleaded with his father that Dermot should accompany him. Tim Molony, later the famous steeplechase jockey, sat in the desk next to Dermot. When asked about his favourite subject, Vincent said at once, 'Mental arithmetic! But I couldn't settle down there. The confine-ment was more than I could stand.'

Mungret College had an excellent reputation and was not cheap. The school fees of all the boys – the older four went to boarding school in Pallaskenry in Co. Limerick – were aided by the substantial legacy left to Dan by his brother James. Kathleen O'Brien had sensibly kept her brother-in-law regularly informed by post of the doings of the family. Father James died in 1925, before the Wall Street crash, but it took a long time to get the estate wound up, and some of the money leaked away to lawyers. Kathleen was continuously fearful that her cheerful, card-playing, race-going husband was 'frittering the fortune away'. Vincent, all the time he was growing up, was concerned that the bank balance was being eroded with little to show for it.

* * *

Horses galloped through the history of those green fields of north Cork. In 1902 a Churchtown horse, St Brendan, bred by Dan O'Brien's friend and neighbour Edward Flannery, won the Irish Derby at the Curragh. In 1919 Loch Lomond, owned by Miss Cowhy down the road, trained by J. J. Parkinson at the Curragh and ridden by Martin Quirke, won another Irish Derby.

Steeplechasing started close by. The source of the name 'steeplechase' came from the first recorded race across natural fences from one church steeple to another: it took place in 1752, from St John's Church, Buttevant to St Mary's Church, Doneraile. A brass plaque outside St Mary's proudly notes the four-and-a-half-mile cross-country duel between Cornelius O'Callaghan and Edmund Blake on their prized and vaunted hunters, though history does not record who won. A staged re-run of the race was held in 1954 with Irish Hunts providing teams. The course was run backwards from Doneraile to Buttevant and attracted several personalities, including John Huston, the film actor and director who was joint master of the Galway Blazers Hunt. The steeplechase was won by Pat Hogan, a famous Irish amateur rider.

The same delight in chasing steeples burned in young Vincent. Part of the farm's horse business was breaking in young, rough horses bought by Dan, often with Vincent eagerly in tow. The raw material was turned into capable hunters. 'I groomed them, mucked them out, and rode them out every day,' Vincent recalls. 'One of my happiest memories is riding the young horses with three or four of the lads in the yard across country for maybe five miles! Never stopped! We could take a different line of country to the yard and back six days a week. Imagine – a different route every day.'

The countryside whirred with game; pheasant, woodcock and snipe rose from the small bogs. Vincent always had the sharpest sight and was a good natural shot. He and his friends would work the ditches with gundogs, hunting hares, rabbits and pheasants; they would eat the game they brought home as well as the trout and salmon they caught. They learnt to 'tickle' trout in the small streams. Dermot says Vincent was 'great with a spear!' Both Vincent and Phonsie started hunting from the age of about eight with the Duhallows – the oldest pack of foxhounds in Ireland.

The 1930s, though, were cruel years for Irish farmers, for this was the time of the 'Economic War' when England, seeking repayment of its mortgage loans to tenant farmers, imposed tariffs of up to 20 per cent on Irish agricultural produce. The Irish farmers were unable to sell their cattle. Vincent remembers big bullocks weighing ten to twelve hundredweight being sold for ten shillings, and calves for as little as five. The farmers would skin the animals and sell the hides, leaving the valueless carcasses in the ditch. But thanks to the priestly legacy the O'Brien family did not suffer too severely during these years.

As a result of continually begging his father, Vincent was allowed to leave Mungret College in Limerick when he was fifteen. 'My father sent me off for a year to learn training under Fred Clarke, who trained at Leopardstown racecourse which his father had owned,' Vincent says. So he at last achieved what he wanted: he had escaped school and was working with racehorses. That one year at Leopardstown was the only professional tuition Vincent ever had in the complicated art of training racehorses, though Clarke often said later that he did not remember teaching Vincent anything. Vincent continued his studies at night-school in Dublin, and probably benefited from the new and challenging training environment. Compared with the experience young men gain today learning the profession as pupils of, or assistants to, leading trainers, Vincent's formal education was minimal. In later life, he made it plain that he thought of education as an unnecessary interruption in a working life. He had managed perfectly well without one; why couldn't everyone else? But he had been learning the ways of horses and the wiles of the racing world since his childhood. Working in the yard at Clashganiff he learnt swiftly, as 'hands on' as any youngster could be. 'I loved work,' says Vincent. 'Work was never any problem to me. And especially with the horses.'

Vincent remembers going to the opening of the Killarney Racecourse in 1936. Cahirmee Fair was on, and his father took five horses there to be sold. He managed to find purchasers for two of them and then went off to Killarney, leaving a friend of his, Jack White, a well-known horse dealer, to dispose of the others. Vincent travelled their three runners – Solford, Greek Belle and Ballysax – to Killarney, leading one himself to Buttevant station four and a half miles down the road to catch the train. During the trip Solford 'got a colic' and was not able to run at the meeting. He was the first horse Vincent felt he had 'trained'. 'Solford was bought as an unbroken three-year-old,' he recalls. 'The day my father did the deal for him he jumped a wall into a graveyard. Fortunately he didn't hurt himself, but later on his legs gave trouble. I blistered him myself and knew he had to be rested. When he was ready to be ridden I rode him every day to a particular area of the farm down by the river where the ground was spongy – every day for weeks and months. I brought him back really slowly. His legs never gave trouble afterwards, even on the hard ground.' All his training life Vincent exemplified such patience. Solford won over hurdles and six flat races for the O'Briens. In 1938 he put up a gallant performance to win the Irish Cambridgeshire, ridden by Jack Moylan under top weight of 9st 9lb and on a rain-sodden track. Cheerful Dan O'Brien loved victories and entertaining friends, and winning the Cambridgeshire was a great excuse for lengthy celebrations in Churchtown. Solford was afterwards sold to The Hon. Dorothy Paget and won the Champion Hurdle at Cheltenham in 1940.

Vincent had also organized the training of Astrometer to win the Irish Cesarewitch of 1941. The *Cork Examiner* described Astrometer's win with these words: 'The winner was owned by Mr Dan O'Brien, the popular Churchtown owner, farmer-breeder and businessman, who everybody knows and whom everybody likes, as was pleasantly in evidence when he had to undergo the seemingly endless ordeal of handshaking and congratulations after he had unsaddled this good winner.'

These two wins, the Cambridgeshire and the Cesarewitch, were a dress rehearsal for the now famous Drybob and Good Days double which Vincent brought off in 1944, and which landed him his first vital working capital. Those who were amazed by this, especially the bookmakers, did not realize that this young, little-known farmer's son from Churchtown was already an experienced trainer with some successes when he set out for the Curragh that year.

The war years were, of course, a difficult time for racing in Ireland. The country was divided into several areas, and only for big races were trainers allowed to bring horses out of their area. Petrol was rationed, though farmers enjoyed special dispensations. Bookmakers were often known to have 'funerals of family members' and to share a hearse to get to a race meeting. Contemporary photographs show stacks of old black, upright bicycles parked against racecourse railings.

Things were far worse in England. The critical year for the Allies was 1940. France had fallen in June. De Valera, who founded the Fianna Fáil party and governed the Irish Free State from 1932 to 1948, had firmly established Ireland's neutrality. On the opposite side of England from that of neutral Ireland a huge German army stood just twenty miles away across the Dover Straits. Despite Ireland's neutrality, supported by both parties in the Dáil, thousands of Ireland's sons and daughters crossed into disrupted, dangerous Britain to join her armed forces, to act as nurses or to work in armament factories. Vincent's wife Jacqueline recalls, 'On our honeymoon Vincent and I disagreed strongly over Ireland's wartime neutrality.' She, as a loyal Australian ally, criticized it; Vincent supported it, because of what he saw as the 700 years of oppression Ireland had suffered at the hands of Britain. But he was in favour of all possible assistance to the Allied war effort. They resolved never to discuss or even to refer to the subject again. They never have. Jacqueline later researched Ireland's bitter struggle for freedom for her books on Ireland, and came to see how much Ireland had suffered.

Dermot was a first lieutenant in the Southern Command of the Irish Army, and he spent most of his time at Waterville and Valentia, where the vital communication cable link between the UK, Ireland and America had to be guarded. Donal and Vincent were members of the Local Defence Force which sometimes joined the regular army for manoeuvres. One night, a plane crash-landed in one of the Clashganiff fields. It had to be guarded all night, and it halted work for the horses the next day.

During that critical year, 1940, Vincent rode his first winner at Limerick. An early photograph shows a happy moment on that 7 November day when Vincent was led in by his father on the home-trained Hallowment. The terms of the race were unusual. It was for amateur riders, but professional jockeys could ride by carrying a mere 5lb penalty. Vincent was delighted to defeat Charlie Smirke, the famous English Classic-winning flat jockey who had a retainer in Ireland while waiting to be called up. 'My father didn't have many horses suitable for me to ride,' Vincent recalls. 'They were mostly racehorses that ran in races for professional jockeys, but I did have a bit of riding and rode a few winners.' It was already becoming clear to Vincent as well as to the rest of his family that all he truly wanted to do was to train racehorses, not necessarily to ride them.

But, again, training horses, let alone moving them about, was not easy during the war years. As assistant trainer to his father he would walk his horse to the railway station at Buttevant, probably the evening before a meeting, leading him and pulling his bicycle on the opposite side. The horse and bicycle would be loaded on the train and taken off at the Curragh. The horse then had to be walked to the racecourse and stabled. It would be Vincent's responsibility to see that he was fed and bedded down comfortably for the night. Vincent was just twenty-one when Solford won the Cambridgeshire. He would have looked after Astrometer in the same way three years later.

But it wasn't all winners during this period. Vincent received an early shock and accepted a timely warning when Astrologer ran at Mallow on Easter Monday in 1942 in a three-year-old maiden. Vincent and Dermot put all they possessed on him. He was beaten a length and a half by Grand Inquisitor, who went on to finish second to Windsor Slipper in the Irish 2,000 Guineas and the Irish Derby. This was a lesson to the two young men: never to underestimate the opposition, even at a country meeting. Astrologer won next time out at the Curragh, but neither Vincent nor Dermot had any funds left to back him.

There were occasional misunderstandings at home. 'Sometimes Vincent and his father had differences of opinion about nights out,' Dermot says. 'God bless his heart, my father never knew when the pictures were over, so we always "went" to them when going out at night. Our great friend was Sean Hughes, the Garda superintendent, and we could always tell Dad we had been with him.' Dermot vividly remembers pushing the car in silently lest the engine noise give them away. Dan O'Brien always slept with the door open, so Vincent would make conversation, enabling the others to tip-toe in undetected.

To fund such nights out, Vincent was able to get a 'first bit of money in my pocket' courtesy of a well-bred greyhound bitch his father gave him. 'I mated her with a pretty good dog and she had nine pups – eight dogs and a bitch,' he recalls. 'When they were twelve to fourteen months old I wrote to a leading greyhound owner on the London tracks at the time, George Flinton. He came over to see them and bought them all. After that I started to buy dogs. I would keep them for a while and give them some trials on a track. If they showed up well, I'd sell them to England. I had a man who would take them, and if they were satisfactory we would figure out a price and he would send me a cheque. It worked well during the thirties, until war broke out. After that there was no dog racing. I had sent four dogs to England but the buyer sent them back. I finally got rid of one, but the man refused to pay. It was the first court case for Matt Nagle, father of David Nagle, who later owned a share in The Minstrel. Matt succeeded in getting me £4, which I later bet on White Squirrel [his father's grey point-to-point mare]. That was all I had in the world at that time.'

It might prove surprising that Dan was not paying Vincent a weekly wage for all the work he was doing. But it was the custom in Ireland, then, and sometimes now, for young members of the family living at home on a farm to get their bed and board without financial payment. Vincent, if questioned about this, would always say, 'Growing up, I wanted for nothing.'

He soon realized that the only way he could make a living was to prepare horses for gambles and to land them success-fully. At that time he was preparing White Squirrel for a few fancied runs in local point-to-points. Then foot and mouth disease caused all point-to-points to be cancelled, though regular racing was permitted on racecourses. Vincent comments, 'We'd only had foot and mouth twice in Ireland up to that time, and that was during the two wars. A strange coincidence. Some said the Germans spread it!'

A new opportunity then appeared and, true to Vincent's style, it was seized upon and exploited. 'One morning I was short of something to lead a couple of our flat racehorses so I rode White Squirrel myself. I was very surprised how well she worked with them. A week later I worked her again with the same horses. She did even a little better. I thought to myself, "This is rather good. We'll have a little gamble on this mare."' As Dermot remembers, 'Our father enjoyed his small wagers. He was very outgoing, and it gave him the greatest pleasure to tell his friends that his horses had a chance.' Vincent takes up the tale again. 'I didn't say anything to my father then, because he'd get quite excited and pass the news all round and the price would be gone. If it worked out, I'd tell him at the right moment, which was as near the race as possible!'

Vincent took over the mare himself, grooming her and riding her daily until the day for the gamble at Clonmel. 'The day the grey mare was due to run I got a very good friend of mine to come to the races with us. I told my friend, "Just before the betting opens on the race, go to my father and tell him he ought to have a bet on this mare." My father gave my friend a tenner and he got 20–1. There was a scramble after that. The best they could do for my £4 was 10–1. But we won, and it was great. That was my first little gamble, and it was quite a bit of money for me to win in those days. My father was not pleased that I had prepared his mare to win without telling him.'

Those early successes and the happy years were threatened by his father's death from pneumonia, suddenly contracted after racing at the Curragh on 2 May 1943. Kathleen had cautioned Dan against taking off his coat as he had had several bouts of pneumonia from wettings at fairs. He went home by train, unusually refusing to play cards, fell ill the following morning and died the next day. Vincent was at home at the time and was deeply shaken by his much-loved father's sudden demise. More than that, it seemed at first that Vincent would have to give up training and start another trade. The forty or so horses had to be sold, and what they made, together with the remainder of the legacy, was divided between the eight children.

'I found myself more or less without a home and with very little money,' he says. 'Farming was in a very bad way due to the war. There were four in my father's first family and four in the second, and there was very little for any of us when everything was divided. Phonsie was only thirteen, and I had my mother to look after. So I knocked about for several months wondering what to do. With the war, the money had gone out of cattle. Top-grade beasts were selling for as low as thirty shillings each. But nobody knew me. I'd no idea I could set up as a trainer. I was prepared to do anything to get started in life. Fortunately I was able to get horses to train, and was also able to train on the farm, which on my father's death, due to the marriage settlement, passed jointly to my elder half-brothers Donal and John.'

Vincent's gambling successes enabled him to give Donal the money to acquire John's share of the farm, which was valued at £3,500. 'I was able to give Donal the capital to buy John out, as he didn't care for farming,' he recalls. 'Fortunately for me, Donal had no interest in horses, so in return I had the use of the stables and gallops. Clashganiff remained home to all the family. John preferred to work with the bank in Dublin and stayed in banking there. He followed the racehorses and was a keen student of form.'

Vincent now had a base to start his own fully fledged training career, but what he urgently needed was to find owners who would send him horses. In December 1943 Vincent set off for Newmarket. 'Jackie O'Brien was a dealer in horses, and a very good friend of mine. I said to Jackie, "Would you come to Newmarket Sales with me?" I had never been there before, and he came. We stayed in London at the Great Eastern Hotel and went to Newmarket by train.' Vincent had to carry his khaki travel permit card, marked 'Business Visitor' and stamped with a British visa. On it were marked where and when he drew cheques.

Jackie O'Brien had already introduced Vincent to Mr Frank Vickerman, a wealthy wool-broker who had moved his business from Yorkshire to Dublin. Vickerman had not been interested in racing himself but thought a few young horses might make a welcome homecoming present for his soldier son, who was with the British Army in North Africa. Sadly, his son fell fatally ill out in the desert. O'Brien had bought five or six cheap yearlings in 1941 in Dublin, and in 1943 he urged Mr Vickerman to put them into training with young Vincent. Vickerman agreed. 'He was my first owner and sent me three of the horses,' says Vincent.

Now aged twenty-six, and facing his first year's training, Vincent bought Drybob at the Sales for 130 guineas as a resubmitted lot. The buyer's intended owner had failed to conclude the deal, and by the merest chance Vincent had over-heard George Everitt, the trainer from the north who had bought the horse, reporting this to a friend. This genuine reason for resale suggested to Vincent that he might acquire a real bargain, since other buyers would be suspicious that something was wrong. 'Actually the horse made more, having been sold for 115 guineas on the first day! He was called Drybob after a good jockey at that time, R. A. Jones, who apparently was fond of his little drop.'

Sidney McGregor from Warwickshire, who had bred the 1932 Derby winner April the Fifth, owned and trained by the West End light comedy actor Tom Walls, met Vincent at the Sales. He found Vincent a buyer for half of Drybob, Norman Wilkinson, who had a few horses in training with Willie O'Grady in Tipperary. Sidney, liking the look of Vincent, decided to send him a horse of his own called Good Days. 'I am sending him,' he said, 'with a view to the Cesarewitch next back-end.' This attitude pleased Vincent just as much as the offer of the horse. 'At least this is a man who is prepared to wait for a year and take a pretty long view, which is always good.'

Without capital, betting was the only way for a young trainer to build a training establishment. 'I started off with those horses in my first year training, and my first runner was Good Days in

May [1944],' Vincent says. 'I ran him in a bumper at Limerick Junction, and in those days you could bet substantially at starting price. In England bookmakers were prepared to take quite a bit of money on Irish racing. English racing was so limited at the time that they could make a market. So we had a pretty good gamble on him, and that came off as he won quite easily. And then my next effort at a gamble was in August with Drybob, again at Limerick Junction. We had another good go at SP that day, and he won. This was all to my advantage from the point of view of publicity and getting in the picture a bit. I was able to collect some more owners and, consequently, more horses.'

Round the circular gallop on the farm and up the little straight he had laid out – he was already concentrating on speed – Vincent prepared the two horses for an audacious attempt on the Irish Autumn Double, then a betting medium which attracted heavy gambling and thus a chance of getting good odds for a bet. Vincent knew that one of his two horses was a miler and that the other stayed. McGregor had formulated the strategy. The Warwickshire breeder had aimed correctly and had entrusted the plan to the young Irishman.

So Vincent prepared Drybob for the Irish Cambridgeshire and Good Days for the Irish Cesarewitch. These two races were exceptions to the wartime restriction that horses from the south could not run in the Metropolitan area. 'Luckily for me,' he recalls, 'Frank Vickerman had asked me, "How about a bit ante-post on the double?" I very modestly said, "Have me £2 each way." Frank had £10 each way and stood to win £5,000, and I stood to win £2,000 with odds of 800–1. Good Days won and Drybob dead-heated, halving his odds. But it was a wonderful beginning!'

CHAPTER 2

COTTAGE RAKE AND HATTON'S GRACE

'I've got to wake up and move pretty quickly'

Now what Vincent urgently needed was a good horse, preferably a jumper, to make his name. By good fortune he came across Cottage Rake, who would make him famous, and not just in Ireland but in England too.

During the spring of 1945 the war in Europe was drawing to an end. Cottage Rake's first owner, Dr 'Otto' Vaughan, was anxious to sell the horse, which had been bred at his brother Dick's Hunting Hall Stud not far from Churchtown. Dr Vaughan's surgery was in Mallow's main street and he kept the horse in a yard at the back. He had sent Cottage Rake up to Goffs Sales at Ballsbridge in Dublin as a five-year-old but failed to sell him. When Cottage Rake was six, Vincent got a call from the doctor. 'He said to me, "I've got a Cottage horse. Would you like to take him to train?" I said, "Right, I will. Where is he?" He said, "Not very far away from you." I discovered he was only a couple of miles from where I lived, and running out on an actual bog! I mean, for a thoroughbred horse to be out on a bog at that time of his life was incredible!'

Phonsie O'Brien set off in a pony and trap to collect the horse and lead him home. Phonsie laughs at the recollection of this humble start, for over the next few seasons the horse who arrived at Churchtown would win the Naas November Handicap (a good Irish punting medium in which he started as 3–1 favourite), the Irish Cesarewitch, the Leopardstown Chase, the King George VI Chase at Kempton Park's Christmas meeting in 1948, and three Cheltenham Gold Cups in successive years.

Vincent vividly remembers Cottage Rake's arrival in 1945. 'I thought, "This horse is going to take time to build up!" But, coming up to Christmas, Dr Vaughan kept asking when the horse was going to run. So I felt I'd better run him at Limerick on St Stephen's Day in a maiden hurdle, because there was no doubt the doctor was getting very impatient. So I put one of my boys on – actually it was Danny O'Sullivan, one of the best work riders I ever had, who later became my head man. The horse jumped off in front and won unextended at 10–1. For his next race, the bumper at Leopardstown [in February 1946], I got Pat Hogan, nicknamed "PP", to ride him. There was no better man to hounds, and he excelled as an amateur rider.' Ireland's 'bumpers', two-mile National Hunt flat races are, even today, shop windows for potential Irish chasers and hurdlers. Leopardstown was one of Ireland's classier tracks. 'Cottage Rake won so well that he impressed a lot of people,' Vincent says. 'There were a number of them trying to buy the horse.'

The first intending purchaser at £3,500 was Tony Riddle-Martin, for Major 'Cuddie' Stirling-Stuart. The horse would have left Churchtown and gone to be trained by Riddle-Martin.

But Maxie Cosgrove, the expert vet who later looked after the great Arkle, failed the horse for his wind, so the major rejected the horse. Within three years he had to watch the reject beat his Cool Customer for the prize he most highly cherished – the Cheltenham Gold Cup. The second intending purchaser appeared in the summer. It was a partnership between Mr 'Jock' Skeffington, later Viscount Massereene and Ferrard, and his mother-in-law, Mrs Lewis. Had they accepted their vet's report, that though the horse 'made a noise' it was unlikely to affect him unless he caught a severe cold, the horse would have been destined to go to that crack English trainer Captain Ryan Price, in Sussex. Mrs Lewis decided she would take a third share herself.

Dr Vaughan remained a definite seller. He liked hunting and point-to-pointing, and had only sent his horse to young Vincent down the road to try to market him. Vincent was desperate not to lose such a potentially good horse out of his small yard, but the doctor would not be dissuaded from selling. 'It suddenly struck me,' Vincent says, 'I've got to wake up and move pretty quickly to try to find someone to buy Cottage Rake and keep him with me.' What really hustled O'Brien was hearing that 'the doctor was making enquiries in England as to how much they'd charge to train the horse over there!'

Through skill and a brave wager, Vincent had achieved his first large capital sum, which was the foundation of his fortune. Moreover, he had made his first contact with an owner of means. That prime need of any trainer touched him forcibly when he realized that unless he could persuade Mr Vickerman to stump up for Cottage Rake he was going to lose the best horse to fall into his hands so far. Yet Frank Vickerman only bought the horse from Dr Vaughan through Vincent, and for Vincent to train, because the prosperous wool merchant had been too businesslike in his first venture into the inexact science of private horse dealing.

Something else had gone wrong with Cottage Rake since the vets had rejected him for making a noise. Vincent had already cleared with Mr Vickerman the possible risk with the horse's wind. The horse would be sold with this affliction for £3,500. 'The money would come out of what Frank Vickerman had won on the double on Good Days and Drybob,' Vincent remarks. 'But then, just at that time, the horse wasn't pulling out a hundred per cent sound in the mornings. So I thought I'd better have an opinion on it, in fairness to the purchaser. I got a vet to have a look at him. He said, "I think he's suffering from slight rheumatism in his shoulder," and I told Frank Vickerman. Vickerman asked me, "Well, what are we going to do about it?" ' So Vincent had to say to the man who had come to his rescue, 'Well, the vet says he's got rheumatism. It's hard for me to advise you to take him.' 'In that case,' said Mr Vickerman, 'we'd better leave it.'

Sixty years later, a wide smile lights up Vincent's face at the recollection of another happy roll of the dice. For Frank Vickerman couldn't 'leave it'. Before receiving the vet's report he had already written out his cheque for £1,000 to Dr Vaughan in part-payment for the horse. When Vickerman went to cancel the deal, he found that Dr Vaughan had already put the cheque through and considered the payment had sealed the deal. Mr Vickerman had no option but to take the horse. 'And of course, it was the luckiest thing that could have happened,' declares Vincent, 'because

Cottage Rake proved to be one of the greatest chasers of all time.'

* * *

Phonsie recalls riding work on Cottage Rake at home. 'You could hear a little roughness at the start of the season, before the horse was fit,' he remarks. Then, with a delighted smile, 'But wasn't it a great thing the noise put off those other buyers?' As for the rheumatism, Phonsie remembers 'getting hold of some poteen to rub into Cottage Rake's shoulders to ease the rheumatism or arthritis or whatever it was. After you'd been in the stable, you'd come out with your head reeling, the smell was so strong. We didn't continue with this treatment.'

Cottage Rake won the Naas November Handicap in 1947, and the two-mile Irish Cesarewitch a year later, in addition to four wins over fences in the 1946/47 season. These victories consolidated the growing domestic reputation of the young man from Churchtown in Co. Cork. Vincent then decided to run Cottage Rake in the Cheltenham Gold Cup of 1948. The most astonishing thing about this decision was that 'the Rake' was Vincent's very first runner in England, and Cheltenham was Vincent's first sight of an English racecourse. He had selected the highest-class steeplechase in Britain, the Gold Cup, on a particularly difficult course. The brazenness of it, the confidence behind the attempt, still astonishes, more than half a century later.

On his first visit to Cheltenham Vincent was even uncertain about where to stand. He was watching by the last fence with a big crowd around him. Happy Home came to the last a good length and a half in front. 'I was particularly concerned as my father had sold Golden Emblem, the grand-dam of his good horses Astrometer and Astrologer,' Vincent says. Michael Magnier, grandfather of John, Vincent's future son-in-law, had bought her for small money. He mated her with his great sire Cottage, and bred Happy Home. 'And here was I,' says Vincent, 'standing at the last fence at Cheltenham watching my horse being led over the last by a horse whose dam my father owned and sold, and I thought, "Wouldn't it be an ironic thing if that horse beats me today?"'

He could not see what happened after the horses had gone by him, and it was in the days before the public address system. 'I didn't know who had won, and it was no use asking anyone around because they knew no more than I did. I made my way across the course and up the back of the stands to the old winner's enclosure, and it was not until I saw Aubrey on Cottage Rake putting his hand to his cap acknowledging acclamations that I thought, "He must have won!"' The Rake, ridden by Aubrey Brabazon, had given Vincent his first English victory by beating Dorothy Paget's Happy Home one and a half lengths after the latter had led him fully that distance over the last fence. 'Cottage Rake,' says Vincent, 'was very well bred on his dam's side. She traced to Stella, one of the great foundation mares. There are very few chasers with the speed to win a top-class autumn flat handi-cap over one and a half miles, and he was capable of really quickening up the long hill, after jumping the last at Cheltenham.'

Churchtown lit the welcome-home bonfires. Vincent was carried shoulder-high through the crowds thronging the village. Stout, provided by Mr Vickerman, flowed freely.

The children wrote essays about Cottage Rake, and the Vickermans visited the school and praised the pupils for their compositions.

Three and a half weeks later Cottage Rake was second in the Irish Grand National, carrying 12st 7lb and trying to give three stone to the winner, Hamstar. 'At the time I had him,' comments Vincent, 'most chasers were pretty strong horses. Cottage Rake was unusual. He was rather lightly built and finer. He showed more quality than the average chaser, but then he always had much more speed than the average chaser!' Jockey Tommy Burns, known as 'TP', had been associated with Vincent from his beginnings. 'I even rode the odd horse for his father.' TP was Vincent's assistant at Ballydoyle after he gave up riding until Christmas 1983. He ended their thirty-five-year-long association to become assistant to Dermot Weld on the Curragh, where he could live with his family. Sitting in front of the fire in the study of his bungalow on the rim of the Curragh, Tommy reminisces, 'Cottage Rake wasn't the most robust horse. In handicaps he couldn't give the weight away. Not like Arkle. I think he never really liked the Irish Grand National course at Fairyhouse. It didn't suit his class, his speed. But how few horses win three Gold Cups! He had to be great!'

After that first Gold Cup Frank Vickerman seriously considered selling his horse at a profit. He had prolonged discussions with Vincent over the Rake's value and the question of buying out the share in the horse which Mrs Lewis had previously bought (this was the lady who had been an early contender to buy Cottage Rake with her son-in-law Jock Skeffington; she had afterwards joined with Vickerman). In July, he told Vincent that Mrs Lewis could dispose of her one third for £5,000, but he wanted £16,000 for the whole horse. 'Dorothy Paget is definitely interested,' he wrote.

This was an ominous threat to any trainer. The Hon. Dorothy Paget, the immensely rich and eccentric daughter of Lord Queensborough and cousin of American multi-millionaire Mr 'Jock' Whitney, could buy any horse she liked. Since she often slept all day when her horses were running she was permitted by her trusting bookmakers to back her horses after they had run. She dominated jumping with her vast string. She had already won five Gold Cups with Golden Miller and one more with Roman Hackle; she would win yet another with Mont Tremblant in 1952. Fortunately for Vincent and Mr Vickerman, the nocturnal Miss Paget, with her bevy of secretaries, her room full of back numbers of the *Sporting Life*, and her night chef to cook her great meals at three a.m., was kept at bay.

* * *

Cottage Rake's objective in 1949 was a second Gold Cup, and on the way he won two of the most important chases then in England. In November 1948 Aubrey Brabazon won the Emblem Chase at Manchester, a good, fair, flat galloping track with a splendid old stand before it was all sold off for housing. In a tremendous finish Aubrey lost his whip racing over the last against Lord Bicester's Silver Fame ridden by Martin Molony. 'The Rake made a slight mistake . . . Martin had two lengths on me. I urged the Rake on with hands and heels and just got up to win by a neck.' The next step was the King George VI Chase at Kempton in December. In this race Roimond, another of Lord Bicester's top chasers, landed over the last fence in front of Cottage Rake, but with a devastating burst of speed the Rake overtook Roimond in mid-air at the last and Aubrey won as he liked. 'Poor old Lord Bicester,' Aubrey wrote afterwards. 'He had pitted two of his star chasers, Silver Fame and Roimond, against us to no avail. He must have wondered what it would take to beat the Rake!'

So different are the racecourses of Kempton and Cheltenham that very few horses can win the two great classics of the steeplechasing season. There is no comparison between the flat, easy three miles around right-handed Kempton and the climbing, dipping and struggling uphill finish of the three and a quarter miles left-handed around Cheltenham. Cottage Rake was one of the rare stars who could win both great races, and his battle song preceded him to Cheltenham in 1949, correctly enshrining his partnership with Brabazon:

> *Aubrey's up, the money's down,*
> *The frightened bookies quake,*
> *Come on, me lads, and give a cheer,*
> *Begod, 'tis Cottage Rake.*

* * *

With Cottage Rake's first victorious assault on English racing accomplished, Vincent had decided on another astonishing step: he would run three horses at Cheltenham. Hatton's Grace would run in the Champion Hurdle, Castledermot in the four-mile National Hunt Chase, as well as Cottage Rake in the Gold Cup again. To get to England, for the first time ever, air transport was used for racehorses. Vincent hired a former RAF transport plane, referred to by the lads who travelled the horses as a 'bomber'. The flight had its alarming moments. Twenty minutes out of Shannon 'Cottage Rake went mad', recalls his lad. There was great rejoicing and swigs of whiskey when they landed safely in Gloucestershire.

Hatton's Grace was bred by the Victor Stud in Co. Tipperary and sold at Goffs for the princely sum of eighteen guineas as a 'store'. The buyer was trainer J. Irwin, who afterwards sold a half-share to Colonel Dan Corry of the Irish Army's international show-jumping team. 'Moya Keogh first shared the horse with Dan who won a bumper on him,' says Vincent, 'and then she bought Dan out and sent the horse to Barney Nugent.' Before Vincent trained him he had won three hurdle races between 1946 and 1948, and had run unplaced at 20–1 in the 1948 Champion Hurdle. The horse had been with two good trainers: the great Dan Moore, father of the equally skilful trainer Arthur Moore, and Barney Nugent, who trained successfully near Dublin Airport. Both were experts, yet O'Brien produced an astonishing improvement. Aubrey Brabazon went even further. He declared in his posthumously published book, 'When Vincent got the horse in the summer of 1948 he effected an almost miraculous transformation.'

Ridden by Aubrey, Hatton's Grace showed that improvement on only his third run for Vincent by winning the Champion Hurdle at the age of nine, when most hurdlers are losing their speed. Indeed he was described in an Irish newspaper as 'Mrs Keogh's old horse' and criticized for his unprepossessing, scraggy appearance. However, after the victory the ugly duckling had suddenly turned himself into a flying swan. The Irish, recognizing this, flung hats in the air and shouted their delighted acclamations of glee. What was

more, the horse he beat was none other than National Spirit –
a year younger, the winner of the previous two Champion
Hurdles, and the darling of English crowds. Hatton's Grace
jumped the last flight in front and shot away up the hill to win
by six lengths from National Spirit, ridden by Martin Molony.

Vincent says of Hatton's Grace, 'He was a perfect horse to
train and easy to ride. He was small, not imposing at all. His
neck was rather light and short, but he did have good limbs and
a good depth of heart. He never had leg trouble. He was a great
jumper and had such a wonderful heart; after he jumped the last
at Cheltenham nothing could beat him up the hill. He was eight
when I got him and nine when he won his first Champion
Hurdle. I remember reading in one paper that National Spirit,
who had won the two previous Champion Hurdles, was eight
and perhaps too old to win again! Hatton's Grace was the oldest
of the triple scorers.'

Photographs of Hatton's Grace easily winning the
Champion Hurdle in 1949 show no signs of scragginess. But
in the paddock he still looked small and light-bodied, compared with the massive seventeen-hands National Spirit.
Between that Champion Hurdle victory and his repeat in 1950,
Vincent ran Hatton's Grace on the flat in two contrasting races,
proving the little horse's versatility. He won the one-mile Irish
Lincoln in the spring and the two-mile Irish Cesarewitch that
autumn, then the Cesarewitch again the following year. 'It says
a lot for the skill and daring of his trainer that he should ever
have even contemplated such a diverse programme,' Aubrey
notes.

Vincent's other entry for Cheltenham in 1949 was
Castledermot, who had been prepared for the four-mile-one-

furlong National Hunt Chase. In those days this 'amateur Grand National' for novice horses took an undulating rural ride round behind the stands and through the far edge of the present car parks. It was very often the scene for well-backed Irish gambles, and Castledermot proved no exception. 'In biting cold here today,' wrote Michael O'Hehir, racing correspondent of the *Irish Independent*, 'owner Mrs Moya Keogh and trainer Vincent O'Brien, who had won the Champion Hurdle with Hatton's Grace yesterday, made history when their Castledermot, starting at 6–4, shortest price in the history of the race, romped home by four lengths in a field of seventeen, the easiest possible winner.' Castledermot had been ridden by Lord Mildmay, called 'Lordie' by the English crowd, champion amateur five years in a row, who the following year tragically disappeared when swimming off the coast of Mothecombe, his Devon estate. While staying at Windsor Castle for Royal Ascot, he had introduced Queen Elizabeth the Queen Mother to the thrill of steeplechasing, her greatest sporting passion. Vincent has letters from Anthony Mildmay written from Fairlawne, Peter Cazalet's home in Kent. 'Lordie' had come originally to stay a weekend with Peter, his close friend and companion-in-arms in the Welsh Guards, but ended up staying for thirteen years.

Before Cottage Rake's second and hardest Gold Cup victory, the horse experienced a grave setback. In February his preparation was seriously held up by a cold and a dirty nose, at exactly the wrong time for a horse attempting steeplechasing's crown within four weeks. And there had been those dire veterinary warnings about the dangers of him getting a bad cold. O'Brien recalls, 'I considered that the Gold Cup might come too soon for him, but' – a typical shrug and flick of his hand – 'the horse was at Cheltenham and we were hoping for the best.' But would Cottage Rake, with the roughness of his wind and the warned risk against catching a bad cold, be fully fit for his second Gold Cup? Cottage Rake needed time, and time, for once, was granted by a quirk of nature.

After the first two days and the double with Hatton's Grace and Castledermot, a severe frost gripped Cheltenham. The turf turned rock-hard and Gold Cup day was lost. The Rake received an extra vital month in which to get fully fit for the toughest race of his life. The race was eventually run on 11 April. This time he started 4–6, although there was an even better horse than Happy Home to take him on. At the elbow before the last fence Cool Customer held three advantages: he was almost two lengths ahead; he had the inside; and 'the Brab' with the delicate hands had gone for his whip on the Rake.

This pressure before the last seemed certain to drain Cottage Rake's final speed, but to the joy of the Irish throng, Cool Customer's commanding lead over the last was first nibbled away and then gobbled up as the Rake flew up that hill. He caught Cool Customer and went away. He won by two lengths. He had now proved himself to be a great horse, and in that toughest struggle of his life, Aubrey's strength, coolness and exquisite timing were magnificent. His defeat of Cool Customer made this one of the greatest Gold Cup battles ever.

But Aubrey had also been Cool Customer's regular jockey. To commemorate Aubrey's victories on Cool Customer, Major Stirling-Stuart had commissioned a special pair of cufflinks. He did not wish to post them; 'We'll meet at Cheltenham, of course, Aubrey!' said the major. And in the sweat of the old unsaddling pen behind the wooden changing room, the major left his Cool Customer in second place to cross over to congratulate Aubrey and to hand him the cufflinks.

So Vincent's second raid on Cheltenham produced the great Gold Cup and Champion Hurdle double, plus what was known as 'The Amateurs' Grand National'. If the race had been run in March, would Cottage Rake have beaten Cool Customer? Perhaps. Certainly in April, aided by luck, he had proved himself, like his trainer, to be something special.

* * *

On 9 March 1950, Cottage Rake won his third successive Cheltenham Gold Cup. This time everything was easier, though superstition had filled Mrs Vickerman with pre-race doubts: Cottage Rake was number 13. He thrashed, by ten lengths, Lord Bicester's top-class and very fast chaser Finnure, who had been undefeated all season until that day. Only four other horses dared take on the Rake; he was the Best Mate (who was the winner of three consecutive Gold Cups in the first few years of the twenty-first century) of his era. Cottage Rake's late start in racing may have helped extend his career, but the essence of his success was Vincent's skill in training older horses.

Hats were flung into Cheltenham's cheering air to celebrate the Rake's hat-trick. There was another bouquet of plaudits for Aubrey Brabazon, for in Vincent's words 'he rode perhaps the brainiest race of his career'. Meyrick Good, who wrote for the *Sporting Life* for fifty years, commented, 'Never in my life have I seen the Gold Cup won with greater ease. "The

Rake" beat Lord Bicester's brilliant Finnure (Martin Molony) by a mocking ten lengths, Aubrey Brabazon having cunningly slipped his field on the descent for home, half a mile away.' The Finnure camp had planned, by setting a doddling pace, to blunt that famous Cottage Rake final thrust, which he could produce when others could not, at the end of a hard-run race. But their plot rebounded and Aubrey's warm and gentle smile as he sailed at ease over the last fence reflected his pleasure in his tactics and the glow of riding a comfortable winner. After the race, the *Life*'s Tom Nickalls reported that 'Cottage Rake would not have blown out the proverbial candle'. And that of a horse whose wind had proved dubious enough in his youth to put off two eager purchasers.

O'Brien, outwardly as cool as always in the winning enclosure, said, 'Cottage Rake came back today as I expected.' Then, perhaps subconsciously aware that the Rake's great days were over, he added, 'No plans at the moment. We've lived only for this week.'

That same week, Hatton's Grace came to the last hurdle again pressing National Spirit, who blundered and became unbalanced. Aubrey seized the advantage and won. 'It's an extraordinary thing that two old horses should have come to the last flight in two Champion Hurdles in exactly the same way,' he said. Peter O'Sullevan called them the 'two Peter Pans', because they didn't seem to grow any older. Aubrey did not complete the treble in 1951. Due to an unfortunate disagreement between the owner and jockey, Tim Molony got the winning ride on Hatton's Grace – the first horse to win three Champion Hurdles and the first eleven-year-old to win. It took nearly thirty years for the next eleven-year-old, Sea Pigeon, whose pedigree was good enough, to win the Derby. Michael O'Hehir described Hatton's Grace as 'a great-hearted and brilliantly versatile star in action on the racecourses of England and Ireland'. He won six flat races including two successive Irish Cesarewitches and a Lincolnshire, and scored twelve National Hunt victories including a steeplechase when aged thirteen. After that, Hatton's Grace was retired to Ballydoyle where he was allowed to turn schoolmaster, leading the younger horses out to jump hurdles.

As for Cottage Rake, Vincent, looking back in retirement on the great chasers since the war, believes his triple winner of the Cheltenham Gold Cup 'ranks with Prince Regent and Arkle as the greatest winners of the Gold Cup. However, in my opinion, neither of the others had the speed of Cottage Rake, who won the one-and-a-half-mile Naas November Handicap when he was a novice chaser, in addition to the Irish Cesarewitch.' Aubrey Brabazon, in his excellent memoirs *Racing Through My Mind*, which features an affectionate foreword by Vincent, says, 'I rode the Rake in twenty races, winning ten, and yet I cannot recall ever hitting him.' What a moral there for lesser jockeys and the whip-happy few from the man of whom O'Brien thought, 'when it came to riding a finish, he had no peer'. Vincent reminds us that Aubrey, who rode easily at nine stone, was 'equally top-class on the flat. In 1948, after he won the Gold Cup on the Rake, he won the Irish Oaks on Masaka. In 1950, he topped this with a unique treble: the Cheltenham Gold Cup, the Champion Hurdle and the Irish 2,000 Guineas.'

Aubrey Brabazon went on to Hurst Park on the Saturday after those three triumphant Cheltenham days in 1950 a little fatigued by both rides and by celebrations. Aubrey lived life fully; his candle blazed at both ends. At Hurst Park he dropped his hands on an odds-on favourite when looking like winning easily and was beaten. He was marched before the Stewards to be fined. 'Brabazon Caught Napping' bawled an evening paper headline. 'If so,' said Vincent O'Brien quietly, 'it was the only sleep poor Aubrey got all week!'

Vincent considered Aubrey Brabazon, Martin Molony and his brother Tim a trio of brilliant young Irish jockeys who dominated National Hunt racing in the early post-war years. When Bryan Marshall was demobilized as a captain in the British Army, he made up a famous foursome. Of this shining quartet, all of whom rode for Vincent, some experts of the day rated Martin Molony on top for style, timing, strength and courage, despite Tim Molony being champion National Hunt jockey five times running from 1948. Martin won top-class races on the flat and was third in the 1951 Derby on Signal Box. An usher at Vincent's wedding, he was to have ridden Hatton's Grace for the third victory in 1951 but contracted the measles. He was retained by Lord Bicester for his top chasers and commuted from Ireland, recording in England an astonishing 33 per cent winning strike rate. However, a terrible fall at Thurles, Co. Tipperary, in September 1951 cut short Martin's career. 'We were so glad that he had recovered from his fall in time to propose the first toast at our wedding in December of that year,' Vincent remarks. Martin, a quiet, religious man, retired to run his Rathmore Stud in Co. Limerick with his wife Julia and their family.

The Gold Cup of 1950 was the last race Cottage Rake won, though he followed his third Gold Cup victory with a gallant fourth under a crushing 12st 7lb in the three-and-a-half-mile Irish Grand National. 'Each season when the Rake finished,' Vincent reports, 'I'd let him out every day at Churchtown on the Lawn Field with a donkey for a companion. This is the meadow between the farmhouse and the road. Each night there were cattle put in the field to graze it. In the morning, the cattle were driven down the back of the farm to the fields by the river. One morning, the chap in charge of the cattle did not show up, and they were not taken out of the field. The horse was let out as usual and started to graze. The donkey, meanwhile, had wandered in amongst the cattle. When the horse put his head up he couldn't see the donkey. He was so upset at losing his friend that he went round the field at a hell of a rate, got too close to a corner and did some damage to a tendon. It was got right, but sadly he was never the same horse again. It upset Vickerman very much, but' – Vincent clicks his tongue, as horsemen philosophically do – 'it was just one of those things. When we patched him up, Vickerman took him away and sent him to England to be trained. He won nothing over there.'

The Rake had launched his trainer. His first Gold Cup had brought enquiries from other owners, like the Keoghs with Hatton's Grace and Knock Hard. Cottage Rake's third Gold Cup made O'Brien's name feared by other trainers and famous in both Great Britain and Ireland. The trumpets sounded in the English press. Fame touched O'Brien early. Other clients began to ring and write, eager to meet him.

Half a century later, the Rake's trainer looks back to compare the first Gold Cup winner he trained with the second, Knock Hard, in 1953. 'Cottage Rake was a very good-legged horse with quality limbs – much more quality than you'd see in other chasers in the old days,' he says. 'He stood over a good deal of ground. He had a grand bold head on him. I liked him very much. He stood over much more ground than Knock Hard. Knock Hard had a short back, and for me, with that short back he could never be a really proficient jumper at speed.' Here O'Brien humps his right hand in a hopping motion. 'Cottage Rake was a shade long over his loins and could do that' – a long swoop, bending his wrist to show the bent back jumpers need – 'and Royal Tan was the same. They were the best two jumpers I ever trained. I maintain that jumping at racing speed comes easier to horses who are not short over the loins.'

CHAPTER 3

MASTER OF CHELTENHAM

'Over they went to Cheltenham, and they'd
win there'

In the decade between 1949 and 1959, to Vincent O'Brien's 'Super Seven' Cheltenham Festival winners – four Gold Cups and three Champion Hurdles – must be added an extraordinary flow of other Cheltenham victories. Most of these came from his domination of the novice hurdling crown, then called the Gloucestershire Hurdle and known as 'The Gloucester'. It was split into two divisions each year to cover the large number of entries. In the seven years from 1952 Vincent won ten Gloucesters, four ridden by his amateur rider brother Phonsie.

It was surprising that each year so many other trainers believed they had a chance with their best young novice hurdlers when the feared M. V. O'Brien stable was almost certain to win one or even both divisions of the season's novice hurdle championship. In 1954 Vincent won the Spa Hurdle (three miles) with Lucky Dome ridden by T. P. Burns, who was one of four of Vincent's horses whose 'inconsistency' was called into question by the Irish Stewards. He also succeeded in winning the 1952 three-mile National Hunt Handicap Chase, a good guide for the Grand National, with Royal Tan, ridden by Phonsie. Two years later Royal Tan and Bryan Marshall did indeed win the Grand National. Castledermot, ridden by Lord Mildmay, had won the four-mile National Hunt Chase for amateurs, and Vincent took this race again in 1954 with Quare Times, ridden by Mr 'Bunny' Cox. The following year Quare Times became Vincent's third consecutive Grand National winner. Finally, Ahaburn (T. P. Burns) won the Birdlip Hurdle in 1955.

Vincent's successes at Cheltenham were remarkable for the wide variety of races contested at different distances. Many of these same horses won top flat race handicaps too. But Vincent had, after all, started in a very mixed yard: his father had big handicap winners on the flat as well as chasers, hurdlers and point-to-pointers. The Irish have always tended to switch their horses between different codes far more frequently than their British competitors. In Britain there is generally a progression from flat to hurdling to chasing, only reverting when there's a very-long-distance flat race on offer, or when a horse has displayed a distinct dislike for fences.

* * *

Until 1951, when Vincent moved to Ballydoyle to lay out a top-class training establishment, his runners were trained far more rustically around the family farm. Phonsie, a regular work rider, recalls the Churchtown training methods, which closely resemble those currently used by 'horsey' farmers both sides of the Irish Sea, not those of big professionals in organized training centres. There was plenty of what could loosely be called 'road work', the four- to six-week period of walking and trotting conditioning for jumpers at the beginning of the season. 'We had plenty of dirt roads and tracks,' Phonsie remembers, and perhaps they were like the few 'green lanes' of England which still linger between hidden hedgerows. 'We'd go about four miles out, walk, trot, sometimes even canter along these tracks, getting the young horses fit, and then ride back again.'

Vincent started expanding the yard at Churchtown almost immediately after he made arrangements with his half-brother Donal to remain at Clashganiff. Initially he rented a yard in Churchtown from John Flannery, and then, in 1948, he began building seventeen boxes. 'It said something about the ambition and determination of the man that he would build all these boxes knowing that he would be leaving them in a couple of years,' Dermot comments. 'He didn't let expense stand in the way of what he was hoping to achieve.'

In 1945 Vincent had twenty-five horses in training; by 1949 the number had increased to thirty-two. Jimmy Gordon started as one of Vincent's first stable lads and now has horses in training himself. He was the first owner of the promising young trainer David Wachman, now married to Vincent's grand-daughter Katie, the daughter of Sue and John Magnier. Jimmy, who still lives in Churchtown village – 'We were the first house to sell ice cream in Churchtown!' – came from Wexford in May 1948 to join Vincent. 'Why? Cos I'd heard from Nixie Halley [a famous horse dealer in those days] that there was a young man near Churchtown making a name for himself. I did three horses, as we all did – three plus a "spare". Then Hatton's Grace came and I got him to do! Three times I went to Cheltenham with him and all three times he won. Oh, he was small indeed, but he was good.

'Vincent and his two brothers, Dermot and Phonsie, and their half-brothers were all living here in the farmhouse. I started work on four shillings a week. We'd go back to the village where we lived to have breakfast. We started at six in the summer. Sometimes there'd be pies cooling on the outside window ledge of the old kitchen facing into the yard and the young lads would pinch one. We'd go home for lunch – off at one p.m. and back by 2.30. Fit! We were as fit as racing greyhounds for we'd have to run both ways twice. Vincent was very strict on time!' This was said with beaming admiration. 'Vincent insisted everything had to be done right. He seldom rode out himself. Phonsie rode everything. Dermot was the man to speak to if you wanted something from the Boss.' He added proudly, 'I was leading point-to-point amateur down there in 1958. No, I got no rides from Vincent. It was always hard to get a ride from Vincent!' And he laughed.

'Maurice O'Callaghan was doing the feeding – oats and bran and powdered milk and Equitone. The Boss would buy the best hay from the local farmers. There were only two wireless sets in Churchtown in 1948 and 1949 so when we were over at Cheltenham they were put out on the windowsills on the village streets. Everyone would crowd around them in the street and listen to the commentators, d'you see? And cheer. And celebrate – we all did. After those winners, the Imperial Hotel up the road at Charleville would put on a Free Night and we'd all go. And when Hatton's Grace won,' continued the lad who 'did' the little horse fifty-six years earlier, 'why, Vincent himself was so excited he danced around the yard here.

Danced around with all of us, so he did!' This celebratory revelation suggests that the outwardly cool O'Brien façade was occasionally dropped.

It was generally believed that Vincent brought over to Cheltenham the local Cork water in milk churns so that his horses would not be digestively disadvantaged by changing to the English stuff. Jimmy Gordon shook his head. 'No, but we brought our own oats. And we'd bring pairs of nylon stockings and rashers of bacon to swap with the poor English during their post-war shortages!'

'The weekly routine devised at Churchtown by Vincent,' Phonsie reveals, 'was Mondays up the dirt roads, cantering up hills, perhaps five miles; Tuesdays and Fridays, schooling; Wednesdays and Saturdays quick work at home – one and a quarter miles would be the longest. And working them for speed.' If there was one rule in Vincent's book, there it is. His stable lads, his assistants, his jockeys, all repeated it consistently – speed, speed, speed. 'We'd ride out at seven a.m. There was the one gallop round the fields, about seven furlongs to a mile in the circle, and a straight of not quite four furlongs on grass, and a strip of plough too. We did an awful lot of slow work in those days. Then we'd ride the horses in the river, the Awbeg, at the back for twenty minutes. I've no doubt at all that the cold water did their legs a power of good. There were only two horses broke down, as I remember.'

What was noticeable at Churchtown – and it was by no means the rule at other successful stables – was the wonderful state of the old meadowland gallops. 'Vincent made us keep these to perfection, stopping tracks every day,' declares Phonsie with a groan at the hard work entailed. 'The fences were moveable so that the ground was not cut up. Vincent's idea was that the horses had to be schooled often. When a horse became proficient over fences he was then schooled over hurdles regularly from then on, except perhaps for one school over fences again just before he ran in a steeplechase.' Phonsie adds, in a statement which may surprise some horsemen, 'We schooled all the horses every Tuesday and every Friday twice over four hurdles or four fences – so long as the ground was not hard.'

Phonsie's wife Ann, an excellent horsewoman herself, was Vincent's stable secretary. She recalls that discipline was tight. 'If Dermot and Phonsie came in late,' she says with awe, 'what Vincent didn't say!' She quakes at the memory and remarks tellingly, 'Vincent was firm with the staff. He did not fuss over them in any way. Yet, they would die for him.'

'I don't think anyone to this day has got near our record for those Gloucester Hurdles at Cheltenham,' Phonsie comments. 'We'd run the horses first in two "bumpers", the first for experience and I'd win the second one. Then we'd run them in two hurdles, the same result, and over they went to Cheltenham, and they'd win there.' He beams, and recalls in particular one dazzling Christmas weekend in 1948. 'One of Vincent's greatest feats was one St Stephen's Day meeting. I went to Limerick with seven horses. It was a two-day meeting, and one of the horses ran twice. I rode seven winners and was second in the other race to Martin Molony. Dermot went to Leopardstown with three, and all three won. And Vincent won at Kempton Park with Cottage Rake. That was some week-end, wasn't it? And at the most only thirty-two horses in the yard.'

* * *

Harry Keogh, whose wife Moya owned Hatton's Grace, 'liked to have a bet', says Vincent. In those days O'Brien himself was a powerful gambler, as his betting books show. 'It was a matter of survival. Owners liked to have a bet and I had to come up with the goods to stay in business.' He needed capital. Without a rich and generous patron, successful betting is still the only way a young trainer can set himself up.

Vincent's link was the man, visibly triumphant in winner's enclosure photographs of the time, who used to place commissions for both O'Brien and Harry Keogh. Nat McNabb knew exactly how well O'Brien was doing. He strongly urged Keogh to move his horses to this outstanding young trainer in Co. Cork. One of them was Knock Hard. 'He had a flat race pedigree,' says Vincent. 'He was a chestnut gelding foaled in 1944 by Domaha out of Knocksouna by Beresford. He had speed enough to win the Irish Lincoln.' In the war's shattered sales he made just seventy-five guineas as a yearling.

The first attempted gamble on Knock Hard was in the Irish Cesarewitch in November 1950. He had been tried at home with Hatton's Grace, and, in Vincent's words, 'smothered him for speed'. So he was specially prepared for the coup. But Knock Hard was not to be the hero of the day. 'Vincent and the owners had a huge bet on him,' says Phonsie. 'Hatton's Grace was run in the race in order to get a better price. They went in first and backed Hatton's Grace which pushed Knock Hard's price out in the market, and then they poured a flood of serious money on Knock Hard.' Phonsie ruefully recalls the day. 'I had £116 saved up when I left Churchtown for the

Curragh. I had £100 on Knock Hard at 10–1. He came down to 6–4. After having my £100 on, I had £16 left, so I had £5 each way on Hatton's Grace. Herbert Holmes rode Knock Hard and Martin Molony rode Hatton's Grace. Holmes's instructions were that he was not to go to the front till he was inside the last furlong. Mr Holmes goes to the front before he even got to the straight at the Curragh! Sitting there as if he's got the race well sewn up. Then along comes Martin Molony on Hatton's Grace, catches him in the last furlong and beats him. If Knock Hard had been ridden in any other way, twenty-seven out of twenty-eight times he'd have beaten Hatton's Grace eight lengths. And Mr Holmes said afterwards he was going so easy he thought nothing in the world could catch him.' Phonsie groans, then laughs. 'The result of my bet was that I won £1, instead of the £1,000 I was supposed to win!'

The only voice from the O'Brien stable cheering for Hatton's Grace was that of his owner, Moya Keogh. 'He is only a little bit of a horse, but wasn't he splendid?' Few from the O'Brien betting group would have agreed on that particular day. Vincent admits he made a lot of money betting, 'but it was entirely confined to the horses I trained myself. I learned the lesson, luckily for me pretty early in life, that betting on other people's horses wasn't exactly a paying game.'

The attempt to recoup the Knock Hard losses in the Cesarewitch was made the following spring in the Lincoln over a mere mile. This was a good race for a gamble, a competitive handicap at the start of the Irish flat season with a big field. But the event picked by Vincent for Knock Hard as his prep race for the Lincoln was an odd one. 'I ran him in a novice chase at Naas,' says O'Brien, 'only two weeks before, the object being to extend his price. Few would believe that a horse that had just run over fences could win a Lincoln! He won the chase, incidentally.'

'I won the Irish Lincoln on him by six lengths,' says TP, remembering a race from early on in his thirty-five-year-long connection with the stable. 'He was six lengths up after he'd gone three furlongs and stayed there. There was great talk of Arkle coming to the Curragh and winning a two-mile race. But our fellow was winning over one mile! He was a fine big chest-nut horse, a lovely horse, classier even than Cottage Rake. Knock Hard was more or less a flat horse that was turned to chasing. I rode him in a five-furlong race myself and then, at the other end of the scale, over the longest distance. They always reckoned that Knock Hard was never really in love with jumping.'

Another coup was planned for the autumn. Phonsie O'Brien had, in under two years, become Ireland's top amateur rider under National Hunt Rules. He was at school during the early days at Churchtown, 'and Vincent wouldn't let me ride in point-to-points in case I got injured', so he only started riding in races in 1949. 'There was a decision taken that Knock Hard should go for the Manchester November Handicap,' Phonsie recalls, 'and to be eligible to run in England the horse had to run on the flat there. So I was the jockey to get him handicapped! Several amateur flat races in England were selected, and I rode him. At Lewes he coasted in at long odds on.' At Worcester they met a very good hurdler, Noholme, ridden by Teddy Underdown. 'Vincent, Harry Keogh and Sidney McGregor had a massive gamble on Knock Hard,' Phonsie continues, 'something like £14,000 to £8,000. I was meant to hold him up, which I did. When a gap appeared, I coasted up on the inside of Mr Underdown and sat there. He appeared to have the race won. I waited and waited, then gave my fellow one crack and we won by a neck. Oh, he was a class horse, a brilliant horse. The speed he had! Of course, at Worcester I'd had a bet myself. Amateurs are allowed to bet, aren't they?'

But the gamble in the Manchester November Handicap failed to come off: Knock Hard was beaten a neck by Summer Rain. Harry Keogh then said to Vincent, 'If you could run Knock Hard at Kempton in the King George VI Chase, it'd be great.' Vincent replied calmly, 'It would give you a chance to get your money back.' This astonishing statement is unlikely ever to have been made before, or contemplated again, by any trainer of racehorses. Here is a man who, having prepared a senior gelding for a gamble over one and a half miles on the flat in one of Britain's most competitive handicaps, coolly resolves that the just-lost thousands might be regained six weeks later over three miles of fences in one of Britain's classiest steeplechases.

'For the Manchester race,' says Vincent, 'the horse had to find a fair bit of speed so we brought Knock Hard back here, and I took him easy, trying to get him to relax again. He went to Kempton and Tim Molony rode him. He went into that first fence taking a really strong hold – he took off boldly and jumped so strong that on landing his forelegs went straight out in front and his hind legs shot straight out behind along the ground. Tim said if he'd tipped a little bit to right or left, he'd have gone, but he just went straight on and got back on to his feet again. The horse got a bad fright. Tim said he was never the same through the race after that.' In spite of the mishap and three miles of uncertain, unenthusiastic jumping, Knock Hard had the class and final speed to finish third to Halloween and Mont Tremblant. 'A month after the race Tim said to me that if he had really got at the horse he would have won, but he was easy on him because he had been frightened.'

After Kempton, Knock Hard ran at Leopardstown in January 1953. His running there, coupled with other races, raised the suspicions of the Irish Stewards. Vincent tells the story. 'Knock Hard was handicapped to give Lord Bicester's good horse Mariner's Log 20lb. That was quite something, though we didn't realize at the time what kind of horse Mariner's Log would turn out to be. P. J. Doyle rode Knock Hard – he was retained by the stable at the time – and I said to him, "I don't want this horse to get a hard race. He's got a lot of weight. But, you know, be there to win if you can." Doyle had the reputation of really getting at a horse and could have given him a very hard race. The horse, after his fright at Kempton, wasn't inclined to jump his fences boldly. He was drawing back a bit. As a result, Mariner's Log beat him, and there was a good deal of chat that day that the horse wasn't trying.

'At that time Judge Wylie was a steward of the Turf Club. With his experience on the bench he virtually ran the club; a few well-chosen words and he was in command. Later in the year I went into the St Stephen's Green Club – the judge was a member and I was too. It was the year Paddy Prendergast was in trouble with the English Stewards over the running of his horse Blue Sail at Ascot. The Irish Stewards didn't agree with the English Stewards' findings. They held an inquiry themselves in Ireland and found no discrepancy between Blue Sail's running in Ireland and his running at Ascot. When old Wylie walked into the club, I knew he'd been at the Turf Club, so I asked him if there was any news on the Prendergast case. "Oh, yes," said the judge, "we could find no discrepancy there." Then he said to me, "If it had been me, I'd have warned you off over Knock Hard last January at Leopardstown." '

This offensive remark led to trouble. Judge Wylie, a power in the world of racehorses, had suddenly declared himself to be an enemy of Vincent's. This was November – ten months after the race. Wylie was a close friend of up-country trainers, owners and jockeys who were not very happy with the success Vincent was having. 'That shook me a bit,' Vincent goes on, 'so I came home and thought about it and decided to ring him up and ask if I could meet him. I sat down and talked to him about what had happened in the King George VI at Kempton. But I don't think he believed me, so anyway the horse went off to run in the Great Yorkshire Chase at Doncaster and Tim Molony was at him, pushing and niggling at him all the way. Then when he jumped the last and saw a clear way ahead of him with no fences there, he just sprinted home. After the race Tim said to me, "Don't have any doubt about it: he doesn't like jumping after the fright he got at Kempton. He doesn't like it."

'To be sure there wasn't any other problem, I decided to get a vet to do a cardiograph on the horse. I'd a feeling there could be something wrong with his heart. I was in the box with the vet and saw the reading coming out of the machine. The vet shook his head at me and said, "I'm sorry to have to tell you that Knock Hard has a faulty heart and could drop dead at any time. Or, on the other hand, he could be all right." ' The gravity of this report burst like a bomb. 'Incidentally,' Vincent comments, 'I told Wylie this as well, but he just . . .' And Vincent shrugs. 'Of course I told Harry Keogh too, and he said finally, "Well, he's got no value now. We can't sell him. The diagnosis could be wrong, so we might as well go on with him.' Back in those days equine medical diagnosis was not as advanced as it is now. O'Brien's other duty was to warn Tim Molony or any other jockey who would ride the horse. 'I told him exactly what the vet had said. But Tim was a very brave man. He just laughed and said he wasn't worried. He had heard that kind of diagnosis before!'

Knock Hard therefore set off for Cheltenham in the early spring of 1953 to contest his second Gold Cup with some peculiar qualifications: he did not enjoy jumping, an activity somewhat necessary for any steeplechaser, let alone one attempting the Classic; and he was allegedly suffering from a bad heart. For the race, the ground was fast and the weather foggy. Rose Park, Mont Tremblant and Galloway Braes loomed out of the mist together down the hill; Knock Hard was a long way back and seemed to be struggling. It would have occurred to any jockey with a trace of caution that this horse with a bad heart might be feeling it and be on the point of collapsing. Not so the heroic Molony. 'Tim was at him, driving him, kicking him, pushing him all the way,' Vincent recalls clearly. 'Then he jumped the last like that' – his hands sail smoothly up and down – 'and he was up the hill and away – once he saw there was no obstacle ahead of him.' That renowned final acceleration again burst like a rocket. Knock Hard was at the post an amazing five lengths ahead of Halloween; Galloway Braes was third again, and the 1952 winner Mont Tremblant was fourth.

That race was the zenith of Knock Hard's erratic but dazzling career over fences – the brilliant chaser who could win over distances between one mile and two miles on the flat.

Knock Hard ran over seven seasons, mixing flat, hurdling and chasing. He won the 1950 Irish Lincoln, and the same month, with Aubrey Brabazon riding, won the two-mile Champion Chase at Naas under 12st 5lb.

'Frankie More O'Ferrall bought Knock Hard afterwards for little money, taking a chance on him,' Vincent says, 'but when his form began to deteriorate I felt we'd better not persevere with him. There was a girl in the north of England who'd been over here a couple of times, Lord Scarborough's daughter, Lady Lily Serena Lumley. I said to Frankie, "How about giving her the horse to hunt, for she's very keen on hunting." Frankie thought it an excellent idea. Lily Serena was fully acquainted with the vet's report on the heart. She hunted him for a couple of seasons, and by God, didn't he drop dead under her one day!' Lady Lily Serena, fortunately, was shaken but uninjured.

CHAPTER 4

BALLYDOYLE

'We had to make gaps in all the fences'

By 1950 Vincent had decided to set up a new training establishment. He wanted a permanent place of his own, rather than using the stables and gallops of his eldest half-brother Donal. It was not as though he was planning a complete switch to flat racing; he was already running and winning with many flat racehorses. Plainly, though, he was thinking ahead, for a stable of classy horses to win the rich prizes on the flat. Dermot, Vincent's constant companion and support, says, 'We must have looked at twenty-five farms in Kildare, Limerick and Tipperary.' They certainly spent a great deal of time and energy in finding a place that would be suitable for training top-class horses.

Vincent chose Ballydoyle in Co. Tipperary, an ordinary farm of 285 acres in rolling countryside ringed by mountains and with plenty of uphill ground on which to work the horses. The farm, which cost £17,000, lay north-east of Churchtown, the other side of the Galtee and Ballyhoura mountains, beside the village of Rosegreen. It had belonged to an auctioneer,

Mr Sadler, who had lived there for many years with his wife and six daughters. Mrs Sadler was an invalid who lived in a room downstairs that later became the drawing room; she had a mirror positioned so that she could see the comings and goings outside. Every time Mr Sadler had a good sale they planted a copper beech in the garden. The garden is still famous for its copper beeches.

'It took a year or so to be ready to train horses there,' Vincent recalls. 'First we had to make gaps in all the fences for the horses to work. The fields averaged twelve to fourteen acres with, between them, substantial banks with stone wall facings and hedges on top. Quite a job to start; I don't think I'd like to attempt to do it again! All this was carried out in the days of shovels and muscle – no power-assisted machinery to make the work faster or easier. Phonsie stayed in Tipperary supervising the construction, which was done by John A.Wood from Cork, owner of many of my National Hunt horses, including Lucky Dome.' Vincent and Dermot moved in with the horses after the end of Cheltenham week in 1951. The Cheltenham runners went straight to their new home in Ballydoyle.

But the most influential thread in a man's life is not one that ties him to land, but which, for good or ill, binds him to a woman, and long are the coincidences as a result of which Vincent O'Brien from Co. Cork met Jacqueline Wittenoom from Perth, Western Australia.

Ireland might seem an unusual country for an academic young girl of twenty-two years – after university and a scholarship studying industrial relations she worked as an economist – to visit in Europe, but Jacqueline, whose father was an Australian MP, had Irish relations in Belfast. Moreover,

Ireland in the immediate post-war years was a happy-go-lucky, well-fed, party-going place to be. Britain, greatly weakened by the war, was still suffering with rationing and high taxation, and the Dublin Horse Show week in early August was, in those days, invaded by British debs and their 'deb's delights' – young men passed as suitable by mothers and chaperones. The young were intent on attending seven hunt balls in five nights and behaving wildly in the beautiful Georgian houses still flourishing in a land that, to visitors from Britain, seemed a booming, beaming, carefree and prosperous place. Visits were a joy.

Her great-great-grandfather the Rev. J. B. Wittenoom, Jacqueline explains, 'was the first chaplain of the Western Australian colony. His wife, to whom he was deeply attached, had died suddenly in England. He then applied for and was given the job of chaplain to the new colony founded in 1829. With his sister and four sons he sailed for five months from Southampton to reach Fremantle, Western Australia. The chaplain built the first church and school, with his sister acting as bricklayer's mate.' In St George's Cathedral, Perth a plaque erected after his death reads: 'The Rev. John Burdett Wittenoom, who for a quarter of a century discharged the sacred functions of Chaplain to this Territory . . . and under whose ministry, amidst the struggles and privations of an infant Colony, a scion of the Church of England was planted in a remote wilderness. This tablet has been erected by members of the flock of which he was so long the respected Pastor.' To her amazement, only in 2005 did Jacqueline discover that an Australian relative, after many years in the bush, had returned to his birthplace, Fethard, Co. Tipperary, in the 1880s and had owned and died in the property Coolmore, which Vincent would later purchase. It is now the home of their daughter Sue and John Magnier, and the base of the bloodstock empire which Vincent, John Magnier and Robert Sangster built.

Jacqueline's introduction to Vincent came through the hands of a notable Irish character, Waring Willis, who rode in races as an amateur with success, bred a few, trained a few, and sold several good jumping horses. Vincent takes up the story. 'I left Ballydoyle one afternoon to go to Dublin, for racing the following day at the Curragh. I dropped in at the Russell Hotel, intending to have a quick meal to get to bed early and do some work next morning, before going racing. But while I was having a drink in the Russell before my meal, Waring Willis, a great friend I'd known for many years, came in with Gerry Annesley from Castlewellen in County Down, and they had this girl with them. They introduced me to the girl and asked me to have a drink. I said, "Well, I'm just going to have a meal," but they persuaded me to have a drink. Then they persuaded me to have dinner with them. And during dinner I just started to look at this girl . . .

'After dinner we went across to the Shelbourne Hotel. Waring wasn't feeling too well – I think he'd had a succession of late nights – and he went to bed rather early. So did Gerry Annesley, and I got talking to the girl . . . I asked her if she'd like to come racing next day at the Curragh, and I said I'd pick her up at the Shelbourne at a certain time. I came round but I found that Waring Willis was right back in the picture again! However, she came racing with me. After racing, we went across the Curragh and had drinks with Aubrey Brabazon . . . and it went on from there. That was May [1951] and she was going back to Australia on the fourth of July. I had to think pretty fast. I'd not much time.'

Jacqueline remembers, 'I must have been very taken with Vincent, but I felt it was all too much of a rush. We said good-bye and I set off for England where I was going to be presented at Court, as was the custom for young ladies from the far-flung colonies, and then, from Southampton, to take the boat to Australia.' Vincent hurried after her and proposed in the Park Lane Hotel, where Jacqueline was staying. Jacqueline accepted. They returned to Dublin and they celebrated their engagement at Jamet's, the top restaurant in Dublin at the time, over strawberries and cream.

She arrived in Perth with an engagement ring and had to tell her family that she would be returning to Ireland. 'I was quite frightened at the thought of leaving my family and friends,' Jacqueline recalls, 'especially as there was no air travel at that time; the trip to Perth took about four weeks by boat, and berths were scarce. Now that it's easy to fly, we spend part of each year in Australia. And breaking the news to my father was a little daunting as he wasn't too pleased with horse trainers. As an MP, several years earlier he had decided he should have a race-horse because it would win him more votes. The horse was called St Paddy, and the first time out he streaked thirty lengths in front and dropped dead of dope. My father was furious. So I told him I was going to marry an Irish farmer!

'As children, my brother and I spent part of the year on our sheep station of 250,000 acres of red-earthed, rough, dry scrubland near Yalgoo in the Murchison district of Western Australia. We were twenty miles from the nearest neighbour and did our lessons by correspondence. Surprisingly, the sheep produced top-quality merino wool. My father was very knowledgeable about them. To the end of his life he remained astonished that the rich green pastures of Ireland would carry only ten sheep to the acre, even though ours back home needed about twenty acres per sheep.'

The engagement was announced in August 1951, and Vincent and Jacqueline were married on 29 December in the University Church, Dublin, with the reception, suitably, in the Shelbourne Hotel. More than half a century on Vincent recalls, 'That afternoon when I set off for Dublin and met Jacqueline for the first time, I had originally intended to turn right out of the gate and go south to Waterford to meet a girl with green eyes who I had been seeing. Something made me turn around and head north for Dublin!'

Before her marriage, Jacqueline had had nothing to do with racing, and all her relations, friends and contacts lay on the far side of the world. A trainer's wife at any level of the game can ease, speed, handicap or sabotage his prospects. Like a husband-and-wife team running a pub or corner shop, a trainer and his consort must work in complementary harmony to prosper. A surly wife loses owners and irritates the staff; a good one removes all the necessary social duties of a trainer's toil. 'It was different to anything I had known before,' Jacqueline says. 'We had spent part of our honeymoon in France walking racetracks as Vincent wanted to see what the steeplechase tracks were like. The first year we were married, we slept from one room to another with gaping holes in the floorboards while the house was modernized, and heating was put in, but we stayed there because Vincent wanted to be near the horses. The furnishings were modest and the dining room and drawing room curtains were the same, made by me from a large roll of chintz bought at a sale.'

Jacqueline now plays an increasingly important role in the story. She watched – 'with hands trembling so much I couldn't hold my binoculars' – Knock Hard win the Great Yorkshire at Doncaster. Her first National Hunt Meeting at Cheltenham saw old Hatton's Grace's swan-song, the fall of Knock Hard in the Gold Cup and the rise of Royal Tan, whose second Grand National loomed. What did she do to help Vincent? 'Well, just about everything,' Vincent declares. 'So far as my personal work's concerned, she was of the greatest help. I'm always glad to be able to consult her. It doesn't take her long to get to grips with whatever the trouble is and to help me out with it. She's been of tremendous assistance in my life.' 'At Ballydoyle,' Jacqueline says, 'I was partially secretary, partially cook, partially anything that needed doing. We didn't have any spare people; it wasn't a smart set-up with people delegating from one to another. It was very much a home affair, like most National Hunt operations were in those days. We had one person in the office, Dick Rogers, who was secretary for a long time, and he did everything – accounts, telephone, entries and forfeits – and I helped. Vincent and I did most of the letters together. Later Denis Hickey became racing secretary and stayed with Vincent for 25 years. Out of the confusion on his desk he performed astonishing miracles of efficiency. If Vincent wasn't there, I would look at the horses with the vet and take notes so that I could tell him the situation as soon as he arrived back. It was a much smaller operation – about twenty people, and around forty horses – and everybody helped.

'But I found my complete ignorance of horses a handicap when looking after Vincent's clients. On my first visit to Ballydoyle just after Vincent had moved in, he left me sitting in the only furnished room and vanished for hours. There was obviously a problem in the yard. Geoffrey Gilbey, a senior and rather crusty racing correspondent, arrived on a visit to look at Cottage Rake. After we had discussed everything possible and the time of his train departure drew ever nearer, I decided to take him into the yard and show him Cottage Rake. I thought I knew where his stable was. Geoffrey wrote later that he was surprised how different the horse looked on and off the racecourse!'

'In the beginning it took a lot of work to get Ballydoyle into shape,' says Jacqueline. 'I went racing often with Vincent, but on arrival at the racecourse he would disappear into the weigh room and arrange to meet me after our last race. Knowing hardly anyone, I found the periods between races interminable, and in the uncomfortable racecourses of those days there was nowhere for a lone person to sit. Race meetings then were quite lonely. I have always tried hard since to look after visitors who are strangers to a racecourse.'

CHAPTER 5

EARLY MIST AND ROYAL TAN

'He wasn't a jumper as such ...'

The first of Vincent's three Grand National winners, Early Mist, came just after his marriage in 1951. Early Mist's previous owner was Jimmy Rank, the millionaire miller whose dream was to win the Epsom Derby, the Grand National and the coursing Waterloo Cup. He won none of them before his death in 1952, and all his horses were sold. Early Mist cost 625 guineas as a yearling and had won six of his races when J. V. Rank's executors held a total dispersal at the Curragh on the day of the Irish Derby in June 1952. The horse was described as 'a washy chestnut, but a fine, big, raking gelding'. At the sale Vincent O'Brien bought him for 5,300 guineas on behalf of Joe Griffin.

Joe Griffin was newly into racing. He had built a substantial fortune after the war by adding dried fruit to sweetened fat, so that it became 'mincemeat', and therefore avoided the strict regulations on the importation of fruit into the United Kingdom – hence his nickname, 'Mincemeat Joe'. When Vincent told Joe that Early Mist could win the 1953 Grand National, Griffin went and backed the horse to win £100,000 in two bets with English bookmakers, Wilf Sherman and Jack Swift. Swift framed his pay-out cheque and hung it in his office; but before the year was out, it was said that Joe owed him £56,000.

'Early Mist wasn't altogether an easy horse to train,' Vincent reflects, with typical understatement. 'After coming to me he gave trouble with a splint, which was so bad that it appeared on both sides of his cannon bone, affecting the inside and the outside of his foreleg. So he had to be fired for it on both sides of the leg, which was most unusual. A splint is usually one-sided; it appears as a bony enlargement either on the outside of the cannon bone or on the inside, but not on both. Any rate, [vet] Bob Griffin pin-fired him and did a first-rate job, and I was able to train him for the 1953 National.'

Early Mist's struggle back to fitness just fitted Vincent's tight timetable, but it did not impress observers. On 7 February that year, Early Mist reappeared in a handicap hurdle at Leopardstown, but he blew up and, finished, tailed off. After running in the Ballydoyle Handicap Chase he went to Naas, where he was so tired that, although he finished first, he staggered across Southern Coup and was disqualified. Racing journalist Tim Vigors wrote, 'For eighteen months I opposed Vincent's confidence in his ability to win the Gold Cup with Knock Hard, so it is with some hesitation that I decry the chances of his two Grand National candidates.' Tim Vigors was Vincent's great friend. He had flown with the RAF in the Battle of Britain, and his narrow escapes were as legendary as his bravery. When asked why he thought he had survived when so many of his comrades had been killed in combat, he gave an intriguing explanation: he had flown as an Irish neutral and had the Irish tricolour painted on his Spitfire. He was deeply proud of being Irish. His family had owned large estates in Co. Carlow for centuries. 'If I'd been fighting over the green fields of my Ireland,' he said, 'I'd probably have been killed, because I'd have taken even more unnecessary risks.' On 19 June 1940, after returning from a night out somewhat the worse for wear, Tim took to the air in response to the scramble signal. Still wearing his scarlet pyjamas under a green silk dressing gown, he shot down his second Heinkel.

Vincent chose Bryan Marshall to ride Early Mist. Bryan won his first race on the flat when he was just thirteen. Brave and tough, he was commissioned in the 5th Royal Enniskillen Dragoon Guards, the 'Skins', and survived a sniper's bullet through his neck at Dunkirk. But he broke his jaw in three places at Kempton the Saturday before Cheltenham so was not able to ride at the meeting. With the National only three weeks away he was worried Vincent would think he wasn't fit to ride Early Mist. 'So I begged an easy old ride from Fulke Walwyn at Hurst Park the weekend after Cheltenham to show Vincent I was still capable,' Bryan said. To keep his jaw stable he rode in the National with a head sling and two hooks that clipped under each side of his mouth.

Vincent felt that Early Mist was not a natural jumper. Bryan suited him well as he liked to gather his horse at each fence and ask him to jump. 'Early Mist, who had fallen at the first fence the year before, jumped well for Bryan, obeying his instructions,' Vincent recalls. 'At Valentine's he took off a bit far back, but he made it all right. And he brushed the last. But he still went on and won by twenty lengths.' Surprisingly for one of Vincent's horses, Early Mist won at 20–1, carrying

11st 2lb, against Mont Tremblant's brutal burden of 12st 5lb.
Irish Lizard was third. 'Early Mist made several blunders
during the race,' says Vincent, tapping his forehead, 'because
he didn't have it up there. But he did have speed. He wasn't a
jumper as such.' This is a remarkable statement to make about
a very easy winner of Britain's most difficult steeplechase. But
Vincent is firm. 'He had a bit of class, and of my three Grand
National winners, if one was to win a Gold Cup, it would have
been him.'

Early Mist did run in the Cheltenham Gold Cup, two years
later. Ridden again by Bryan Marshall and strongly fancied by
the Irish, he started at 5–1, and finished fourth. After snow,
then frost, then thaw, the ground grew glutinous and the race
went to the 33–1 shot Gay Donald, who won with sauntering
ease at the longest price ever then recorded for the race. But
Early Mist's training had suffered further interruptions. He
developed a splint which might have left him crippled, and
he then had trouble with his feet.

Jacqueline listened to Vincent's first Grand National win on
a radio in Dublin with Moya Keogh, owner of Hatton's Grace.
'Before Early Mist had reached the winning post,' she says, 'we
headed for the airport. Planes were few in those days, but
we caught a small one, the first that went in the Liverpool
direction. We reached the celebration dinner in the Adelphi
Hotel banqueting room not quite in time for the first course,
but we enjoyed the dessert and speeches. No-one knew we
were coming. The decorations were in Joe Griffin's lively
colours. Red, blue and yellow streamers billowed over the giant
chocolate horse on the main table. Two hundred guests had
been gathered – not difficult in those days of slow travel, as

most of the Irish attending the Aintree meeting stayed at the Adelphi.'

Their return home was to an extraordinary reception. 'We all came back from Liverpool by ferry to Dun Laoghaire to be met by three hundred employees from Joe's firm, Red Breast Preserving Co., and a band,' Jacqueline continues. 'Then Early Mist was put into a horsebox and walked down Dublin's O'Connell Street where he was followed by a fleet of the firm's lorries decked with red, blue and yellow streamers, hooting cars, messenger boys on bicycles, staff from the Griffin factories, and cheering crowds on foot. This ended with a reception by the Lord and Lady Mayoress, Senator and Mrs Larkin, at the Mansion House.'

In Cashel that evening bonfires blazed from the ancient Rock, lit up for the occasion. The houses were decorated with the national tricolour, red, blue and yellow bunting, and messages of congratulations. The town was awash with rain mingled with the froth of the barrels of free porter. The Christian Brothers' Flagelot Band and the Bansha Boys Pipe Band played the procession into the town, and the local TD, Michael Davern, welcomed Vincent on behalf of the citizens from the balcony above his pub. There was great cheering. In those days Irish victories in England were rare and the cause for great celebration.

John Stapleton, Early Mist's faithful lad who had shared the magnificent triumph at Aintree and the celebrations, did not leave his charge until he was back in his stable, No. 18 at Ballydoyle.

In 1953, Vincent topped the National Hunt list in England, and the year yielded an astonishing treble: he won the Gold

Cup with Knock Hard, the Grand National with Early Mist and then the Irish Derby with Chamier. Chamier, owned by the Vickermans, won on an objection against Premonition, trained by the imposing Captain Cecil Boyd-Rochfort, later Sir Cecil, trainer for royalty and grandees, who was so incensed at losing that he hired the cinema in Newmarket to show his friends a newsreel of the race; it was, however, not the one seen by the Stewards.

* * *

Vincent's second Grand National winner, Royal Tan, was bred fewer than two miles from Ballydoyle, as Vincent recalls. 'He was bred by the Tophams, an old hunting family from Tullamaine, close to Ballydoyle. Tim Hyde senior bought him and trained him for Ben Dunne together with Des Darragh, who'd been his partner in the earliest Dunne's Store. Harry Keogh, owner of Knock Hard, wanted a horse to follow in the footsteps of Castledermot, who'd won the National Hunt Chase at Cheltenham in 1949.' The Keoghs bought Royal Tan and the horse won his novice chases, progressed the next year to handicaps, 'and then,' says Phonsie, 'he ran in the Irish National, giving away 23lb to Icy Calm, and in the English National of 1951. I rode him in both races and was second in each. All in the space of ten days.'

At Aintree that year the heavily backed seven-year-old Royal Tan faced a field of thirty-six runners. He had been flown from Dublin to Liverpool for the race – a most unusual step then. It was the year of disasters. Thirty-four of the field failed to get round after a dreadfully ill-timed start which caught many of the riders off their guard and caused havoc at the first fence.

Two survivors came to the second-last together. As they landed, Phonsie called across to Johnny Bullock, 'What's that you're riding?'

Little Johnny shouted back, 'Nickel Coin.'

'Well, I think I've got you cooked,' cried Phonsie, and on they strode to the last fence.

'At the last,' Phonsie continues, 'Royal Tan was a stride in front. But he hit the top and he went down and down. Right down so that his nose got to one and a half inches off the ground.' With balance and strength, Phonsie stuck to the horse, but his chance of winning was gone. He followed Nickel Coin home, beaten six lengths by the 40–1 mare; the O'Brien camp was sure that, barring that last-fence blunder, they would have won the duel. Vincent recalls, 'Royal Tan was a brilliant jumper. My brother gave him a kick with his heels coming to the last, and the horse seemed to resent it. I think it's true to say that he did not want to be told how and when to jump! Royal Tan made a mess of the fence and he was on the ground literally. But by some extraordinary effort he got back on his legs again and my brother was still on his back – a truly incredible performance on his part.'

Of his instructions from Vincent, Phonsie jokes, 'When I rode for Vincent, I was like 007! He'd write down the instructions and almost say, "When you've read this, swallow it!" Every occasion they read: "under no circumstances jump the last fence in front".' Vincent felt the run-in was very long, and the horse would be in front for too long, but Phonsie, with hindsight, maintains that if he had gone on the horse might not have made the error.

After Royal Tan's dramatic and expensive disappointment

at Liverpool's last fence in 1951, he was still qualified to run in a two-mile 'bumper' flat race at humble Listowel in October. Phonsie again rode Royal Tan. 'And I think Vincent had a sizeable, oh a very sizeable bet in view of losing so much on the horse before. And I happened to scrape home on him by a neck. It was a lot more difficult than we thought it'd be, I can tell you.'

Royal Tan was to go to Cheltenham in the autumn of 1951 to run in the three-mile Cowley Novices Hurdle. It was Vincent's policy to run his National horses in hurdle races after Liverpool as he hoped this would make them forget about the stiff fences. Royal Tan made the crossing from Waterford to Fishguard but refused to get off the boat. Phonsie recalls, 'It took the man in charge a hell of a time, at least an hour, to get him to step off the boat. No way did Royal Tan want to land in England after what had happened to him in the Grand National.'

Phonsie O'Brien had some horrible minutes during that Cheltenham hurdle race. 'The most terrifying race I've ever ridden in my lifetime,' he says. 'About twenty-eight runners, and there was a grey horse that fell early on. We met him coming towards us on the second circuit, really galloping at us! People were terrified. Bad enough meeting a hurdle at speed, but you meet another horse rushing towards you ... Anyway, we avoided him and went on and won easily. Royal Tan was a thinking horse. We always had lots of problems with him in the saddling stalls on racetracks. After his first National he would never walk out of a saddling stall once you'd put the saddle on. You had to get on his back in the stall and ride him out.'

That last fence proved disastrous to Royal Tan again in the 1952 Grand National. 'He came to the last again,' says Vincent,

'Phonsie again riding him, lying third. I don't know whether Phonsie gave the horse a kick or not. He was very close behind the leading pair, and the horse made the same mistake, only perhaps a little worse, and that was that.' Although Royal Tan was right on the ground he never toppled over. He got back onto his feet again from an impossible position, but Phonsie came off. Phonsie would often say, 'Royal Tan didn't have only four legs. He must have had six!' The race was won by Teal.

In those days O'Brien's jumpers were schooled up the gentle slope which lies on the right-hand side of the drive to Ballydoyle House. Phonsie and the lads with tweed caps turned back to front would school the jumpers up the hill. Royal Tan would never go down unless he had a lead, and something else. 'All you had to do,' Phonsie fondly remembers, 'was to tap him down the mane with a little stick. Just stroke him down the mane. That's all, and he'd go anywhere you'd want him to go. But if you put a guy on him who started kicking and driving him, he'd stand straight up on his hind legs and go nowhere.' T. P. Burns, who rode Royal Tan in hurdle races, says of him, 'He was a typical Liverpool horse with a lovely, kind and generous look. Not too heavily built, and a long-backed horse. He was a real character schooling at home. If you asked him to jump he'd bloody kill you.'

Leg trouble kept Royal Tan off the racecourse during the 1952/53 season giving Early Mist the opportunity to win the 1953 Grand National for Vincent. Bob Griffin, the vet, and Vincent had a struggle to repair Royal Tan's damaged tendon. Then, in the summer of 1952, the horse developed splints as well, described by Vincent as 'more than usually troublesome'. Royal Tan was therefore off the course from the spring of 1952 until he ran in a hurdle race at Limerick more than one and a half years later, in October 1953. In addition, and at an advanced age, Royal Tan developed sore shins, an inflammation of the membrane between the skin and the cannon bone to which delicate two-year-olds are often subject. 'I should think,' jokes Dermot O'Brien, 'he should be in the *Guinness Book of Records* for getting sore shins as old as he did.' The maddening complaint makes it extremely painful for a horse to stride out, let alone jump. It holds up training until the inflammation disperses and the membrane hardens.

With Early Mist sidelined for the 1954 Grand National, a replacement was waiting in the wings. The Keoghs were anxious to sell Royal Tan and Vincent advised Joe Griffin to buy him as a National prospect. Bryan Marshall had won on Early Mist the previous year so it followed that he took the ride on Royal Tan. 'Bryan had been riding him in his prep races for the National,' says Vincent, 'but somehow he wasn't getting along with the horse.' He adds, again with typical understatement, 'We were getting quite concerned about it.' (Vincent has always shown almost no emotion in either victory or defeat – 'I don't believe it's the thing to do.') 'In Royal Tan's race in Ireland before the Grand National, the Thyestes Chase at Gowran Park in January 1954, Bryan rode him,' Vincent continues. 'Going into the open ditch second time round, Bryan picked him up approaching it and gave him a couple of kicks. Well, the horse simply left Bryan sitting on his backside on the landing side of the fence. Bryan was big enough to say when he came in, "Well, he got rid of me . . ." We were more worried than ever.'

Time was fast running out; the horse's timetable had, as

usual with Vincent, been carefully planned. Surely it was too late for a change of jockey? Yet for sure the horse would blunder if you tried to master him; Bryan Marshall, after years of forceful riding, was unlikely to change his style. 'Then,' says Vincent, 'my brother Phonsie, who had been riding the horse and knew so much about him, said, "Why not just tell Bryan to sit still on the horse and leave him be?" So I got permission from Gowran Park to take Royal Tan to school after racing between that meeting and the National. I asked Bryan to come over and told him to leave the horse alone at his fences.' During that day's schooling, carried away with excitement as he passed the stands where some friends were watching, Bryan gave Royal Tan a show-off kick as the horse thundered down on the third fence. 'He nearly came down,' Marshall said with a grimace, 'then up came his neck again and smashes me in the nose!' To O'Brien's firm instructions was now added the horse's own painful lesson. For the rest of the schooling session Marshall sat as still as a mouse, and Royal Tan jumped perfectly. Vincent remembers happily, 'Bryan came back with a grin from ear to ear and said, "Now I've got it."'

After Gowran Park, with Bryan riding him, he was unplaced in a two-mile-one-furlong handicap chase at Baldoyle, and then he went to Cheltenham to finish second in the three-mile National Hunt Handicap Chase, ridden by Pat Taaffe. That Cheltenham handicap chase was Royal Tan's last race, two weeks before the Grand National, and an excellent portent for Liverpool. Still, in view of Royal Tan's unhappy memories of the Aintree track, Vincent separated the horse from his four other runners at the 1954 Grand National meeting and sent him to be stabled twenty miles away from the scene, in the peace of the deserted racecourse stables at Haydock Park. Royal Tan's psychological as well as his physical disabilities had to be overcome.

Bryan Marshall started Royal Tan on the wide outside and held him up until he was nearly last. This was directly opposed to contemporary tactics which held that, due to the risk of fallers, you should jump the first four fences as close to the front as possible. On the second circuit, in poor visibility, Royal Tan could be glimpsed steadily picking his way through the fallers (twenty starters failed to finish) and making his way up to the vanguard, jumping magnificently. He was in front between the last two fences – 'Bryan did go on,' says Phonsie, 'in spite of the instructions.' And he jumped his bogey fence perfectly; it was his challenger Tudor Line who screwed at the last. Royal Tan fought off Tudor Line's long, strong challenge all the way up the run-in to hold on by a neck. Irish Lizard, favourite at 15–2, was third. Only five of the twenty-nine runners completed the course.

It was one of the most exciting Nationals ever seen. One sports writer declared, 'The titanic struggle between the two chestnut horses over the last quarter of a mile was racing drama unsurpassed.' Another turf historian pronounced, 'Not since Battleship and Royal Danieli in 1938 had such a grim tussle has there been such a finish.' One paper rightly commented later, 'Vincent dispelled the belief that had persisted so long in the world of racing, that Ireland is the only place to breed racehorses and that England is the place to train them.'

When Joe Griffin went bankrupt in 1954, Prince Aly Khan bought Royal Tan at the disposal sale, and it was in the colours of this dashing gentleman that Toss Taaffe, Vincent's jockey, rode the old horse, then twelve and carrying 12st 1lb, to third in the 1956 Grand National. He put up a very good performance to be beaten ten lengths by ESB (11st 3lb) and Gentle Moya (10st 2lb). But it was the mysterious collapse of the Queen Mother's Devon Loch, clear in front on the run-in and passing the water jump, within sight of the winning post, which filled the minds and still puzzles the memories of all observers. A horrified silence fell on the gigantic crowd. It was as if the horse had been shot.

Between 1951 and 1956 Royal Tan ran in the Grand National five times and was first, second and third. Prince Aly Khan retired him and gave him to the Duchess of Devonshire, at whose family property, Lismore Castle on the Blackwater, she would occasionally hack out the famous old horse. The Grand National hero who always insisted that things were done his way enjoyed his retirement. But he was inclined to stop dead with the duchess in Lismore town. She asked Vincent to come and ride the horse through the streets and see what the problem was. Vincent was very nervous, terrified he might be dropped in the middle of Lismore, but all went well. Vincent advised 'Debbo' to do as the horse pleased and avoid the town.

Comparing his first two Grand National winners, Vincent says, 'Royal Tan was a brilliant natural jumper, so clever. He was like a cat, and all his jockey had to do was to sit on him. Early Mist was exactly the opposite and needed assistance from his jockey. He was the classier of the two.'

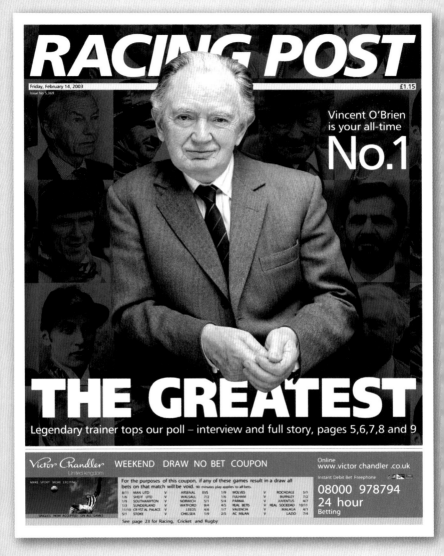

The votes are all in and counted.

ABOVE RIGHT: *The Boss, as he was known.*
ABOVE LEFT: *Vincent's parents, Kathleen and Dan.*
FROM LEFT TO RIGHT: *Vincent, Dermot, mother Kathleen, Pauline.*

Vincent outside the front door, riding the donkey as if landing over a big drop.

ABOVE: *Cottage Rake and Aubrey leading to win their third Cheltenham Gold Cup.*

RIGHT: *Father Dan and Jimmy Canty congratulate each other after the Irish Cesarewitch, 1941.*

LEFT: *Vincent rides his first winner at Limerick in November 1940 – his father's home-trained Hallowment.*

RIGHT: *Vincent with brother Dermot, his friend, aide and assistant trainer for so many years.*

BELOW: *National Spirit stumbles and allows Hatton's Grace to race on and win his third Champion Hurdle victory.*

FROM LEFT TO RIGHT: *Dermot, Vincent and Jacqueline, Phonsie, Evie Magnier (mother of John), Ann (later Phonsie's wife), Wendy Hall, Anthony Fogarty.*

ABOVE: *Early Mist (Bryan Marshall) has won the 1953 Grand National. Head man Maurice O'Callaghan leaps with joy. Owner Joe Griffin leads in his winner, followed by his brother. Vincent, unusually showing delight, on the right.*

LEFT: *'The Liverpool feat of all time': Three different Grand National winners in three consecutive years. Vincent carries Liz and holds Early Mist (left) and Royal Tan. Jacqueline has Sue on her arm and Quare Times on her left.*

Royal Tan (B. Marshall) just beating
Tudor Line for the 1954 Grand National.
Two chestnuts, two white blazes, inches
apart at the finish after 4½ miles.

Phonsie O'Brien on Royal Tan amazingly did not fall at the last fence
but got up to finish second to Nickel Coin, a 40-1 shot.

CHAPTER 6

SCANDAL

'I assumed the inquiry was a routine matter'

O n 28 March 1954, Vincent returned from a victorious Aintree meeting with his four winners: Royal Tan (Grand National), Stroller (the Coronation Hurdle), Evian (the Mildmay Chase) and Galatian (the Liverpool Hurdle). It was a great triumph. The homecoming was exuberant, with fireworks, speeches, receptions and parades. 'The Irish,' Jacqueline O'Brien remembers, 'went just delirious.'

But Vincent had been summoned to attend a Stewards' Inquiry five days later into the allegedly inconsistent running of four of his horses over the past two seasons. These were Royal Tan, Lucky Dome, Early Mist and Knock Hard. Galatian was originally listed too, but the Stewards later said they did not want to include him. 'I assumed the inquiry was a routine matter,' Vincent relates, 'and I considered that the explanations I would give the Stewards were so conclusive that I could not even be cautioned.'

His expectations were not realized. After the inquiry the

verdict was 'that the Stewards of the INHS Committee could not accept Mr M. V. O'Brien's explanations and when considering what action to take on these findings the Stewards had before them the fact that Mr M. V. O'Brien had been warned and cautioned on several occasions as to the running of his horses.' The Stewards, under Rule 16(II) and 104(VII), withdrew his licence to train for three calendar months from 2 April 1954. Vincent released a statement: 'I am completely in the dark as to what, if any, offence I am alleged to have been guilty of. No suggestion was made against the manner in which the horses were ridden in any of their races. In fact, no specific charge of any kind in respect of the running of any horses in any of their races has been made.'

Vincent was shocked beyond belief, but he had been aware for some months that there was ill feeling towards him from Judge Wylie, the senior flat racing Steward. Wylie had arranged that the Stewards of the Turf Club (the body that controls flat racing in Ireland) sat in with the National Hunt Stewards on this inquiry. The stewards were Mr P. Molony (chair), Mr G. V. Malcolmson and Lord Fingal, who administered the rules under the INHS; and Judge Wylie, Sir Cecil King Harman and Major Dermot McCalmont for the Turf Club. Wylie ran the meeting from the start, despite the fact that Pierce Molony was in the chair. Vincent's feelings on the matter are best given in his own words, exactly from the notes that he made before, during and after the inquiry.

> *The charge against me was that four horses ran inconsistently.*
>
> *Inconsistent running is not an offence. A horse is*

not a machine and may run inconsistently without blame to anyone, as all owners and trainers know.

Atty Persse said that if he only backed 'the certainties' in his own stable he would be bankrupt. [Persse, a tremendous punter, was Irish, but trained in England with great success into his eighties. He had three Royal Ascot winners in 1951.]

A trainer becomes culpable if he deliberately causes his horses to run inconsistently by

1 *Stopping them during a race. Here, he must have the co-operation of his jockey.*

2 *Running them unfit.*

3 *Administering some stimulant or deterrent to affect the horse's speed during a race.*

A trainer is not to blame if a horse runs inconsistently due to natural causes outside his control, e.g. bad jumping due to a fright.

If a horse runs badly and is not backed, and shortly afterwards runs well, backed, it seems to be assumed that the trainer or jockey has deliberately stopped the horse. It is just as likely that a trainer will back a horse after a bad run if he feels that for some reason or another the first race did not show the horse's true form, e.g. distance may have been too short, going unsuitable, also pace. These factors are perfectly visible to the racing public.

'Over many years,' Jacqueline points out, 'one of the most surprising things I have found is that Vincent will watch two or three of his horses doing a final piece of work which has gone badly wrong, as work frequently does, and yet draw a quite different conclusion from everyone else watching.'

Vincent continues, 'As there had never been any suggestion to me that I was administering anything to affect the horses' speed, and no questions had ever been asked me by local stewards regarding the running or behaviour of my horses on the days any of the four horses ran, I prepared my case on the basis that the issues were to do with stopping the horses during the race, or racing them unfit. The English Stewards must have been satisfied with the English running or they would have made inquiries on the spot. It was only after the inquiry that I realized there was no suggestion that jockeys had stopped these horses or that the horses had run unfit. Therefore the Stewards' case had to be that I had been able to control the running of my horses in some mysterious fashion. It is very hard to disprove something that is not even hinted at except in a negative way, especially when no questions were asked on the days the horses ran. This would have given me some chance to have the saliva of the runners tested.' Vincent points out that urine or blood testing was not done at that time.

Vincent's notes go on to address each horse separately, and he considers that they explain the differences in the horses' performances. Leading up to an important objective, it is frequently difficult to find races that are suitable.

LUCKY DOME

Comparison of the two races the Stewards were questioning:

1. Completely different types of races – one a two-mile hurdle race at Baldoyle, the other a three-mile hurdle race at Cheltenham. Lucky Dome is a horse that is a proven stayer.
2. Difference in course: Baldoyle a small, sharp track and Cheltenham big, wide galloping course for stayers.
3. Difference in going. The heavy going at Cheltenham assists a stayer.
4. Lucky Dome got a bad fright steeplechasing. The Baldoyle hurdle race was after his first steeplechase for ten months and in this he was pulled up. Remembering the fences, he jumped his hurdles slowly and was never well placed in a big field on a fast track.

I did not bet on Lucky Dome at Baldoyle because I did not give him any chance. I had my smallest bet of any of my horses on him at Cheltenham because

a) The poor race it was. This is proved by the fact that John Wylie, the handicapper and son of Judge Wylie, did not put Lucky Dome up one pound in the Irish Handicap after the Cheltenham race. He should have gone up ten pounds if it was the good race the Stipendiary Steward, Dan Bulger, tried to make it out to be.
b) The distance suited.
c) Heavy going for a horse that likes the soft.

It was rumoured that the stable had won a fortune on Lucky Dome at Cheltenham. This was not true. Bulger said he 'heard' Lucky Dome had run a good race in England but he had not 'heard' it officially.

During the course of the discussion on the bets I asked Bulger what was the source of the Stewards' information regarding these bets, and he replied, 'There is no smoke without fire.' Judge Wylie stressed that the amount of £2,500 my stable had won on Lucky Dome at Cheltenham was a very big amount. I would like to point out that it was a wrong basis to stress that amount of money won. The amount actually wagered is the important thing because it reflects the degree of my confidence in the ability of the horse. Bulger then tried to lump together both win and place bets on Lucky Dome. This also was wrong because place bets are really made as 'savers' as far as my stable is concerned. Bulger then tried to lump the owner's bet with mine in the case of Lucky Dome. This was also a wrong basis as the owner's bet was independent of mine, and in the case of the other horses the owner's bet was not taken into consideration at all. He tried to establish that with the owner's bet there was £800 on the horse whereas the total amount wagered was only £670.

I am convinced that both Judge Wylie and Mr Bulger had heard rumours and had their minds made up against me on this point.

ROYAL TAN

Stewards compared a two-mile steeplechase at Baldoyle

and three-mile steeplechase at Cheltenham. Between the races there was

1. *Difference in distance of one mile.*
2. *Difference in pace as a result.*
3. *Difference in course.*

With Royal Tan, I consider that I could have been asked for an explanation if the horse had won at Cheltenham – an explanation does not mean a warning off. At Baldoyle the race was too short and too fast for the horse to ever have a chance. The Grand National film shows that Royal Tan was nearly last for a mile in the Aintree race. If he could not keep up in a four-and-a-half-mile race he had no chance in a two-mile race. The pace upset his jumping, which was very poor at Baldoyle.

The fact that he was well beaten at Cheltenham was not noted.

I did not bet on Royal Tan at Baldoyle because he is not a betting proposition at two miles. I had a bet at Cheltenham (which I lost) because

1. *He had won this race before: liked course and the going.*
2. *More suitable distance.*
3. *On his Gowran performance he had a chance.*

EARLY MIST

Baldoyle, handicap chase, two miles, unplaced; won at Naas three-mile handicap chase.

1. *Difference of one mile in the distance of two races.*

2. *Difference in pace and course.*
3. *At Baldoyle, Early Mist was having his first outing over fences since the Grand National the previous year – ten months earlier. He jumped carefully in what Taaffe said was one of the fastest races for some time.*

Next time out he was backed because

1. *He had had a previous race over fences.*
2. *Difference of a mile in the distance.*
3. *Naas was a stayers' course for a horse that was being trained for the National.*
4. *Poor-class race.*

KNOCK HARD

Leopardstown three-mile handicap chase.

Knock Hard ran poorly at Leopardstown. I consider that this was due to the fact that he had got a bad fright at Kempton Park in the King George VI Chase and was frightened of jumping. I did not realize this and do not consider that Doyle rode him out as Molony rode him when he won at Doncaster.

'With Knock Hard,' Vincent explains, 'I gave the Stewards details of my bets, and the positive proof that I did not stop the horse was that I had the *biggest bet of the season* on him at the shortest odds. This was ignored by the Stewards, but it was proof that his running as far as I was concerned was genuine. And this was the race that Judge Wylie said he would have warned me off for and which I had already tried to explain to him.

'The Stewards' case was based on the assumption that four cases of similar inconsistent running of horses in two years cannot be a coincidence but had been caused deliberately. As Bulger stated, he was absolutely satisfied that the jockeys rode the horses out: unfitness was not an issue.

'At the inquiry there was a lengthy statement from Bulger, who said that in all the races in Ireland the horses were dead, listless or tired, whereas at English meetings from ten to fourteen days later they showed marked improvement and either won or were placed second. I maintained there were perfectly logical explanations for the form of the horses, and in this I was supported totally by jockeys and owners. It was only Bulger and Judge Wylie who argued against the form of the horses.

'The meeting was wound up and I was given the verdict as above. In my opinion it was totally unjustified, and the whole proceedings, controlled by Judge Wylie, were the result of prejudice and dislike. Even before the inquiry he was hopelessly biased against me. He had stated directly to me his desire to put me out of racing indefinitely. Judge Wylie in a telephone conversation after the inquiry said to me, "If Royal Tan had won at Cheltenham you would have been off for good. You were lucky your suspension was so short." On another occasion he sent his son John Wylie, the handicapper, to tell me that if I came up before him again he would put me off.

'The whole inquiry appeared completely lacking in integrity. Mr Pierce Molony came to see me afterwards on 7 April deeply distressed, and said that he had not realized how far the matter had been taken; nor had he seen the original copy of the official statement. He had apparently threatened to resign if the penalty had been any more severe. I consulted counsel, but under the terms of my licence agreement with the Turf Club I had no legal rights.'

The relevant *Racing Calendars* referred to reveal Vincent's previous record. He had been before the stewards six times in all between 1949 and 1953, and the worst case was hardly heinous: in 1951 there was an inquiry into the running of The Dapper, belonging to Frank Vickerman, at Listowel, after which Vincent was severely warned over the future management and running of his horses. The other five cases, for the record, were: a 1949 inquiry into the running of Alberoni (explanation accepted); an apprentice weighing out in 1952 without a surcingle (fined ten sovs); Silk Cottage late into the parade ring in 1952 (fined twenty sovs); in the same year, Vincent was blamed for putting an inexperienced apprentice on Alberoni; and in 1953 he was found to have raced Churchtown unfit. 'In 2005,' Vincent says, 're-reading my old notes, I still feel the intensity of the injustice. As for giving anything to a horse to affect his running, I never did and never would.'

In looking at that 1954 suspension, it is important to consider the attitude of some racing authorities and powers towards this extraordinarily successful young trainer. He had started in the rustic fields of Co. Cork. He had moved to a remote farm in Co. Tipperary. His good farming family had never been part of Dublin society and had nothing to do with the Anglo-Irish ascendancy. Vincent had not applied to train with 'all the other flat race trainers' on the Curragh, which was then regarded exactly as Newmarket was in England, as the official headquarters of racing. It was a centre where the authorities could 'keep an eye on young trainers'. Dermot O'Brien explains, 'Before Vincent began to make headlines training in the South it was unheard of for a trainer from there to make an impact up-country at the Curragh, Leopardstown or Phoenix Park. As the people who controlled racing, and their trainers and friends, resided up-country, jealousy was rife. They began to say he has got to be giving his horses something.' Some of these trainers and owners could not believe that Vincent could be 'that good'. He was bound to attract jealousy, particularly because his stable was so successful when it came to betting. Success in betting always generates envy and suspicion. Within ten years Vincent had won three Cheltenham Gold Cups, three Champion Hurdles, two Grand Nationals, the 1953 Irish Derby with Chamier, and innumerable other races. Hopes of putting him in his place, smouldering below the surface, had, it seemed, burst into scandalous flames.

CHAPTER 7

QUARE TIMES

'The greatest bit of training I've ever known'

After Royal Tan's victory in 1954 and before he finished third in 1956, Vincent produced his third successive winner of the Grand National in Quare Times, making it three Nationals in consecutive years with three different horses. This triumph of training was a feat which by 2006 has not been equalled.

Quare Times was bred by Phil Sweeney, a great Irish breeder living near Thurles in Co. Tipperary. 'The English,' says Vincent drily, 'used to think that the name was Latin, and some pronounced it "Quaray Timees". But in fact Quare Times was called after a famous greyhound owned by Bill Quinn of Killenaule, near the horse's birthplace.' When Quare Times was a yearling in 1947, Sweeney sent him to the Ballsbridge Sales. He was beautifully bred for jumping, and he was bought by Mrs Cecily Welman for 300 guineas. 'A goodish price for a yearling at that time,' comments Vincent. 'She gelded him and let him run out.' Mrs Welman allowed the youngster to grow and develop at her stud farm, Gaybrook, near Mullingar in Westmeath. She had the horse broken and only sent him to Vincent when he was five. Vincent shook his head and murmured to Mrs Welman, 'He will take a long, long time.' Looking back now, Vincent says, 'He had trouble with his knees, and various other leg problems which didn't make him the easiest horse in the world to train.'

Quare Times was six years old before he first ran, and in that year he was unplaced in all of his three races: on the flat, in an amateur maiden hurdle, and in a novice chase at Gowran Park. He then ran into training difficulties and could not run between November 1952 and December 1953. It was an inauspicious start, but over the winter of 1953/54 the horse's strength finally grew to match his size. Vincent had told Mrs Welman ten months ahead of the race that this horse was the right type for Cheltenham's four-mile National Hunt Chase for novices, which the stable had won in 1949 with Castledermot. 'He will win the race,' he said.

The horse won a £100 two-and-a-half-mile novice chase at Gowran Park in January 1954, and went on to Leopardstown with his Cheltenham rider, Mr Bunny Cox, on board. He was brought down in that race by a loose horse, but he was going so well at the time that he started as flaming-hot favourite at 5–2 at Cheltenham in a field of twenty-six on desperately heavy ground. He won so impressively that racegoers that day felt they had seen yet another Grand National winner for O'Brien. Bunny Cox, winning the race for the second successive year, was described by a lyrical Irish sports writer thus: 'Once again he treated the huge crowd to an exhibition of horsemanship that without doubt makes him the uncrowned king of the amateur riders.'

But Quare Times suffered a setback before the 1955

National. Vincent remembers a journalist coming to the yard 'when I didn't want to show the horse, because all was not well with him, and I didn't want it to get into the papers before the Grand National'. The problem was a bruised foot.

Quare Times was only one of four O'Brien entries that year: he had included the last two National winners, Early Mist and Royal Tan, with Oriental Way as his final entry. Jacqueline relates, 'We came to Quare Times' Grand National full of tension as the chance of a third consecutive victory was hanging in the air. Nobody mentioned the possibility,' Jacqueline says. 'Vincent had collected all four jockeys the night before the race and they had watched films of previous Nationals. His usual instructions were to keep out of trouble on the outside for the first part of the race and then make steady progress.'

After three days of almost continual rain the ground was so wet that the Grand National was in doubt. Near the water jump the ground was flooded, and at noon there was still fear that the race might be cancelled. Vincent had said after Cheltenham that he had hopes for Quare Times in the National provided the going was not heavy. The rain sluiced down from clouds so low that one Irish wit exclaimed, 'There's hardly falling space for the rain.' Jacqueline recalls that day well: 'It looked as though racing would be called off. We went early to the track and walked it to see how bad was the ground. The water jump was railed off. I am sure racing would have been abandoned but the Queen Mother and Princess Margaret were there, and royalty had not been at the National since 1950.'

Optimism about Quare Times' chances ebbed away. Early Mist, at 9–1 and again with Bryan Marshall on board, started second favourite to Copp (7–1). Poor old Royal Tan, ridden by Dave Dick, carried 12st 4lb on his eleven-year-old back. The going was so wretchedly wet that the horses stood fetlock-deep in mud and water. The jockeys, delayed at the start for six minutes by an unruly outsider, crouched miserably in the rain.

'But in Pat Taaffe,' says Vincent, 'we had the ideal combination for the horse. Quare Times was a free-galloping horse. He simply jumped over the top of all those fences. Pat rode very short for somebody as tall as he is. He sat up his neck and they got along beautifully together.' Pat's riding style had not endeared him to his father – 'Once I had the notion of breaking him out of it, but he stuck to his own way and he was right!' – and the O'Briens believe that Mr Taaffe told Pat to let down his leathers at least for the National. 'Instead,' says Jacqueline, 'I think Pat pulled them up a hole!'

It was an all-Irish victory, for Quare Times was bred, owned, trained and ridden by the Irish, and five of the first six horses home were Irish-bred. Tudor Line, beaten by O'Brien's Royal Tan the previous year, headed Quare Times over the third-last fence, Jacqueline remembers, 'But George Slack knew from the smile on Pat's face that Pat could beat him whenever he liked.' And so he did, by twelve lengths. Vincent says proudly, 'The horse never put a foot wrong and Pat won easily on him.' At the races were the jockey's mother and father and his fiancée, Molly Lyon. Pat's brother 'Toss', who was also in the race, finished third riding his father's first runner in the Grand National, Carey's Cottage. Toss was Vincent's steeplechase jockey at this time, and Vincent has happy memories of him. Riding Sam Brownthorn at Naas in January 1957 after a collision at the first fence, Toss landed with both feet on the ground, held onto the saddle and after walking a few steps vaulted back up, rodeo fashion, and was able to retrieve his irons before the next fence. Vincent remarks, marvelling, 'I never saw such an acrobatic performance on the racecourse. The Taaffe brothers certainly can ride!' Pat's son Tom, carrying on the family success story, saddled the outstanding Cheltenham Gold Cup winner Kicking King in 2005.

Quare Times returned to Dublin by boat. He was paraded through Mrs Welman's local town, Mullingar, led by two bands and rapturously escorted by several thousand local fans. 'He had two more receptions,' says Jacqueline, 'one in Thurles and one in Cashel, before Vincent finally got him back in his box at Ballydoyle. Vincent felt the receptions were more nerve-racking than the National!'

In the history of the Grand National, no other trainer has ever saddled three different winners in consecutive years. Fred Rimell's four Grand National winners, another great achieve-ment, came in 1956, 1961, 1970 and 1976, while the only other trainer to win four Nationals is Ginger McCain, most recently with Amberleigh House in 2004 and before that three with the great Red Rum. The backgrounds of Vincent's three National winners were even more remarkable, for they were all of contrasting characters and build. Even odder, the horses were all so plagued with mishaps at various stages in training that it seemed unlikely they would even get to the starting post at Liverpool, let alone win that gruelling race. It should also be remembered that the fences at Aintree in the 1950s were the fearsome, unsloped, upright, thicker obstacles which every year prevented most of the field from completing the course. Ossie Dale, who worked on the Aintree fences for thirty-five years, confirms that the fences now have been eased considerably. They are no longer upright, bushing out towards you; they are invitingly sloped away so that the horse can no longer get too close or even under them. The top twelve inches are now spruce, which can be brushed through.

Bob Griffin looked after all three winners. He had known Vincent's father, and in particular his two horses Astrometer and Astrologer. 'Those three National winners were the greatest piece of training I've ever known,' he said. 'All three gave serious trouble. All needed severe treatment. Vincent would say to me, "I'll want to canter them on a certain date, gallop them on a certain date and give them their first race on a certain date to have them in peak condition for the National. Can you do it?" I'd say, "With that time-frame, I think I can." The dates, the times they cantered or galloped, were practically to an hour. In each case the training programme was different for each horse.' The expert vet remained astonished by this for the rest of his life. 'Whenever I suggested to Vincent something would be a good idea for the horses, if he agreed, expense never mattered. Nothing ever stood in the way of what was best for the horses.'

And Griffin added a revealing light on the trainer's philosophy, possibly surprising those who believed O'Brien concentrated only on the crème de la crème. 'All through the years I've felt that Vincent always liked to think that there was good in every horse. He never discarded the horse and said, "You're no damn good." The attention he paid to the least important horse in the stable always appeared to me just the same as it was to the best.'

CHAPTER 8

BALLYMOSS AND GLADNESS

'Dear Mr McShain'

W hat sets Vincent O'Brien apart is his super-abundance of triumphs in the two branches of horseracing. Only seven years separated the last of Vincent's three consecutive Grand Nationals from the first of his six English Derbys. In the years between Quare Times winning the rain-soaked National of 1955 and little Larkspur surviving a swelling on his hind leg which kept him box-bound seven days before the 1962 Derby, Vincent swung the balance of his horses from steeplechasing to flat racing. In concentrating on flat racing he would move into the big money, in terms of prizes won and earnings from stallions he had trained. The prize money for Cottage Rake's third Cheltenham Gold Cup, in 1950, was £2,936; the first of Vincent's six English Derbys in 1962 was worth £34,786, and in jumping any residual stud earnings are rare indeed.

Vincent now required a new richer type of owner. He realized early on in his career that America was the source of tough horses of the highest class and the progeny of a huge pool of blue-blooded mares bought from England and Ireland over many years. America was also the home of owners richer by far than the now dwindling band of British and Irish aristocratic landowners who kept a diminishing circle of top-class stud-farms.

His first contact with a rich American owner came when he made the acquaintance of the master-builder millionaire John McShain of Philadelphia. Vincent says, 'I found out early in life that you have to move out and meet people; they don't come to you. With that in mind, with no orders and no-one in particular to buy for, I set out in 1955 for Tattersalls' September Sales, then held at Doncaster during the St Leger meeting. If you're in the business, you'd better be around where things are happening.'

O'Brien's contact in Doncaster was a Yorkshire solicitor, Hedley Nicholson, with whom he had sometimes stayed when running horses in the north of England. Nicholson did not own racehorses, but he enthusiastically followed racing, knew the form, and enjoyed an occasional bet. His bets on the O'Brien raiders at Cheltenham had proved resoundingly profitable, and a warm friendship had developed between the English lawyer and the Tipperary trainer. Nicholson was also a close friend of the then head of the National Farmers' Union in Britain, James Turner, afterwards elevated to the peerage as Lord Netherthorpe for his services to agriculture. On a visit to America with a group of farmers, Turner, who was not a racing man, had stayed in the Barclay Hotel in Philadelphia, owned by McShain.

'John's father had emigrated from Northern Ireland and raised a family in Philadelphia,' Vincent explains. There, John worked his way up in the building contracting business to become one of the biggest builders in the United States. He built the Pentagon, with its one-mile circumference and eighteen miles of corridors, in fourteen months. He restored the White House too, taking it apart brick by numbered brick, and putting in a reinforced bombproof floor for additional accommodation. He also built the Jefferson Memorial, the Kennedy Center for Performing Arts, the airports of Washington and Philadelphia, the Catholic Cathedral in Washington and much more.

The American gave James Turner and his group a typically good time in Philadelphia. Turner, when thanking him, asked McShain to let him know the next time he came to England. When McShain later told Turner he would be over in September for the Doncaster Sales, Turner regretfully had to be away in Italy. Fortuitously, he asked Hedley Nicholson to look after McShain.

'When I met him at the races,' Vincent continues, 'Hedley was quite excited. He said to me, "Look here. I have this American and he wants to buy yearlings!" I thought to myself, "Well, I've heard all about rich Americans and yearlings." I took it with a pinch of salt. But Hedley introduced me to John McShain at the sales on the first evening after racing. McShain was quite definite that he wanted to buy some yearlings, and that I should buy them for him. But his idea was that he would take the yearlings immediately to America.' This was not at all what Vincent wanted. He bought the yearlings as if for racing in America, but he set about trying to convince his new patron that this would be a mistake. 'During the sales over the next few days I introduced him to various people, breeders mostly, and when they heard he was going to take horses to America, at once they all said, "For heaven's sake, don't do that! Keep them here for at least a year or two and you'll give them a much better chance." Breeders feared the difficult racing conditions in America would break their own animals down. So he listened to what these people had to say.' McShain made a cautious reappraisal. He would at least let Vincent take the eight yearlings back to Ireland to be broken in; he would consider how well they went and decide later when to take them back to the United States.

McShain was a careful and outstanding businessman. He critically examined the economics of racing, and Vincent learned from him. He told Vincent that as a boy he had always kept his pocket money to lend his brothers when they had run out of theirs – and he lent it with interest. Jacqueline remembers John McShain very well. 'You had to respect him enormously for what he achieved,' she says today. 'People who succeed as well as he did perhaps aren't the easiest. He could be very nice, and his wife was always lovely, and most generous to the children, but John definitely would always look for the things that were wrong rather than appreciate the good.' This is perhaps why he was so successful in business.

During the early years at Ballydoyle there were no hotels where visitors could stay, so Vincent and Jacqueline went to great trouble to entertain their eminent American owners, often with very little staff. 'We used sometimes to vacate our own en suite bedroom,' she remembers. John Stapleton, one of Vincent's best riders, was roped in to act as butler. He couldn't resist shocking John McShain when he brought him hot water for shaving by saying that he 'did two of his good horses'.

Much later Jane, their youngest daughter, would put on a dark green uniform and white frilly apron to wait at table when important American guests were entertained. Vincent, otherwise preoccupied, said, 'No potatoes, darling,' as she moved around serving the vegetables.

Vincent now established his own close connection with the distant millionaire. He discovered that McShain liked nothing better than to receive detailed reports on his horses, 'so I took a great deal of trouble from then on in corresponding with him. He enjoyed getting the reports and he promptly replied to every one. He banged them back! He told me he would read my letters first in his office, then he'd take them home with him and read them all over again with his wife, Mary. I've no doubt at all that our association would never have reached the heights it did if I hadn't taken the trouble to write to him constantly.'

And Vincent's correspondence started immediately.

> *13th September 1955*
> *Dear Mr McShain,*
> *The yearlings arrived safely, and are looking well. The*
> *MOSSBOROUGH colt [who was to be named*
> *Ballymoss] is most promising, and is likely to be better*
> *at three years than two. His pedigree, which has top-*
> *class staying performances, entitles him to Classic*
> *opportunities. He has a nice temperament. He is a*
> *strongly built colt and is a good straight mover.*

A few weeks later McShain asked for some advice from Vincent about one of the horses in America.

11th October 1955
I would almost certainly have suggested rest as the
answer, and a change of environment. I think this is
what Mrs McShain would prescribe for you if you
were overworked. In the case of the horse it applies to a
youngster not fully developed, and therefore not yet
reached his full strength.

McShain also pressed Vincent about acquiring a set of starting stalls for practice at Ballydoyle. The horses would then be prepared when they arrived in the US (there were no starting stalls yet in Europe). Vincent replied, 'I met Seamus McGrath [trainer, son of the Irish Sweepstakes magnate Joe McGrath]. He said that his gate cost seven and a half thousand dollars, which rather shocked me! Of course his father is the richest man in Ireland. He has promised to send me specifications and I will see if a smaller one can be made.'

Vincent then made a shrewd move.

24th October 1955
There are some important English and Irish races closing
on Tuesday, 1st November, and I wonder if you would
like any of the yearlings entered . . . If they go to America
or don't look like coming up to Classic standard they can
be taken out. It is difficult just yet to advise you
regarding the best time to take them to America.
However, we will be better able to decide on this about
April time.

He pressed home the point a week later, deflecting a rebuff.

1st November 1955
Of course I absolutely understand about the yearlings
going to America, and fully realize that you would like
them there as soon as possible. When racing is your
hobby you naturally want to see them run. I only sent
the list of races closing in case you might feel like a
crack at one of the good races, before going over, and if
any one turned out particularly well next year you
may consider sending the horse over for the Derby or
St Leger. To win any of the Classics here would greatly
enhance the value for Stud. Also, should one or more
of them prove unsuitable to the American tracks or
starting gate, you might decide to send it back. With
these considerations in mind I took it on myself to
enter the MOSSBOROUGH colt in the English and
Irish Derbys and St Legers . . . I hope you will
understand that I made these entries as a
precautionary measure. These races are now available
to the animals in case you should want them for any
reason.

The letters worked: four yearlings stayed and became two-year-olds. It was time for Vincent to make a compromise.

21st March 1956
I think your decision in taking four of the two-year-
olds to America is the best you could have made.

Vincent had won half his battle numerically, and he had kept Ballymoss. Now he pushed his case for a third year.

15th May 1956
As long as you are associated with horses there are
bound to be odd things going wrong, but no matter
how good the management, care and attention, it is
not possible to avoid them. You can expect
disappointments, but they make the thrill of success
greater. Sometimes for no accountable reason you have
a run of reverses, but I am sure you will find that in
business too. It would be well for you to keep in mind
that even though a horse may not run to expectations
there may be a sound reason for it, so do not be
discouraged until you have examined every possible
reason for his defeat.

The MOSSBOROUGH colt is developing into a
grand individual, and is a beautiful mover. He should
be fit for an easy first run about mid-July, and in the
last three months of the season he may be forward
enough to win.

Vincent would indeed run him, on 21 July. In the meantime he
purchased a mare for John McShain and sought to cast his net
wider, setting out the great benefits of Ireland as the place for
horses.

2nd June 1956
I have been giving some thought to the future of the
mare and foal. I feel that the soil on your farm is of a
sandy nature and would probably be lacking in lime. I
am not entirely convinced that it is the very best place
for high-class bloodstock. I do not think there is any

doubt that the soil on our good studs here is first-class,
probably the best in the world for producing
bloodstock. For this reason big English breeders, also
the Aga Khan, have their studs here. Even the Queen
sends her mares, foals and yearlings over here every
year to a stud near Lord Dunraven's. Would you
consider keeping the foals here until they are yearlings
at least, and leave the mare here altogether? Cost of
keeping horses here is very much lower and top-class
stallion fees more reasonable. If you think well of this
suggestion, tell me as soon as possible as I would need
to be seeing about a stallion in good time.

Vincent was caring when it came to his staff, but it seemed in
July 1956 that Mr McShain questioned an item on his account.

5th July 1956
I think I forgot to mention to you that it is customary
here to give the lad looking after a horse and the head
man a small present when the animal wins or is sold out
of the yard. None of your four that went to America
come into either category. In looking after them however
the boys missed their chance of doing horses that might
have won races. In view of the unusual circumstances I
thought that you would not mind giving the boys a
present when the horses left here. I intended to write to
you about this, but have just found that the item was
included in your account and paid. I am sorry for being
late with the explanation.

Just over a fortnight later, on 23 July, Vincent wrote 'a rushed letter to tell you that I was well pleased with the way BALLYMOSS ran at the Curragh on Saturday. He had an easy race as he was just a little unfit. He showed plenty of speed for four furlongs, and he finished about halfway in the field of twenty-two. He is not a bit the worse for the race. Before running him again I will give him a month or five weeks to develop further.' The great horse who would go on to win two Classics, the King George VI and Queen Elizabeth stakes at Ascot and the Prix de l'Arc de Triomphe, had been ridden for the only time by stableman and future travelling head lad Gerry Gallagher, and had started unfancied at 100–7.

O'Brien produced his first winner for McShain, the two-year-old York Fair at Mallow Racecourse, on 6 August. That bank holiday was doubly happy for Vincent. 'I motored straight to Dublin from the races,' he recalls, 'and in the nursing home I found my first son, David, just born and in his cot. Rather a coincidence.' David would go on to win three Derbys, English, Irish and French, beating Vincent at Epsom, and would then become an award-winning wine grower in Provence. The following month Vincent ran Ballymoss at humble Mallow to finish only second. 'This horse in particular,' he wrote on 28 September, 'I would like to keep over the winter as he is a slow-developing type, and I would like the opportunity of bringing him to his best. With your approval I thought I might prepare him here to run in a grass race in America. We could choose a valuable race, and take him out about a week beforehand.'

Ballymoss won his first race, a £202 maiden at Leopardstown, soon after that. 'I had £20 on for you at three to one,' Vincent informed McShain in a letter dated 1 October, 'which will cover all ten per cents as presents. I would suggest giving £30 to Burns, who rode the horse; I get 10%, which is £20; and £5 each goes to the head man here and the boy doing the horses. The actual value of the race to you is £202. I know this is not much, but let us hope it is the prelude to much bigger things.' But a few weeks later Ballymoss was beaten in a Stayers' Plate on the Curragh, coming second at 5–4. 'I studied the form of the horses very carefully before the race,' Vincent told McShain, 'and decided in view of BALLYMOSS's comparatively limited racing experience that it would not be wise to have a bet for you. At least we have the satisfaction that no money was lost on him!'

Vincent correctly assessed Ballymoss's one weakness: his action was too good for soft ground. 'I hadn't realized then how unsuited he was to heavy ground,' he says. Following Ballymoss's win at Leopardstown in September, Vincent had written to John McShain:

> We know that he stays and he has definite possibilities as a Classic horse, although I would not say this in more than a whisper at the moment. I wondered what you and Mary would think of a try at the English Derby at the end of May [1957] before taking the colt to America? If he won it of course he would be a very valuable horse; his stud value could be in the region of $500,000. I suggest this as he is progressing so well here, and he has a long future ahead of him at three, four and five.
>
> If Ballymoss went to America and by any chance did not prove a success in different racing conditions

there, we probably would be regretting not having let him achieve something worthwhile here.

I hate to be too optimistic at this stage – however, think it over, and if you like the idea you had better make some holiday plans!

* * *

The other champion John McShain owned at Ballydoyle, Gladness, arrived in 1954 as, in T. P. Burns's words, 'a big scrawny t'ing'. There was a connecting thread in her breeding, by Sayajirao out of Bright Lady – 'a top staying filly' in Vincent's words. Gladness was a sister to Good Days who had landed half of that original Autumn Double which launched Vincent's career. Gladness was a year older than Ballymoss but, being big and backward, and having a patient owner, Sidney McGregor, as well as a patient trainer, she ran only once as a two-year-old and then not until November 1955 when, unfancied, she ran unplaced in a maiden plate on the Curragh.

Not only was Gladness slow-maturing, she also had over-round joints. The summer of her two-year-old season was dry. The combination of firm ground and round joints made her hard to train before the autumn, and to make things more difficult the mare got loose one day at exercise, galloped back to the yard and slipped up, injuring herself.

Gladness did not run at all through her three-year-old summer either. 'The ground had been very hard and her fetlock joints would not have stood on the firm going,' Vincent states just as firmly. At last the filly was despatched to Manchester to contest a maiden plate. 'There was nothing left in Ireland at that late stage in which she could run,' Vincent comments.

The season was ending, and it was 16 November 1956 when Gladness ran in the one-and-a-half-mile Broughton Plate, ridden by T. P. Burns. Vincent and the stable had a great deal of money on her, and Dermot travelled with her to get the wager on. Vincent is given to understatement, but in the case of Gladness's first appearance that year on a racecourse he refers to his wager as 'a substantial gamble'. The maiden filly was backed by an avalanche of money down to 8–11, and won. It had been put about that the filly was crossing to England only to return to her breeder's stud in Warwickshire. 'Gladness was the medium of a very big betting gamble,' Burns reflects. 'It was a hush-hush sort of job. She left here as if she was going back to Sidney McGregor's place, d'you see!'

That was Gladness's only race that year. In June 1957 Vincent fell out with her new owners. They had prepared themselves for Royal Ascot to watch the mare run; hats and dresses had been selected, hotel rooms booked. But the ground was firm. Vincent told them that the ground was too hard and that he was not going to run her. They protested fiercely, and Vincent could have lost the mare. He waited ten days, until John McShain came over to watch Ballymoss win the Irish Derby. 'The next day I told him, "If Gladness can be bought, I'd advise you to have her." The deal' – he nods slowly – 'was completed in a day or two.' Jacqueline remembers her price was £12,000.

Ballymoss had run 'deplorably' in his first three-year-old race, the Madrid Free Handicap at the Curragh. 'He finished right out the back door,' remembers Vincent. 'The horse was hating it,' TP adds, 'and we were all a little worried that he was always looking at mares. We wondered whether the bugger should be gelded.' Mossborough's stock were not achieving great success, and their honesty and courage were in doubt. After Ballymoss's poor showing in the Madrid, Judge Frank Tuthill, a great expert, came to Vincent and asked ominously, 'Do you know that over in England they are now gelding all the Mossboroughs?'

To the psychological doubts was now added physical injury. Ballymoss bruised a foot, and his training was impeded. It was without hope of any sort that he was allowed to accompany Gladness to the post for the Trigo Stakes at Leopardstown in May 1957. The filly was red-hot favourite at even money; the unconsidered Ballymoss started the rank outsider. 'The ground was fast, which was all against Gladness,' says Vincent. 'Also they went no pace. And up comes Ballymoss to win at 20-1.'

'There'd been discussion,' says TP, 'between the Boss, Dermot and me whether Ballymoss should take his chance in the English Derby.' The decision to run in the Derby was based on a mixed gallop which took place at the Curragh. 'I rode Ballymoss,' says TP. 'I'd been associated with him from day one. In the gallop there were three or four of Paddy Prendergast's horses, and two of the McGraths, and we galloped about a mile on the inside of the course. Ballymoss didn't just beat them, he trotted over them! We were all amazed. It was then confirmed that he would take his chance at Epsom.' Vincent wrote to John McShain on 30 May:

BALLYMOSS is in excellent form and is definitely entitled to his chance at Epsom. Of course it is expecting a great deal for him to win as it would mean that he is the best colt in Europe. The only thing we cannot be sure about is if he is absolutely top-class. He has all the other necessary qualifications – balance, action, conformation, looks, a liking for the top of the ground, and he is able to act round sharp bends.

BALLYMOSS is crossing over by boat tonight, and he is a very good traveller; it will not take anything out of him. He will go to Gerald Balding's training quarters, which are not far from Epsom, and will complete his final preparations there. Gerald trains for Jock Whitney and is also a close friend of his. They played polo together before the war.

Gerald Balding was the father of two top English trainers, Toby and Ian, and grandfather of another, Andrew, and the excellent BBC commentator Clare. It was with Gerald that Vincent stabled his Cheltenham runners during his Cheltenham years. He and Vincent were very good friends.

In the Epsom Derby Ballymoss beat all but the brilliant Crepello, trained by Noel Murless, the colt whose forelegs were so delicate he lived in stitched-on bandages. 'Ballymoss had a very short preparation for the Derby,' Vincent points out, 'due to the stone bruise in his foot. And I'm sure that he was a much better horse three or four weeks later on the day of the Irish Derby, which he won very easily.' His price for the Epsom Derby had been 33–1; for the Irish Classic he started 9–4 on.

The McShains, sadly, were not able to go to Epsom, so Vincent wrote again on 7 June:

We are home again and the excitement has subsided a little. BALLYMOSS will be back tomorrow morning. Looking at him the evening of his race you would not have known that he had raced. He was certainly the best-behaved horse in the saddling enclosure, and in the parade for the race. He was perfectly calm and unconcerned. I must say that I was not feeling the same way myself.

On 20 July at Ascot, Gladness won the Sunninghill Park Stakes (two miles, £1,178) carrying 10 stone at 13–8. She could not have been more impressive and won without being extended.

22nd July 1957
It was fortunate that we got sufficient rain to make the ground very nice as I would have been very loath to run her on the hard. Tommy [Burns] had to ride for the President at the Phoenix Park, and I engaged A. Breasley [the famous Australian 'Scobie' Breasley] for the mare. He is a top-class jockey, and is noted for being kind to his mounts. This is most important, especially if the jockey is not attached to the stable. Most jockeys getting a chance ride will not take a long-term view where the animal is concerned, and may punish the horse.

Four days later Vincent sent the following news:

GLADNESS came back from England in excellent form and her legs are in perfect shape. I spoke to

*Breasley on the telephone and he told me that he was
most impressed with her, and considers her a top-class
stayer. He said that he thought she should be Cup
standard. This is great news as I needed confirmation
of my opinion of her, and it was a big responsibility
recommending her to you. I expect her to be better in
1958. She has only had five races in her life, and must
improve. At this moment she must be without doubt
the highest-class staying filly in the British Isles. It is
a wonderful thing to have two such animals as
BALLYMOSS and GLADNESS.*

The next month, Ballymoss was second in the Great Voltigeur
Stakes at York.

23rd August 1957
*The ground was unquestionably on the dead side
though it had dried considerably since the previous
day, but we decided that he must have a race before
the Leger. The Leger being his chief objective, I had left
a little to work on where his training was concerned. I
had him at the peak of his form on the Irish Derby
Day and I wanted him that way again on the 11th
September. It is not possible to keep any horse at his
peak for too long.*

And then, glorious news: Ballymoss won the St Leger. This
was the first Classic victory the McShains had been able to see
and Vincent's first English Classic.

16th September 1957
It was most sporting of you to come over, particularly
knowing the uncertainties attached to racing. I have no
doubt that the thrill you got made the trip worthwhile,
and you certainly deserved all the success. You have done
a great deal for Ireland too, which I am sure gives you
much pleasure. The fact that BALLYMOSS was bred in
Ireland, trained here and ridden by an Irish jockey is a
great source of pride to all Irishmen, and it is also a very
big advertisement for Irish bloodstock.

As in most things he did, John McShain wanted to make a
financial success of his racing; he did not want it to be considered a 'hobby' and an indulgence. Immediately after the St
Leger victory he asked Tommy Burns, 'How much money am I
going to win?' Tommy reflected later, 'That's sad when you have
just won a second Classic out of your very first crop of runners.'

The McShains had several jumpers with Vincent. Vincent
never felt that the industrial tycoons who were his owners should
not be party to some of the difficult decisions about their horses;
he felt that their success in their own business demonstrated that
they were perfectly capable of looking at both sides of a case and
coming down on the right one. In the spring of 1958 he summed
up for McShain the jumping situation and his reasons for a
change.

7th March 1958
My runners at Cheltenham are the poorest lot I have
sent there in years [yet Vincent had winners there that
spring]. The fact is that I have been gradually cutting

down the number of jumpers here and increasing the flat racehorses. Financially, both from stakes point of view and a market for horses, there is very little in jumping, and it is only the few rich people still interested in this sport that can afford to keep going. I am sure the position in America is the same.

A few months later, as a four-year-old, Ballymoss triumphed at Epsom in the Coronation Cup over the Derby distance.

6th June 1958
BALLYMOSS put up a delightful performance. I wish you had both been there to see him. The early pace was slow, which did not suit him, but nevertheless when the speed was turned on none of them could worry him. Breasley described him as a grand horse, which undoubtedly he is. Mary [McShain] and I had a very costly telephone call (nearly forty dollars' worth) and I hope she will not mind me blaming her for the extravagance.

Royal Ascot that year also proved a triumph for Vincent. Gladness, ridden for the first time by Lester Piggott, won the meeting's richest race, the two-and-a-half-mile Gold Cup. Only two mares had ever won this race in the previous sixty-four years, the immortal La Flêche in 1896 and Quashed in 1936, who beat William Woodward's Omaha in one of the epic races of the English turf. This was the first time an Irish horse had ever won the race. Vincent also won the Ascot Gold Vase that week with Even Money, a horse he had bought when he happened to be passing Goffs Sales at Ballsbridge. He'd liked him so much at first sight that he'd purchased him after looking at him for only a couple of minutes. The horse ended up at the Magniers' stud, Grange, near Fermoy, as a leading National Hunt sire. Piggott, who rode Gladness beautifully, complained afterwards about the lengthy instructions Vincent had given him. Vincent always retorted that he wanted to be sure that Lester knew exactly what to do. Gladness was well on her way now to becoming the best staying mare of that epoch.

Remarkably, in the spring Vincent had yet again won both divisions of the Gloucestershire hurdle with Admirable Stuart and Prudent King, and in 1959 he won with John McShain's York Fair, who had been Vincent's first winner for the McShains at Mallow the day David O'Brien was born in August 1956.

That summer of 1958 was an amazing one for Ballymoss too. He won four races in succession, all ridden by Scobie Breasley, including the Coronation Cup at Epsom, the ten-furlong Eclipse at Sandown, and one week later the King George VI and Queen Elizabeth Stakes at Ascot. When Queen Elizabeth presented the Gold Cup (which she personally approves for the winner of the race) to John McShain, she told him how impressed she had been with Ballymoss's win. She felt that he would be a great asset if left to stand at stud in England. At Ascot, the Queen Mother supported the Queen's plea. The royal appeals influenced McShain in his later decision to accept a substantially lower figure for Ballymoss than he could have secured in America.

In Vincent's next letter, dated 2 August 1958, he reported on the mare's next victory, the second of four successive wins, pointing out that Gladness had 'once again confirmed what a great mare she is by winning the Goodwood Cup on Thursday. As you will see by the photograph of the finish she won with considerable ease, and the crowd gave her the reception she deserved. Her performance was so much more meritorious because she had to take up the running before they had gone two furlongs, and she was never headed afterwards.' He added, 'It is most gratifying that she has now won £18,443, which is more than she cost.' Trainers need to be businessmen too.

Both Gladness and Ballymoss were then sent to York for the rich and famous Ebor handicap. The ground was soft so Ballymoss was not started, but Vincent pleased the crowd by parading him. 'Gladness carried nine stone seven and won by six lengths in a canter ridden by Lester Piggott,' Vincent recalls. 'I remember William Hill, the big bookie, telling me that the performance Gladness put up that day was the greatest he had seen in a handicap in his lifetime.' In the century-old history of the Ebor, Europe's richest handicap, only two horses had previously carried 9st 7lb or more and won. This result was a triumph for Major Leslie Petch, clerk of the course at York, who had been criticized for putting up £10,000 for a handicap. It was felt by those in authority that valuable handicaps encouraged mediocre racing. Vincent enclosed a few newspaper cuttings of the Ebor Handicap win in a letter dated 21 August. 'Gladness got a wonderful reception,' he reported, 'as befits the great mare she is. It is very likely that there has never been one like her before, and how lucky we are to have been associated with her.'

Just over a week later, on 30 August, Vincent was able to write to McShain, 'It was most generous of you to decide to leave BALLYMOSS here, and if the deal materializes I know there will be great jubilation.' His sale before the Prix de l'Arc de Triomphe (part of the deal was that Ballymoss would run in the McShain colours in the Prix de l'Arc de Triomphe) was financed by William Hill, the bookmaker, and Sir Victor Sassoon, owner of Crepello, who had just beaten Ballymoss in the Derby. The National Stud had tried to buy the horse but the government could not come up with the money. Ballymoss stood at Banstead Manor Stud near Newmarket. When he retired, he was then the highest money-winning horse ever in England, only eclipsed in Europe by Ribot.

The following month the suggestion was put to Vincent that he might move to England – something not many people know even today. He informed McShain.

10th September 1958
Hedley Nicholson [the solicitor who had introduced Vincent to McShain at Doncaster in September 1955] got in touch with me about Druid's Lodge, which is one of the leading private training establishments in England. I understand that James Turner is interested and that he has told you about it. Their idea is that he would farm the land, you would have the training establishment, and I would train there. I am very seriously considering this and will write you or ring you in the next few days.

The remote establishment was originally famous for being the scene of many successful secret gambles executed by the Druid's Lodge Confederacy. It was said that stable staff were locked in when coups were being plotted. What particularly interested Vincent, however, was the excellence of the old turf gallops and the fact that he was finding the travelling from Ballydoyle for horses and himself something of a burden.

'The outstanding feature of Ballymoss,' Vincent pointed out in a letter of 19 September, 'is that he has now been sold, and as we both agreed, his programme takes on quite a different aspect. I think we may as well run for the big money in France and America, provided that I am satisfied with the horse and ground on the day.' First came the Prix de l'Arc de Triomphe. Ballymoss's preparation for the Prix de l'Arc de Triomphe was handicapped by soft ground, which even for Ireland was particularly heavy, so Vincent sent the horse to Newmarket where he lodged with the leading English trainer Noel Murless to enable him to work on better ground. 'I was very confident of his chances,' Vincent recalls, 'and I had quite a substantial bet on him which I had asked my great friend Peter O'Sullevan, later Sir Peter, the brilliant commentator, to place. On the day of the race itself, about noon, it began to pour and never let up. My hopes sank. I managed to find Peter again and I asked him, "Is there any hope at all of laying off the bets?" Peter said he would try. The start of racing was postponed for an hour to escape the downpour.

'In the second race Scobie rode a filly for Alec Head, which finished last. Scobie came in looking very depressed. Shaking his head at me, he was giving the soft ground as the cause of the poor performance. I thought, "Oh my God." Just before the Prix de l'Arc de Triomphe I found Peter again, and he said, "I am sorry but I couldn't do anything about the bet. It's too late. It is impossible here anyhow." I just thought, "Well, that's that," and I forgot about my bet.' But Scobie comforted Vincent by saying, 'Don't worry. The horse handled soft ground in the

Leger and if I find he can't handle it here you know I won't knock him about.'

7th October 1958
I was so glad to be able to talk to you on Sunday night after the race. It was a little sad not having you, Mary and Jacqueline to share in the tremendous success of our wonderful horse. Of all his victories this surely was the greatest, particularly with the ground so much against him. Breasley rode in the previous race and finished last on Alec Head's filly. When he came in he said the ground was very bad indeed, and I am sure he would have agreed if I had said BALLYMOSS ought not to run. However, it cheered him up considerably when Alec Head told him that the filly had burst a blood vessel, which of course accounted for her bad performance and not the ground, as Breasley thought. I thought he rode a wonderful race and showed great courage in the way he progressed steadily through the field all the way down the long hill for home.

I've never heard anything to equal the reception he got and was only sorry you were both not there to witness it. French, English, Irish and goodness knows how many other nationalities all paid tribute by surging in around the horse, cheering and clapping as he walked from the track to the winner's enclosure. BALLYMOSS ought to have gone crazy with all the excitement, but on the contrary he could not have been less perturbed. What an incredibly cool and calm horse he is. There is no doubt that these qualities have a lot to do with his greatness.

8th October 1958
I want to thank you again for your great kindness in
giving me a share in BALLYMOSS. It was a most
generous gift, and I cannot tell you how much I
appreciate your goodness. You have been so kind to us
always that I really do not know how to thank you.

An unsuccessful trip to America followed (of which more later), then Ballymoss was sent to stud at Newmarket. Vincent noted in a letter dated 9 December that he saw the horse there 'and he looked very well . . . It was a great relief to me that he came out of training absolutely sound without ever having a day's sickness in my care. The bruised foot as a three-year-old was his only hold-up in work.' A few months after that, he and Jacqueline took a well-deserved break in America. On 19 March 1959 he wrote to McShain, 'It did us both no end of good, and I feel a hundred per cent fit again. This was the first holiday I had had entirely away from horses since 1951.'

But that spring Mr McShain delayed showing gratitude to all Vincent's staff. Because of the bad ground conditions in Ireland Vincent had of course sent Ballymoss to Newmarket for the final two weeks of his preparation for the Prix de l'Arc de Triomphe. Mr McShain had therefore concluded that the horse had not been looked after by Vincent's staff. Vincent deftly pursued the matter.

15th April 1959
You'll remember I mentioned to you before leaving
America in November about a present for the staff out
of the Prix de l'Arc de Triomphe win. You said at the

*time that you considered the horse was not trained
here and therefore the staff were not entitled to
anything out of the win. Whatever your views about
this, the horse was never managed, fed or ridden by
anyone outside this stable. The boy looking after him
and the travelling head lad were with him all the time.
Yesterday, the boy who looked after BALLYMOSS gave
me notice because he had no present out of the race or
the sale of the horse. As the Prix de l'Arc de Triomphe
is the richest race in Europe you will appreciate that
these lads felt pretty badly not getting a penny.
Although one could say that they did rather well last
year, apart from this we would have not felt too pleased
with the French Jockey Club if they refused to pay the
stake money, because we had already won so much!
Also it is customary for the lad and head lad to get a
present when the horse is sold.*

*I probably should have mentioned all this to you
before, but I had not realized how much feeling there
was here about it. I intended to talk it over with you
when you came over. If you give the staff no present
out of the Prix de l'Arc de Triomphe it will naturally be
discussed in every stable, and I know you would not
want this. I have told Tuohy, the lad who has given
notice, that I have written to you. He had looked after
BALLYMOSS right through since the horse was a
yearling, and is a very good lad.*

*5th May 1959
Regarding staff presents out of the Prix de l'Arc de*

*Triomphe – I appreciated very much your fair
comments as it was a matter I hesitated to mention to
you. I do feel it would be most important to give a
present to the head lad, travelling head lad, and the boy
doing the horse. No matter how small the race, these
three would always be given a present. For a local race
the travelling lad would be excepted.*

The correspondence between the two shows the skilful way in
which Vincent could handle a man as tough as John McShain.
Above all, of course, Vincent had managed to keep the best of
the yearlings he had bought for McShain to race in Europe. The
ploy was a total success.

As was the choice of jockey for Ballymoss. The remarkable
Scobie Breasley was closely associated with the colt, riding him
in almost all his races as a four-year-old. Vincent's letters show
how highly he regarded the Australian's quiet style. 'If a horse
didn't enjoy being ridden by Scobie Breasley,' he wrote, 'forget
him.' Tommy Burns, who had ridden Ballymoss in all his races
as a two- and three-year-old bar two, was second on him as a
four-year-old in the Ormonde Stakes at Chester but then had
a dreadful fall in a hurdle race at Clonmel and suffered severe
back injuries and a broken breastbone. As a result, Scobie got
the ride on Ballymoss in the 1958 Coronation Cup. 'O'Brien
rang to ask me. I happily obliged, and we had the others
cold in a few strides after Tattenham Corner. It was the start
of a great partnership between us!' Together they won the
Coronation Cup, the Eclipse, the King George VI and
Queen Elizabeth Stakes at Ascot, beating the Derby winner
Hard Ridden, and the Prix de l'Arc de Triomphe. Scobie, after

his long career, rated Ballymoss the best horse he ever rode.

Scobie always said that he wished Ballymoss had ended his season with the Prix de l'Arc de Triomphe and not run in the Washington International at Laurel Park. 'That's when the Ballymoss fairy story turned into a nightmare,' Scobie would sadly reflect. McShain had arranged for Vincent and Scobie to watch previous tapes of the race, and had also brought two of his American horses to the course so that Scobie could ride them in preliminary races for experience. In addition he had arranged for Scobie to have a ride from another trainer earlier on in the day. Scobie declined to accept any of these invitations. Vincent, discussing the race beforehand, said to Scobie, 'You will have to lie up.' Vincent remembers Scobie's retort: 'Don't worry, he'll win swimming up a river.'

America was the only country using starting stalls at that time. In an effort to be fair to horses of other nations, including the Russians, who came for the first time, a tape start was used. Six times the horses started and each time they were brought back by the starter, unfortunately named Eddie Blind. 'It was chaotic,' Jacqueline observes.

Scobie feared that round the very sharp seven-furlong track at Laurel he could run into traffic problems. Sure enough, Orsini II, ridden by Piggott, crashed into the hedge which served as the inside running rail and barged into Ballymoss, 'turning him sideways. He was never going on an even keel after that.' By the time he was round the bend Ballymoss started to make up ground in the back straight. Eddie Arcaro, famous American jockey, knew that his horse was finished, and shouted across to Scobie, 'How are you going?' Scobie yelled back, 'Good!', to which Arcaro replied, 'You'd better be kicking on then.' Sadly it was too late for Ballymoss – the two leaders had gone.

Ballymoss finished a reasonably close third, and after the race Scobie said, 'In the circumstances he ran pretty well,' but Vincent knew, and had said to his jockey, that waiting tactics were seldom successful in American racing, particularly on a track as sharp as Laurel. Scobie also said, 'I wasn't hard on him when I knew we couldn't win.' This particularly annoyed John McShain because there was a successful objection to the winner, Tudor Era. Had Ballymoss finished second he would have been given the race.

Despite McShain's reputation as a hard-headed business-man, nearly half a century later O'Brien stressed the American's great generosity to the nation. 'Well, you know he bought the entire Killarney estate in the lovely south-west of Ireland,' Vincent points out. 'He spent part of each year there with his wife Mary and their very special only child, Polly, who became a nun, Sister Pauline McShain, in the Holy Child Order in Philadelphia. Then John and Mary gifted the estate to the Irish nation. The beautiful lakes and surrounding country-side had been presented to the Kenmare family by Queen Elizabeth I in the sixteenth century. So Killarney House, Ross Castle – a nineteenth-century castle on Innisfallen Island – the lakes and about 10,000 acres, instead of being in private hands, now belong to the Irish people. There was a famous song, "How Can You Buy Killarney?" John McShain did, and the nation benefited enormously.' It was a lucky day for Ireland when Vincent O'Brien met John McShain.

Then Vincent nods and emphasizes the other side of 'Dear Mr McShain'. With a wry smile, he adds, 'But he took his horses away from me and sent them to John Oxx [Snr, the father of the current trainer John Oxx]. He was delighted to find that John's training fees were about half mine! John McShain found great difficulty in accepting the European policy of a "retained" jockey and felt that if he contributed the bulk of a jockey's annual retainer he should have the jockey riding whenever one of his horses ran. Also he did not want to have to put up the retained stable jockey, especially abroad, if a better rider was available. He had the same difficulty with John Oxx apparently, and decided to run down his horse operation.'

It would be nice to record that Ballymoss, by Lord Derby's sire Mossborough, proved an outstanding success at stud. It would make a perfect end if his union with McShain's other superb horse, the remarkable mare Gladness, had produced a super horse. But Ballymoss proved only a reasonably good sire, his best son being Jim Joel's Royal Palace, winner of the Epsom Derby of 1967. Ballymoss's mating with Gladness produced Merry Mate, who won an Irish Oaks. Breeding would be easy if the combination of two alpha-plus animals regularly produced an offspring of their calibre. It does not. Vincent wished that Gladness had gone to a stallion of more quality than Ballymoss. 'Gladness was a big, rather plain, masculine mare, and Mossborough got big, strong and rather plain horses,' he observes.

ABOVE: *Quare Times and Pat Taaffe coming in after their 1955 Grand National. Vincent and owner Mrs Welman lead them in. Maurice O'Callaghan (right), Phonsie (left) and Dermot (behind).*

BELOW: *Quare Times (number 10) ridden by Pat Taaffe on their way to winning the National. Note how short Pat was riding then compared with the others.*

LEFT: *John McShain proudly holding his colt Ballymoss after winning the St Leger, Vincent's first English classic winner.*

BELOW: *Gladness strolls imperiously home in the Ebor at York, 1958.*

ABOVE: *Walter and Lorna Burmann, Phonsie, Jacqueline and daughter Elizabeth with Irish Derby winner Chamour.*

BELOW: *As Chamour was winning the Irish Derby, Vincent, banned from his stables and the racecourse, fished on the Duke of Devonshire's stretch of the Blackwater.*

BELOW: *Raymond Guest leads in Vincent's first Epsom Derby winner (of six). Larkspur was ridden by Australian Neville Sellwood, who was tragically killed in a racing accident soon afterwards.*

Jack Mulcahy, 'Uncle Jack' to the family, gave Vincent advice which changed his fortunes.

From left to right: Vincent, Jimmy Brady, Bull Hancock, Raymond Guest and Tom Cooper, ready for Ascot.

Aerial shot of of Ballydoyle showing the round and straight gallops, said to be one of the finest training establishments in the world.

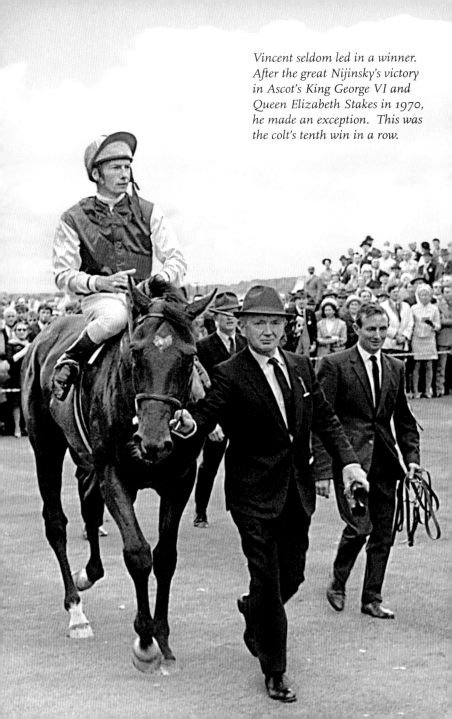

Vincent seldom led in a winner. After the great Nijinsky's victory in Ascot's King George VI and Queen Elizabeth Stakes in 1970, he made an exception. This was the colt's tenth win in a row.

CHAPTER 9

CHAMOUR

'It was like a nightmare'

Between the triumphant years of Ballymoss and Gladness and Vincent's first victory in the Epsom Derby with Larkspur in 1962 occurred the lowest point of Vincent's career to date. The issue was shocking enough to dominate the international racing press.

Monday, 9 May 1960. Jacqueline recalls, 'At breakfast we checked the post collected every morning from Cashel and brought by the stable boys. It was the usual quick look to see if there was anything of interest – the rest could wait until later in the day. The horses were waiting to be worked. We opened an envelope marked "Private and Confidential". It was from the keeper of the Match Book at the Turf Club. We were shattered to read that samples of sweat and saliva taken from Chamour, a recent runner, had been found to contain a drug or stimulant. Copies of the analyst's certificates were enclosed and an inquiry was to be held by the Stewards of the Turf Club five days later.'

The Turf Club had pointed out that there had been three

cases of alleged doping, that two had been cleared, and, in the third case, the trainer had admitted giving a stimulant and was given a year's disqualification. There had been a warning in the *Irish Calendar* that future cases would be dealt with more severely.

The horse, shared in partnership between Walter Burmann and Jacqueline O'Brien, had been routinely tested after the Ballysax Maiden Plate, a £200 race at the Curragh on 20 April, and found positive. Chamour was an improving three-year-old colt and this was his first race of the season. Vincent had stood to win just £20 for his 10 per cent entitlement as a trainer, and though the horse started at 4–6, he had had no bet. The certificates stated that on 20 April two samples from Chamour were received in London by the analysts used by the Irish Turf Club: one said that in the saliva they had found *approximately* one ten thousandth of a grain of an amphetamine derivative *resembling* methylamphetamine, and the other stated that *approximately* one five thousandth of a grain of an amphetamine derivative *resembling* methylamphetamine was found in the sweat. 'Our initial reaction was that the horse must have been "got at",' Jacqueline recalls, 'but how or why? We had never heard of the drug and had no idea of its properties.'

Vincent was summoned to explain the presence of the drug. The Stewards said that the matter was serious but that Vincent could ask for a postponement until 23 May, but the letter concluded, 'I am to add that this matter is entirely con-fidential at present and is known to no-one except the Stewards.' Vincent was very anxious that the allegation of doping would not become public so that the culprit, if there was one, could be caught. He was equally fearful of the terrible harm the publicity could do to his reputation. He settled for the hearing on 13 May.

With only three days to go Vincent had still not contacted anyone. Confidentiality had been stressed in the Stewards' letter and he felt he should go along with that. As the inquiry drew closer, however, the gravity of the situation became more apparent to Vincent. 'Vincent endeavoured frantically to get in touch with the Turf Club to ask for a postponement of the inquiry. When he was able to, the answer,' says Jacqueline, 'was that no postponement was possible as witnesses had been called.'

'Friday the thirteenth arrived, and we awoke at the Shelbourne Hotel to read in the newspapers the shattering news that Prince Aly Khan, aged forty-six, an owner and a friend, had been killed at midnight in a car crash,' Vincent remembers gloomily. 'It was indeed a very black Friday.'

At nine a.m. Vincent hurried to a hastily arranged meeting with his solicitor and counsel (no legal help was allowed at the inquiry). They discussed the fact that the certificates alleged the specimens, marked with the name of the horse, Chamour, had arrived in London on 20 April, which was the day of the race. In fact they had left Dublin by registered post on the evening of the 20th and probably arrived on the 22nd. There was also the question of the lack of security when Chamour was stabled at Turf Club premises at the Curragh.

Then Vincent set off for the inquiry at 25 Merrion Square, the old headquarters of the Turf Club, together with Dermot and Garnie Bougoure, the Australian stable jockey who had ridden Chamour. He met other members of his staff there. In

Vincent's words, 'the Stewards said, "Regarding the certificates, the matter of the dates means nothing to us." When I questioned Mrs Mundy, the English analyst, about this, one of the Stewards hearing the case said I was confusing the witness and that the Stewards had a letter explaining the mistake. I was never shown this letter.' With regard to the adjournment, the Stewards said, 'We are not granting it as we are not concerned whether you give the matter to the police or not.' Vincent then questioned the responsibility of the Stewards when the horses were in their care at the racecourse stables the night before the Curragh meeting. During that period it transpired that the Turf Club employee who was supposed to be on night duty had a full-time job with the army and had been doing his regular duties from early morning. The gates to the stable area had been left open and unattended from 7.30 p.m. to 7.30 a.m. Again this was of 'no interest' to the Stewards.

The verdict, as published in the *Racing Calendar* that evening, was read out to Vincent:

> *The Stewards were satisfied that a drug or stimulant had been administered to Chamour for the purpose of affecting his speed and/or stamina in the race . . . The Stewards of the Turf Club accordingly withdrew Mr O'Brien's licence to train under Rule 102(v), Rules of Racing, and declared him a disqualified person under that Rule and under Rule 178 from May 13, 1960 until November 1961.*

'The most shattering blow was that his licence and disqualification rested on Rule 178,' says Jacqueline. 'Rule 102 makes a trainer responsible at the Stewards' discretion for every-thing connected with the running of a horse trained by him. In Ireland the Stewards did not have to automatically disqualify a trainer for doping as they did in England at that time, and the horse could race again. The Irish Stewards had discretionary powers. Under Rule 178 it has to be established by proper evidence either that the drug was administered by the trainer himself or that he caused it to be administered. No evidence was ever heard or given that indicated any blame attached to Vincent apart from his responsibility as a trainer, yet he was convicted under rule 178 that he was responsible as a trainer.'

Vincent's statement to the waiting media was as follows:

> *The Stewards have withdrawn my trainer's licence and declared me a disqualified person on the grounds that they found evidence of drugs in a routine sweat and saliva test taken from Chamour on April 20, a test to which I knew the horse was liable to be subjected. This horse won a £200 maiden race at the Curragh and neither I nor any person associated with the horse had a bet. My personal gain was £20 – 10 per cent of the stake. I did not drug this or any other horse. I trust my staff and I have placed the matter in the hands of my solicitors.*

'There was apparent comparison as to length of penalty between my case and Hurley's,' Vincent says, referring to a previous case in which a trainer had admitted giving the substance found. 'I took notice of the warning in the *Calendar* that if I gave any medicine or drugs of this kind I would be more severely punished than Hurley. I did not give anything of this nature, therefore the case was not similar. Nor should the penalty have been tied to Hurley's case. In fact, my case was the first of its kind, where a trainer could not be shown to have been guilty in any way and where a severe penalty was imposed.'

So, from the evening of Friday, 13 May, Vincent O'Brien, who had been the idol of the Irish racing public, lost his right to train horses. As a disqualified person he would not be allowed on any racecourse or training ground in Ireland or throughout Europe as the respective racing bodies followed each other's decisions. He faced the break-up of the training establishment which he had built up to be one of the best in the world, he faced personal humiliation for himself and his family, and he could anticipate enormous financial loss.

Rather than break up Vincent's racing establishment, the Stewards then stated that they would permit Phonsie to train the horses at Ballydoyle, provided, according to Vincent, 'that I left home and did not enter the premises again. I was allowed a couple of days to get matters sorted and to get out.' 'We received the verdict that the stable could only stay in existence if Vincent left Ballydoyle,' remembers Jacqueline. 'With only a couple of days' notice we had to try and think where to go with a family of four small children – the youngest, Jane, was only two, the eldest, Elizabeth, seven. Phonsie took us in for a few weeks. We next rented a house in Ardmore. We seemed to go from place to place, children and nanny, until we were allowed back to Ballydoyle on condition Vincent did not enter the yard. It was like a nightmare, especially knowing that Vincent had done absolutely nothing wrong. He really suffered, and it was hard to persuade him that he would ever train again.'

'Dermot and Phonsie were wonderful,' Vincent adds, 'and offered all the help it was in their power to give. The Ballydoyle staff also did everything possible to make the changes work. I had the most loyal support from those around me – a fact I still recall with pride. I would not wish these circumstances to be repeated but there's no doubt it's at times like this you feel humble for the unswerving support people give.'

Vincent's owners were also sympathetic and totally support-ive in leaving their horses in training at Ballydoyle under Phonsie and Dermot's care. Vincent says, 'I don't remember a single horse being taken away from the stable.' Jacqueline adds, 'Walter Burmann, joint owner of Chamour with me, even offered a reward of £5,000 for information which would lead to the identification and/or conviction of any person or persons who administered the drug. Only three nonsensical replies were received, including one from a man who was in prison. A note from the supervisor was appended saying that the prisoner had been nowhere!'

'Then,' Vincent says, 'with the help of Paddy McGrath, who approached his father, Joe McGrath, Senior Steward, present-ing our predicament, I was allowed to resume occupation of my home without prejudice to the continuation of the training. Provided that I did not take part in any work of the establish-ment, I could use Ballydoyle as a residence only for myself and family but I could not enter the yard or have any connection with the training.'

As for Chamour, the Ballysax Maiden Plate was taken from him but he was permitted to continue racing. In May he won the Gallinule Stakes amid wildly jubilant scenes at the Curragh. The excited, cheering crowd simply erupted. But this was as nothing compared with the celebrations that followed the Irish Derby – a triumphant public vindication for Vincent and Chamour.

On that day Vincent, with his small son David, was fishing on the Duke of Devonshire's stretch of the Blackwater, a lonely figure listening to his portable radio. Jacqueline reports, 'I went to the Curragh with our elderly nanny and our daughter Elizabeth. I had not been racing since the ban was imposed and only intended to stay across the course on the far side of the track. As the horses approached the winning post with Chamour in the lead, Nanny and Elizabeth took off across the track in the path of the galloping horses. I followed them into the winner's enclosure, thankful that there had not been a horrendous accident.

'There I witnessed a scene I have never experienced on a racecourse before or since. It was a really hot day and men in shirt sleeves pushed into the winning area. "We want Vincent!" was the chant from thousands of racegoers. Angry people surged into the reserved enclosure and for a period it looked as though the weighing room would be attacked. From all sides came the cry, "We want Vincent!" The sense of fair play of the racegoers and the "plain people" of Ireland was deeply offended. They did not see why Vincent, who had not even been investigated for a crime, should be so drastically and illogically punished. They knew he was innocent. They surely showed their wrath that day, and their dislike of the verdict of the Stewards.'

Two avenues of investigation, legal and scientific, opened up to give the O'Brien family hope. 'We had a great friend with a high regard for natural justice, a Supreme Court Judge, Cecil Lavery, also a member of the Turf Club,' says Jacqueline. 'We will never forget his kindness and concern for Vincent. In fact, without him I know Vincent would never have trained again. Judge Lavery told us that he wrote to the Turf Club pointing out that the Stewards had convicted Vincent of personal responsibility and that they should stand over that or withdraw it. He added, "I think MVOB is entitled to a public admission of this mistake – without any reservation."'

The demonstration of the people's desire for justice at the Curragh, and the action of several of the members of the Turf Club bringing to the attention of the Stewards the real threat of a libel action, prompted them to issue a statement in the *Racing Calendar* of 20 July exonerating Vincent O'Brien of the allegation that he had administered the drug or stimulant or knew of its administration, and 'that any other impression given by the wording of their previous decision was incorrect'. They did not, however, remove his disqualification under Rule 178, which stated exactly that.

Walter Burmann, joint owner of Chamour, was a paint manufacturer and a scientist. He was deeply suspicious about the certificates. A senior scientist at Glaxo emphatically dismissed them as evidence of dope. 'Gradually, the scientific circle opened up and we were able to see through new eyes that the certificates were meaningless,' Vincent says. 'At first it was difficult to get the scientists to state their views in print for fear of an unpleasant libel action being brought by Herd & Mundy, the London analysts; they would not disclose their methods of analysis, which gave rise to grave suspicion in scientific circles.'

With the help of leading world scientists in the field and the encouragement of friends, a body of evidence was assembled showing that the certificates were totally meaningless and did not show Chamour to have been doped at all. Tim Vigors, Vincent's brave Spitfire pilot friend, approached the British Home Office pathologist Francis Camps, the authority on forensic medicine, who reported, 'The position appears to be that it has, in my opinion, been assumed that the certification contained evidence of the presence of a drug when, in fact, it did not.' Dr Brendan Farrelly, later chosen to represent the Veterinary Medical Association of Ireland on the Duke of Norfolk's committee on doping, concurred and wrote a damning denunciation of the certificates, stating that 'These certificates do not contribute any evidence whatsoever that specific drugs or stimulants had been administered to this horse.' The director of the Metropolitan Police Laboratory in London, L. C. Nickolls, reported, 'Before it is possible to be dogmatic in saying that there is a foreign substance present which is characteristic of a horse-dope, it is essential, in my opinion, that the substance should be identified beyond reasonable doubt . . . it is obvious from the certificate that an *unidentified drug* has been found. As one constantly giving evidence in criminal cases, I am satisfied that the information given in the certificate might be valuable to an officer investigating a possible crime, but is valueless as definite evidence as proof of that crime.'

A full report also came from Dr E. Conway of University College Dublin: 'The statement of the results concerns a substance they did not definitely recognize but stated to "resemble methylamphetamine". I am strongly of the opinion that even on that point alone no serious attention should be given to the analytical report, which merely states that minute amounts of this "unidentified substance" were found.' And Dr Peterson, the chief chemist in the State Racing Commission Laboratory, New York, gave his informed opinion: 'It is unlikely that amounts as small as 1/10,000 grains (6.5 micrograms) of methylamphetamine can be detected in a saliva sample, or 1/5,000 grains (13 micrograms) can be detected in a sweat sample.' International evidence stated that it was not yet possible, scientifically, to isolate such small amounts of methylamphetamine, even in a pure solution.

These scientific reports, with others from the leading racing laboratories in France and Germany, and with the permission of their authors, were printed and forwarded to the Stewards. Vincent asked to have his suspension reconsidered in light of this evidence accumulated from leading international authorities. 'But,' says Jacqueline, 'the Stewards refused to consider any of the scientific evidence which was piling up from all sides, including that from their fellow racing bodies in England, France, Germany and America.'

At a special meeting of the Stewards on 25 November 1960, Vincent's suspension was cut from November 1961 to May 1961 – a period of six months. But there was still no refutation of the libellous Rule 178. Vincent pressed for the return of his licence on 1 January 1961 so that he could participate in preparing his horses for the flat racing season which opened on 17 March. The return of his licence as late as the middle of May meant that he could not study the performances of his horses or decide on entries for races until the season was well under way. The Stewards refused. In a letter dated 28 January, Vincent pleaded again: 'I ask the Stewards to give further consideration to my application and to allow my licence to be restored or, failing that, that my disqualification, which, as I have tried to explain, is still rested on Rule 178, should be removed. The removal of the disqualification would enable me to prepare to resume training in May and help me to rebuild my career.' The Stewards refused.

A trainer, in taking out a licence to train and race horses, agrees to abide by the Rules of Racing set up by the Turf Club, and also by its decisions. Vincent refrained from legal action until it was quite clear that the Stewards would take no action, not even to rescind his disqualification under Rule 178. However, advised that he had a reasonable hope of success in proceeding with a libel case against the Stewards arising out of the inquiry and publication of the result, Vincent had no doubt about the route he must take. As long as the libel against him sat in the record books he could never train again. This judgment could be used against him any time, and added to another offence could ensure that he would be a disqualified person for life. His good name was more vital to him than training again.

Vincent had now put up with being 'warned off' for nearly a year, and had faced personal humiliation, the break-up of his family home, and severe losses sustained as a result of his being away for so long from his business. 'He was absolutely innocent,' declares Jacqueline, 'and he had seen how the Stewards could refuse to see injustice leaping out at them. He could never trust them again. In fact, Vincent said, "I remember my senior counsel saying to me while we were fighting the case, 'Would you apply again for a licence?', and I said, 'No way.'" '

Vincent was advised by Judge Cecil Lavery that he could not let the libel stand and that he must proceed along the legal route. Judge Lavery, writing to Senior Counsel John P. Keane, said, 'I am a man of peace as I hope my efforts for the last year have shown, but there must be an end to "giving in". I would willingly stand aside from the whole business except for the feeling that a grave wrong has been done and that amends should be made generously.'

From a legal point of view, it was Vincent's good fortune that the Stewards had convicted him under a wrong rule, so he was able to take the case to court. Accordingly, the Stewards were served with an action for libel on 5 April 1961 by Vincent's solicitor, Dermot McDowell. In the *Annual Calendar* of the Turf Club for 1960, published after the action was brought, the original statement was repeated (p. 360). The Turf Club tried to recall the book on the grounds that it contained an error, but there was no error as the statement of their decision of 13 May 1960 was correctly reproduced. The grave matter was that it was a repetition of the libel after attention had been brought to it. This only strengthened Vincent's legal case.

He was well aware of the strengths of the authorities. 'There were threats that means would be found to ensure that Vincent's training days were over; that he would never be given a licence again. He was even approached by one of the Senior Stewards who said that all his legal costs to date would be paid if he would drop the case.' The genuine concern for his future among his friends, both inside and outside the Turf Club, was shown in this handwritten letter which Jacqueline received from Lord Dunraven pointing out the dangers of a law case against the authorities:

Killgobbin,
Adare,
Co. Limerick
12th April 1961

My Dear Jacqueline,

Many thanks for your letter, and I am sure you realize that I will always give all my support for what it is worth to Vincent. At the same time I think bringing this case will have a very bad effect. In the first case I doubt very much whether he will get a clear-cut verdict, whatever the lawyers say. The situation then will be quite desperate. You say that he is doing this to clear his name, but the stewards have already stated that they did not accuse him of administering dope or knowing it was being given. With regard to the new rules on doping, these were made to safeguard as far as possible trainers who were accused of doping. And I doubt whether this would be a point, especially as they were made after the case. Anyhow, everybody is waiting for the report which the Duke of Norfolk's committee will publish in a few weeks and which may alter the whole case. I don't suppose the case will come on until the autumn and will be hanging over him all this summer.

How much better would it have been to come back in May when everybody would have been delighted to see him, and if he had won a lot of races (as he will) all would have been forgotten in a few weeks. As it is, I don't think it will ever be finished. I know you feel very strongly about this but my advice would be to withdraw the case. I think most people would be really glad if this was done.

Anyhow, always count on me for any help I can give.

I do hope Travel Light is better.

Love from us all.

Yrs Dunraven.

Jacqueline says, 'I wrote in a reply to Lord Dunraven, "Even in the past few days Vincent has been made very conscious of the fact that he will lose a number of his 'friends' and be made very unwelcome on a racecourse in future. We would only like the people who accuse him of rushing into law to see the correspondence with the Stewards which he has had in an effort to remove his conviction under Rule 178."' She declares, 'To this day Vincent has not been able to understand the thinking of the Stewards. Were they badly advised, or afraid that racing would crumble if they admitted they had been wrong? There had to be some reason to make them so rigid, stubborn and inflexible. What was it?'

Despite the threats, Vincent applied for and was given his licence back on Saturday, 13 May 1961. A newspaper report said that he received 'nearly as many handshakes at Leopardstown as President Kennedy received at his inauguration'. At Limerick Junction, where Vincent had his first runners, there was a record attendance; his return was greeted with rapturous delight by the racing public. 'There was a spontaneous outburst of cheering for his first winner, Mr

Moss,' wrote one account. Another said, 'The roof was almost lifted off the stands when Bougoure landed the O'Brien-trained Mister Moss. There was a tremendous reception and Vincent removed his hat in acknowledgement.'

The libel case was due to be heard on 5 July 1961 in the High Court before Justice Murnagham. Vincent was so relieved to be finally facing a judge and jury and to air the deep hurts he felt the Stewards had so painfully inflicted on him. Jacqueline says, 'On the steps of the Court House John Costello, our counsel, told us that the Stewards, who were inside, had requested a settlement, which followed almost exactly what Judge Lavery had advised us we should accept. The Stewards apologized and paid all the costs of the action. Vincent accepted that they had acted in good faith initially and he waived damages, which he was advised could have been very substantial.'

Chamour, whose performances had done so much to cheer Vincent's miserable sentence, died suddenly at the beginning of 1961. Vincent recounts sadly, 'We were holidaying in Monte Carlo and at a dinner-party of thirteen people, including the two owners of Chamour, Walter Burmann and Jacqueline, and Bob Griffin, our vet. We received a call from Dermot. Chamour was found by the nightwatchman dead in his stable. The horse had apparently become cast in his box and died when the buckle of his rug pierced the jugular vein. It was the most bizarre accident, and a tragic end to a gallant horse.' All rugs at Ballydoyle from then on were stitched together and slipped over the horse's head. The O'Briens now hesitate about sitting down thirteen for dinner.

Changes were made in the efficiency of methods of

detecting drugs in racehorses and the operation of the rules as early as July 1960, a few months after Vincent's case. Two specimens of urine and saliva (sweat was now considered unsatisfactory) were to be collected, one as a check for the trainer; a new analyst was to be appointed for the Turf Club; samples were to be marked in code and not with the name of the horse as in Chamour's case; and racecourse security was to be improved, with identity cards for those with access to stables. The discretionary powers of the Stewards were further expanded.

In England on 5 December 1960, the Duke of Norfolk's Committee, appointed by the Stewards of the Jockey Club to inquire into the question of doping racehorses and the efficiency of methods of detection and of the rules, began its work. The Committee's conclusions were published in March 1961 and the system was set up which generally applies now. A trainer was no longer held to be guilty if his horse was found to be doped unless he could be shown to have been negligent. Before this the trainer resembled the man who is automatically put into prison because his house has been burgled.

'I think it could fairly be said that Vincent's tragic experience led the authorities to a revision of the whole doping scene,' says Jacqueline, 'and perhaps it took the case of someone as much in the public eye as Vincent was to force the changes. The finale to this saddest chapter of Vincent's racing career came when in 1999 he was invited to become an honorary member of the Turf Club. He accepted with pleasure. He and Lester were inducted into the newly established Turf Club Hall of Fame. They were the first people thus honoured, in 2003.'

CHAPTER 10

LARKSPUR

'They asked me a lot of questions and they stole my hat!'

Vincent's first Epsom Derby winner came about because of the interest in steeplechasing and the admiration for Vincent of Raymond Guest, later the American ambassador in Dublin. His father, Sir Winston Guest, was a first cousin to Sir Winston Churchill and served in the House of Commons with Churchill for thirty years. Raymond, tall and genial with glistening white hair, was a noted amateur player of golf, football and polo and he loved hunting, fishing and yachting. He rose to the rank of commander in the US Navy in World War Two and after the war served as Senator for the State of Virginia. He was an admirer of all things Irish.

In the autumn of 1960 Tom Cooper took Vincent to look at a yearling of Philip Love's, bred by him in Co. Dublin. Vincent knew that his stock usually made the top prices at Goffs Sales, then held in Ballsbridge. The yearling Vincent and Tom were interested in was by the 1954 Derby winner Never Say Die. 'Larkspur as a colt was well made,' Vincent remembers. 'He was a nice horse, but his height was the one thing against him.

And we bought him. He made the highest price of the sale, somewhere between 12,000 or 13,000 guineas.' The price was a record for a Ballsbridge yearling and created some excitement. Vincent smiles. 'One English trainer said loudly that we'd made a bad buy, that the yearling was far too small!'

Vincent did not enthuse over Larkspur's first season, with one notable exception. 'He ran a good race in the Timeform Gold Cup, and Tommy Gosling, who rode him, was very adamant that had he had a clearer run, he would have been closer. Tommy was very positive about him, and Tommy was a good judge.' However, Timeform, the sponsors, dismissed his running in their valuable two-year-olds race. 'He made little show in the Timeform Gold Cup,' they stated in their piece on the chestnut colt a year later. Raymond Guest and the O'Briens took a happier view. They returned to London by train and a good deal of champagne was drunk during the journey. 'By the time we got to London,' says Vincent, 'we had next year's Derby winner!' They did not seriously suppose so, but the joys of racing lie in travelling hopefully.

On Larkspur's second outing the following year, he won the Wills Gold Flake Stakes at Leopardstown over one and a half miles. Once again *Timeform Annual*, even with the benefit of hindsight, did not get the race quite right: 'But the bare result of that race was not informative . . . he was not everybody's idea of a Classic winner . . .' A professional handler of horses, the top-class trainer Paddy Prendergast, took an entirely different view. 'Prendergast went to Chester the next day,' Vincent recalls, 'and spread the news that this was a definite Derby candidate, and all his people backed him.'

Vincent's retained jockey, Pat Glennon from Australia, did

not agree with the Boss. He chose to ride the stable's other runner at Epsom, Sebring, who was working more impressively at home. 'But then,' Vincent says, 'Larkspur always took things easy.' They engaged another Australian jockey for Larkspur, Neville Sellwood, a top-class rider nicknamed 'Nifty', one of the prominent Sydney-based jockeys. Vincent recalls, 'Later that year he was very sadly killed in a riding accident at Maisons-Laffitte.' On the Monday of the week before the Derby, just nine days before the race, Sellwood flew over to Ballydoyle from France to ride work on Larkspur. Raymond Guest had come down the night before to stay to watch the gallop.

Then disaster struck. They were sitting over breakfast in the long dining room, which used to glow with pictures of great horses and the gold and silver trophies they had won. The window at the end looked over the main yard. Vincent, from his seat at the head of the table, was looking down it through the window into the yard. To his unease, he saw his head lad, Maurice O'Callaghan, coming quickly across to the house. He got up and went out to meet him. Was everything all right? It was definitely not. A swelling had come up overnight on the outside of Larkspur's near-hind leg below the hock. There was no question of working the horse. The gallop was cancelled. Guest, bitterly disappointed and extremely frustrated, strode off to his car and with a fierce spatter of gravel sped off down the drive. Jacqueline, left with a dispirited group around her dining-room table, suggested to Sellwood, 'Why don't you just sit on the horse while he's walking around the covered ride?' Sellwood happily agreed, and this was the only time he was on the horse before Epsom.

Bob Griffin, the loyal vet, was immediately summoned to drive down from the Curragh. He examined the horse, was by no means discouraging, and prescribed fomentations and two days' complete rest. The Derby runner would thus be laid off work and box-bound until a week before the Classic. 'I'll come down again on Friday,' said Bob, 'and see if the horse can work.'

With Larkspur laid off work, Vincent decided that he should inform the press of the hold-up in the horse's preparation. He said truthfully that there was a possibility that the horse would not run in the race. As a substantial betting man himself at the time, he did not want the public to lose their money and enrich the bookmakers by backing a non-runner ante-post. The extraordinary aftermath of his announcement without doubt coloured O'Brien's future views about giving the press detailed reports on his horses' progress. A good deal of this reluctance stems from the behaviour of the Epsom Stewards in the minutes immediately following the Irishman's first English Derby.

Having re-examined the leg, Griffin said Larkspur could work for the first time in six days. He checked the horse again after the work. The swelling was no worse. 'You can send him to Epsom,' Bob cheerfully told Vincent, and the horse travelled over.

Even before he heard this encouraging news, Raymond Guest, who relished a gamble, had already backed Larkspur. It was this flurry of informed wagering in the same week in which Vincent had publicly pronounced his doubts that led to the Epsom Stewards' suspicious summoning of the winning trainer. Why had Raymond Guest so soon backed his horse?

Vincent shrugs. Raymond liked betting, as he would show again in the case of Sir Ivor. Jacqueline suggests that 'he really didn't want to face the fact that things had gone wrong. He'd been very depressed by the setback that morning at breakfast.' One thing is certain: nobody working in the yard at that time, when asked to rate Larkspur against Vincent's later Derby winners, puts him anywhere but at the bottom of the golden six. Rejected by the stable jockey and box-bound seven days before the Derby, Larkspur was little fancied except by his optimistic owner. He had drifted out in the ante-post market even before Vincent made his announcement. On the day, he started at a longer price than he had opened.

But this was the Derby when 'they all fell down'. To be precise, seven fell, and of the field of twenty-six at least nine or more were impeded, some seriously. King Canute II was too greatly injured to survive and was put down. Hethersett, the favourite, was one of the fallers. Larkspur had been just behind him in the middle of the field when the leaders, disrupted by the crash of the beaten Romulus into Crossen, started to go down like bowling pins. Hethersett was sliding on the ground when Larkspur neatly jumped him. A bigger, clumsier colt would probably have tripped over him and fallen himself. A pack of distraught loose horses pursued the leaders into Tattenham Corner, making Epsom's steep and twisting descent look more like the setting of a bucolic point-to-point rather than that of the world's most famous Classic race. Larkspur, just behind the leaders, moved to the front with the greatest of ease and sailed home comfortably; Arcor was second, and Le Cantilien just about overcame the loose and blinkered Crossen in their disadvantaged race to the post. Well behind came Miralgo, Larkspur's conqueror in the Timeform Gold Cup. Larkspur's more fancied stable companion Sebring did not prove Glennon entirely wrong: he finished fifth. Plainly, Larkspur's swollen leg, still 'up' only five days before the race, had not affected his performance. The press referred to it as a 'thoroughpin'. Horses seldom go lame from a thoroughpin if you stop their work promptly. It can be treated by poulticing or by draining off the fluid.

The Epsom Stewards that day included Lord Derby and Sir Humphrey de Trafford. They should have been busy trying to determine why seven horses fell in a flat race, but first – even before the jockeys had weighed in – they summoned the victorious Vincent before them. They wanted him to explain the money bet on the winner after he had been announced as a doubtful runner. Vincent reported the facts, and the Stewards promptly accepted his account. But Vincent was angry about being so curtly summoned from the winner's enclosure. On top of being deprived of those first glorious minutes after he had won the Derby, Vincent's top hat had mysteriously disappeared while he stood in the Stewards' room. He complained afterwards very crossly to Jacqueline. 'They asked me a lot of questions and they stole my hat!'

Looking back on that first Epsom Derby, Vincent says, 'I do believe that Larkspur on that day was a good horse. He didn't have the soundness of limb – I think the weakness came from Never Say Die – and he was never quite the same horse again. His action was never as good. Racing all the way down the hill at Epsom had its effects. But they did not show up until the Irish Derby. He ran quite differently when Scobie Breasley rode him at the Curragh. Scobie shook his head when he came in and said, "He didn't like the ground, it was too firm. He felt it."' Indeed he did. He was off the course for two months thereafter with sore shins. Vincent comments sagely, 'The Never Say Dies had soft bone.' In the opinion of T. P. Burns, 'On Epsom Derby Day he was better than on any other day. Lucky? Sellwood said he'd have won anyway, no matter how many fell. Oh, he did the job that day all right.'

Larkspur was even more disappointing in the St Leger than he'd been in the Irish Derby. He finally finished sixth, and Raymond Guest decided to retire him to stud. He stood for many years in Japan. But Vincent had won his first Epsom Derby, just as his new American connections had hoped.

* * *

Raymond Guest's success with Larkspur brought Vincent's name and reputation to the attention of some of America's old racing families. Over the next decade he trained for a remarkable collection of outstanding and wealthy people. For Americans, the tempo of racing in Europe was attractive. Despite the poor prize money, the animals were sensitively trained, and racing on grass favoured their development. Young stock were gently brought on, which pleased the horsemen among these families; commercialism was less evident.

James (Jimmy) Cox Brady was one of the first to approach Vincent, and over the years they remained close friends. Jimmy Brady's father, a prominent owner and breeder, had been one of America's top businessmen. All his bloodstock was sold when he died, aged only forty-eight, including Hard Tack, sire of the movie hero Sea Biscuit. On leaving Yale, Jimmy set aside his rich connections and took a job shovelling coal in a Bronx gas plant – nine hours a day for $23 a week; he was determined to rise up the ladder the hard way. By the age of thirty he held directorships in fifty corporations. He was a decorated naval commander in the South Pacific, and after the war took on the job of chairman of the New York Racing Association. Here he waged continual war against New York State in an effort to stop the greedy legislators pulling profits away from racing. Jimmy loved Saratoga and spent August there each year, alternating between the early-morning track trials, the racing, and evenings spent on the shady porch chatting with family and friends. Jacqueline too recalls Saratoga with great affection. 'Saratoga was wonderful in August, with its Victorian houses and wide, tree-lined, shady streets. It was the summer home of the New York Ballet, the Philadelphia Orchestra, and the New York Racing Association. Watching horses and trainers work in the early mornings was a whole new experience for us. We always stayed with the Bradys. They had a lovely house there with a big veranda where everybody sat out on the balmy summer evenings.'

Among the American-bred yearlings Vincent received from Brady was Long Look, a filly by the great Ribot. The Italian government had permitted Ribot to be leased to Darby Dan Farm in Kentucky for just three years, but Ribot refused to get into the plane for the return journey. He was notoriously difficult to handle and stayed at Darby Dan for the rest of his life, unapproachable by anyone but his one groom. Long Look won the Epsom Oaks in 1965, giving Vincent his second English Classic victory. The famous white, black and red Brady colours were now seen on an English racecourse. Paul Mellon, the American philanthropist who did so much for the arts in America, deputized that day for Brady, who was unable to attend due to family commitments.

Jimmy loved Ireland and bought the Cashel Palace Hotel as a place to stay and entertain his friends. It had been the palace of the Archbishops of Cashel, a lovely house designed in 1731 by Sir Edward Lovett Pearce, one of the most famous Irish architects; he also designed the Irish Parliament House. The Bradys hoped to spend more time in Ireland but, sadly, Jimmy died of an aneurysm at the age of sixty-six.

Through the Bradys and Raymond Guest, Vincent was able to meet other potential owners. 'The American owners were most important to the whole concept of Ballydoyle, helping to raise it to the status of an international operation,' Jacqueline says today. 'When you're a trainer, getting horses is the hard part, because you have a job that requires you being around the horses, rather than socializing with clients in restaurants, bars and clubs. If you have to get back to rural Tipperary and are not prepared to stay up after racing and have dinner with owners, it is very hard to keep them happy, especially if things go wrong with the horses. Gathering that wonderful collection of American owners was so good for Vincent at that time.'

Among them was C. Mahlon Kline, 'Kliney' to his friends, who had sought Vincent out to train for him at the end of the 1950s. A bachelor, with a wonderfully dry sense of humour and ready wit, he avoided publicity personally but did not hesitate to use advertising for his company. During his sixty years he built up the huge pharmaceutical company which bore his name, now GlaxoSmithKline, making it one of the largest in the world. In 1967, when he died, it had sales in excess of $200 million.

Kliney bred horses for fifty years. Jumpers were his special interest, and his jumpers were three times voted the best brush horses of their years by the United Hunts in the USA. He won the Irish Guineas with El Toro and had some useful horses with Vincent, including Arctic Sea and Ross Sea. Vincent found him a horse, Adare II, to race in America, and as Kliney was not averse to a bet it gave him great pleasure that Adare won in Florida at Hialeah Racecourse at odds of 103.7–1.

The Oaks victory of Valoris in 1966, following Long Look's win in 1965, brought great joy and tears to Mr Charles Clore, the London property developer. He had suffered a long period of ill luck at the races and had pondered this before the Oaks. He decided that his original green and grey colours must be unlucky and changed them to a confection of blue, pink and white. Either the new colours or Vincent worked the miracle as Valoris won his first Classic for him. 'In work, when Valoris hit the front,' Vincent recalls, 'she would suddenly look around, and if she saw anything anywhere in her vicinity she'd duck away from it – for instance the markers here on the gallops which she must have seen a hundred times. I always figured that perhaps there was something about her sight that wasn't a hundred per cent, although the experts could find nothing wrong. I did say to Lester, "When you do hit the front, just be sure that you catch a good hold of her because with the crowds and the cheering she might easily start to duck around." Lester caught her up and she went on and won easily. The Oaks was her last and greatest performance. After that I think she lost her courage due to her eyesight. Her mother was blind, so perhaps there was some hereditary problem.'

Gaia, a big filly by Charlottesville out of a German-bred mare, Ghana II, won the Irish Oaks in 1969 for Hope Hanes, another of Vincent's American patrons. John, her husband, owner of the huge Hanes clothing business in America, set up the New York Racing Association as it is today, handing it over when he retired to James Cox Brady. The Hanes had a magnificent shoot in Georgia, and Vincent and Jacqueline's visit there was truly memorable. 'The gardens were full of the scent of gardenias and frangipani,' Jacqueline recalls. 'A grey-green moss, special to the Deep South, hung from the trees. Colourful, old-world pageantry, horse-drawn wagons, white-coated handlers threading their way through the still pine forests, and dogs rustling about in the undergrowth looking for coveys of quail. When the dogs pointed, the "guns" would quietly descend from the wagons. It was shooting in a natural way, not like a "drive" on a managed shoot. Liking the birds, I was pleased the tally of quail was small.'

Jack Mulcahy was the American owner whose advice changed Vincent's fortunes. During Ireland's bitter civil war, at the age of fifteen, he had been caught acting as a messenger-boy for De Valera's side, the militant republicans. He had narrowly escaped being shot, unlike his two companions, and was jailed for a year because of his youth. He was packed off to America by his family after that and qualified as an accountant at night-school during the Depression. Working his way up, he eventually owned Quigley & Co. steel company, and was a heavy investor in Pfizer Pharmaceuticals. His brother Dan, then the head cashier in a Munster and Leinster bank in Cork, opened Vincent's first account. Dan promised to look after him if he needed money. 'I still have my account there and never, in all that time, has there been a problem regarding the amount I was overdrawn!' Vincent says.

Jack came back to Ireland a highly successful businessman. A quick introduction from his brother Dan and Jack was interested in investing in bloodstock. He became a close friend of the O'Brien family and was known by them as 'Uncle Jack'. He advised Vincent, 'You must take a piece of the action; get a share of every horse you train.' He could not get over the fact that Vincent was having so much success for his owners without sharing in their capital profits. His advice, adopted without delay, markedly advanced Vincent's fortunes. Among Jack's horses trained at Ballydoyle were the brilliant filly Cloonlara, and the champion miler Thatch.

Other American visitors also had business plans for Vincent. A. B. (Bull) Hancock probably made the greatest contribution of any breeder to the bloodstock industry in America. He inherited Claiborne Farm from his father, nine times the leading breeder of races won, who died at 48, a stern taskmaster who employed Bull as a twelve year for 50 cents a day to sweep out after the yearlings.

Bull said 'I never thought of anything else but horse breeding'. When he took over Claiborne in 1948, Joe Hersch, the famous racing correspondent of the *Morning Telegraph*, described the farm as a 'crumbling dynasty; its renaissance brought about entirely by the genius and perserverance of Bull Hancock and the trusted and knowledgeable employees with whom he surrounded himself. He weeded out all but one mare, Flaming Top, and imported the stallions Nasrullah, Princequillo, Ambiorix and Double Jay. He bred Round Table and Bold Ruler'.

For the following fifteen years a Claiborne stallion headed the American sire roster. In twenty years at Claiborne Farm Bull bred the winners of almost 3,000 races. Bull and Vincent shot grouse together in August 1972, but, returning to America via Ballydoyle, Bull became ill and died very shortly afterwards, aged only sixty-two. He had invited Vincent to train in America, and the year before they had formed a partnership with Bill Perry and Jack Mulcahy in which they would jointly own the yearlings bred at Claiborne. Vincent says, 'Perhaps the greatest compliment I was ever paid was when Bull asked me to train for him in America.'

* * *

Some six years after buying Larkspur, Vincent was convinced of the virtues of American-bred horses. So it came about that when Raymond Guest was looking for another horse to win the Epsom Derby for him, he commissioned Bull Hancock to pick one out at the famous Keeneland Sales. He was prepared to pay much more than the 12,000 or so guineas he had given for Larkspur. The world bloodstock markets had started their upward surge. Vincent recalls, 'Raymond told Bull he could go to around $60,000. The yearling Bull picked out first and tried to buy went for $90,000. He had selected an alternative, a yearling by Sir Gaylord, and got him for Raymond for $42,000. Bull rang me and asked me to train him.' The colt on which Bull Hancock had been outbid went to Charles Engelhard, for whom Vincent, two years later, would be training Nijinsky. 'The yearling,' Vincent continues, 'was Sir Ivor, named after Raymond's cousin, Sir Ivor Guest. Sir Ivor was foaled in 1965 by Sir Gaylord, out of a good American mare called Attica. He was bred by an attractive lady, Alice Chandler, who descends from one of the first white explorers to penetrate what is now Kentucky – that mighty hunter, Daniel Boone. Boone struggled westwards from Virginia over the Cumberland Mountains to find one of the Indians' best hunting areas. 'Kentucke' derives from the Indian meaning 'dark and bloody ground'. A replica of the fort Boone founded against the Indians exists in South Eastern Kentucky. Mrs Alice Chandler's family were also closely involved in the founding of the Keeneland Association which uniquely runs a non-profit taking racecourse, one of the prettiest in the States, and the largest bloodstock sales company in the world.

Sir Ivor's dam, Attica, was a present from Alice's father. She was a top class race mare winning five races at three and four years old and was placed in two American Stakes races. She was by the great Mahmoud's son Mr Trouble.

Alice Chandler says, 'My father gave me Attica and said "someday I think, Al, she may throw you a racehorse"'. She had produced three winners; none of them top class, before Sir Ivor appeared.

Vincent felt he looked rather a backward type for an American sales-produced yearling. American breeders are great stockmen; their yearlings are normally produced in marvellous condition. 'Even as a two-year-old I thought he'd take some time, and I remember showing him to Raymond in April [1967] and he agreed, saying, "Well, we wouldn't expect too much of him until the autumn at the earliest." '

CHAPTER 11

SIR IVOR

'He was as tough as they come'

The initial expectations of both owner and trainer changed rapidly. Even the best judges cannot exactly see the future. 'Remarkable to say,' Vincent says, 'in May and June Sir Ivor changed completely.' The lads in the yard at the time of his arrival recall, 'He was so big and backward – he was bigger than Golden Fleece – that you'd never think he would run as a two-year-old.' T. P. Burns adds, 'As a two-year-old you'd fear he'd grow into a monster . . . but he grew sideways.' The lads remember Liam Ward driving down to ride Sir Ivor a bit of work in May and 'being impressed with him'.

'Come the month of May,' said Vincent, 'he had changed a lot and he came up to his first race on Irish Derby Day, the last Saturday in June, at the Curragh. He was the sort of horse who needed a run, but I thought he'd win, and when he finished fourth I was quite disappointed. But Liam said to me afterwards, "The three that finished in front of him today will never do so again."' And Sir Ivor did win next time out at the Curragh at the end of July. He returned in September for a brilliant victory in the National Stakes, and then flew to France to beat the best of their two-year-olds in the Grand Criterium.

As soon as Sir Ivor won that first race back in July, Raymond Guest boldly struck an enormous Derby wager on his colt. 'Raymond had a friend staying with him,' Vincent recalls, 'called Abe Hewitt, an American by way of being an expert on thoroughbred pedigrees, and so forth.' Presumably Mr Hewitt encouraged Mr Guest, for Vincent goes on, 'Raymond was always somebody who loved to have a bet, and he and Hewitt decided they'd get some money on the horse at long odds for the Derby. They managed to find William Hill who was on a yacht at Deauville, and they got a bet of £500 each way at 100–1.' The bet stood at £62,500, which in today's terms is worth about £750,000.

As William Hill noted Sir Ivor's victories in Ireland's and France's top two-year-olds races, the anxiety of the bookmaker waxed grimly. At Longchamp in the Grand Criterium, Sir Ivor was ridden by Lester Piggott. 'He had the horse five to six lengths behind at the two-furlong marker,' says Vincent, 'and Lester said after the race, "He quickened so fast he nearly ran out from under me!"'

William Hill had already made vain approaches to Guest to get the wager reduced, before O'Brien took a startling new step. This nearly ended in a disaster for Sir Ivor which would have saved the sweating bacon of the bookmaker. Vincent decided to send eight of his best horses to Pisa. The pretty little racecourse and the winter training grounds sheltered by umbrella pines are enclosed on three sides by woods in a quiet, level park on sandy soil not far from the sea and the Leaning Tower. There are two excellent mile straights made from the velvety alluvial soil where the River Arno once flowed. They are, however, some way from the fine stables, standing outside the parkland, and directly at the side of a straight and busy road, noisy with lorries and bordered by a deep dyke.

Work rider Johnny Brabston went out from Ballydoyle to Pisa on New Year's Day 1968. 'The horse got an abscess in the foot which lasted fully three weeks, for sand had got in and he had a terrible leg. The Italian blacksmith wasn't very clever and the leg swelled up like a balloon! Then Bob Griffin came out. He opened the foot up and his advice was to keep him walking and to keep bathing the foot. But, of course, having been idle, Sir Ivor got terribly fresh when we started to exercise him again. You could meet flocks of sheep coming at you with bells on them, on the road to the training grounds. Once I had to slide off him as the saddle went up his neck!'

'The Italians have been wintering their horses in Pisa for generations,' Vincent remarks. 'You get mild weather and none of the cold winds you get in Ireland and England. Sir Ivor did tremendously well out there, so much so that one morning he gave a jump and a kick going down the pathway by the side of the main road and he got Johnny off. I was behind him in a car with my head man. We nearly died of fright! We jumped out of the car and we got our hands wide out round him. But there was that long dyke with water in. If he'd got away from us, he'd have toppled over into that dyke. But the three of us – because Johnny had landed on his legs and kept hold of the reins – luckily managed to stop him from getting away. It was a tremendous relief when he didn't get loose. He could have gone to Rome or anywhere.' Even the recollection of that scramble on the brink of disaster makes Vincent shudder.

The lads recall of this intelligent horse, 'At three years old he'd pull himself up at the same spot on the home gallops where he used to pull up as a two-year-old. It looked as if he wasn't genuine, which was very worrying. But the Boss simply started his work the same distance further back, and all was fine.'

Sir Ivor's prep race for the 2,000 Guineas that spring was Ascot's 2,000 Guineas Trial, run in desperately heavy ground. He only just won, and was nearly caught. Piggott, hard of hearing, reported, 'The horse heard them coming – not me!' Not everyone appreciated Sir Ivor's achievement in Ascot's mud, and Dermot O'Brien remembers that 'he'd been working a bit in-and-out at home, so two weeks before the Guineas we took him and two other horses over to Newmarket. We stayed in the Links Stables and worked there on the gallops.' The lads say, 'The Boss came over to watch his work. Special? The really special thing was the way he worked! The night before the race Lester Piggott said, "Nothing will beat this horse." '

On Guineas Day at Newmarket, many preferred Petingo, the impressive winner of both the Gimcrack and the Middle Park Stakes; however, Sir Ivor, ridden with supreme confidence by Piggott, caught Petingo in the Dip and won going away by one and a half lengths. He was instantly hot favourite for the Derby. The only doubt surrounding Sir Ivor's chances in that race lay in his stamina: could a horse possessed of such brilliant speed stay one and a half miles? The combination of his calm temperament, his relaxed manner of racing and the configuration of Epsom strongly suggested he would.

William Hill then became, in Vincent's words, 'really worried. He tried nearly every trick in the book to try to get Raymond Guest to call off at least a portion of the huge wager. He even told Raymond that if he wouldn't cancel his investment he intended to publish details of it in the *Sporting Life*.' This exceptionally unethical threat was presumably uttered in the belief that the United States ambassador to Ireland might be frightened of having so large a wager publicized. This seemed like blackmail, as if a stockbroker were threatening an ambassador with publication of his private investments in the *Financial Times*. Guest was in no way deterred, and Hill supposedly executed his threat by leaking news about the bet to the *Sporting Life*. O'Brien comments, 'I thought this was very poor form.'

Raymond Guest kept his bet. He could not, however, keep his date at Epsom. On Derby Day he had to go to the opening of the Kennedy Park Arboretum in Co. Wexford to plant a tree to commemorate President John F. Kennedy's birthday. A newspaper cutting from the time reported:

Mr Guest watched the Derby in Ireland on a portable TV, and as his three-year-old swept to victory, Mr Guest was mobbed by hundreds of wildly enthusiastic Irishmen and women. In the excitement, the ceremony, Ireland's tribute to President Kennedy, was forgotten for a while and government ministers, diplomats and bishops gathered around the TV set on the ground, wrapped in brown paper to shade it from the sun. The eminent Raymond Guest knelt on the ground visibly trembling in front of the set.

When Sir Ivor was rounding Tattenham Corner he
whispered to Mrs Eunice Shriver, President Kennedy's
sister, 'We're not well placed! He's going to leave it too
late.'

Seconds later he jumped up and said, 'Where is
he?' Beside him was 12-year-old Maria Shriver [now
Mrs Arnold Schwarzenegger], who kept shouting,
'Hurry up, hurry up!' As his money-spinner went past
the post he bounced up and down shouting, 'Go on
Lester!'

Mrs Shriver gave him a big kiss on the cheek as he
passed the post. Later, when congratulated by
President Eamon De Valera, he said, 'Sir Ivor gave me
so much trouble; I will put you up on him next time.'

With tears in his eyes, Mr Guest said, 'I was
worried until the last step, but now I feel wonderful. I
want to thank my trainer Mr Vincent O'Brien, Lester
Piggott and the Giver of all good things. I am very
grateful.'

When asked about his big win, he said, 'Don't
forget that Uncle Sam will take 77% of the money.'

Raymond's absence from Epsom that day was the greatest
disappointment of his racing life. His wife, Caroline, a descen-
dant of Prince Murat, one of Napoleon's marshals, led the
winner in. At least Raymond made the celebration dinner at
the Savoy Hotel in London.

The American breeder of the winner, Alice Chandler of
Kentucky, decades later reviewed the scene. 'The horse was
tucked in solid on the rails, a hundred yards out, and he had

no shot of winning. Then you've never seen a horse run so fast in your life. We didn't believe he'd won. I've seen that film many, many times and I'll still give you 6–5 he got beat.' Hearing this, Vincent murmurs, 'Started to run? That's after Lester eased him outside Connaught.' One of the lads recalls, 'Poor Sandy Barclay on Connaught looked round and thought he could never be caught, never be beat. He came in crying!' Even the carefully unemotional O'Brien, who himself had hefty bets on the horse, declares, 'Lester rode a spectacular race . . . and I often wonder what the time was for that final furlong.' In America it would have been clocked and illuminated on the track.

In the light of Sir Ivor's subsequent career, Piggott's brilliance that day was in conserving the pounce of what was really a great one-and-a-quarter-miler in a one-and-a-half-mile race. The English Derby, due to its steep and sharp downhill bend, and its generally fast ground, can be won by horses who do not truly stay one and a half miles on a galloping track.

After Epsom, Sir Ivor was ridden by Liam Ward – who had a verbal agreement with Vincent to ride his horses in Ireland – when beaten in the Irish Derby on the wide and galloping expanse of the Curragh, where he was outstayed by Ribero, ridden by Lester Piggott. Ward's comment was firm – 'He died on me' – but Piggott, who was convinced that Sir Ivor was less likely to stay the twelve furlongs at the Curragh than at Epsom, deliberately rode to outstay the O'Brien colt, taking up the running early in the straight and easily repelling Sir Ivor's challenge. Liam had been champion jockey in Ireland six times 'before Vincent'. He smiles. 'I was never champion jockey at Ballydoyle.'

Liam recalls with dry gloom the Irish Derby celebration party Raymond Guest had laid on in the Residency in Phoenix Park prior to the defeat. 'Dreadful. No-one knew what to say, or do. Vincent and I hung back in the bar. The butler comes – "Your presence is requested." As we're going into that cheerless gathering Vincent, who never told me I'd ridden a good race and never told me I'd ridden a bad one, put his hand on my shoulder as we were walking into the dining room and said, "You did everything I hoped you would do on him." And that was that. The whole evening ended miserably before eleven.'

Only a week later Sir Ivor was back in England again for the Eclipse and was beaten by two older horses, the winner being the previous year's Derby victor Royal Palace, sired by Ballymoss. Piggott was criticized from the grandstand for riding Sir Ivor too confidently, but the ground was very firm and the colt came back to Ireland, in Vincent's phrase, 'jarred of his knees'.

On the Sunday before the Prix de l'Arc de Triomphe the much-travelled colt went to France for his prep race at Longchamp. 'He was second,' says T. P. Burns, 'and he blew a lot. We took him down to Lamorlaye and he stayed in a little block of three stables out in the forest. On the Thursday or Friday the Boss came out and Sir Ivor did a good bit of work. And in the Prix de l'Arc de Triomphe, ridden by Lester Piggott, he ran a hell of a race. He was only beaten by a very good horse indeed, Vaguely Noble, who got all the breaks in the race.' 'Vaguely Noble,' says Vincent, 'truly stayed a mile and a half. Also the soft ground was much in his favour.'

Thirteen days later, Sir Ivor easily won the Champion Stakes at Newmarket, after which he flew back to America for the Washington International. This was the second time ever in the history of American racing that an English Derby winner had raced in the US; in 1923, Zev, winner of that year's Kentucky Derby, had defeated the 1923 Epsom Derby winner Papyrus in a $100,000 match at Belmont Park. There was so much public interest that the race was broadcast on the radio – a first for American broadcasting.

The Laurel Race, run on very soft ground, came at the end of an extremely tough three-year-old campaign for Sir Ivor. The American press were very critical of Lester Piggott's riding, although he rode Sir Ivor in his usual style. He was lying only third or fourth swinging round the last bend into the short home stretch. Then the horse, for the last time, flaunted that astonishing acceleration for which he had become famous and won easily by three quarters of a length. Yet the press damned Lester for riding a bad race. He was upset and quite hurt. Then, after a few days, just one of the journalists came out and suggested that maybe he had won cleverly. The following year he won the Washington International on Karabas, trained by Bernard van Cutsem at Newmarket. This time, although the press were more polite, Lester would have nothing to say to them. 'So that year I was branded "a rude bum",' said Lester afterwards, 'as opposed to simply "a bum" on Sir Ivor in 1968.'

Raymond Guest allowed Sir Ivor to stand at stud in Ireland, at his Ballygoran Stud Farm in Co. Kildare, for two years, 1969 and 1970, before leaving for America. This extremely generous gesture enabled European breeders to use Sir Ivor before he went to stud at Claiborne in Kentucky under the care of Bull Hancock, who had chosen him as a yearling.

Vincent says, 'Sir Ivor always had the most wonderful

temperament . . . When he came to racing he was as tough as they come, never got upset, and when he had to get down and really run, he always pulled out all he had to give.' There could be few finer tributes from a trainer to his horse, O'Brien continues, before comparing Sir Ivor, who died in 1995, with Nijinsky. 'Well, of course, they're two brilliant horses, but different in their characters in all respects. Sir Ivor was so self-contained . . . I think Lester, wholly for that reason, would probably lean toward Sir Ivor. Nijinsky was quite highly strung. He wasn't as easy a horse to train as Sir Ivor. He was always on his toes so that he needed much less work. You had to be careful you didn't overwork him. Whereas with Sir Ivor you were completely unconcerned about anything to do with him. So, of the two, he was the tougher horse.' He weighs one against the other and gives a small shrug. 'Two great horses,' he repeats. 'I'd hate to say which was the better.'

Sir Ivor has been a very successful sire of fillies who as brood mares have produced more than a hundred stakes winners. Of his daughters among the best were Ivanjica, who won the Prix de l'Arc de Triomphe, and Optimistic Girl, who raced in America. Sir Ivor was the sire of Lady Capulet, dam of El Prado, who was Champion sire in America in 2003. His best colt at stud has been Sir Tristram, one of the most outstanding sires in the southern hemisphere and, with his son Zabeel, a great influence on breeding there.

CHAPTER 12

NIJINSKY

'Any minute now this will turn into wine'

T
wo things came into Vincent's life by good fortune and his own acute eye and decisiveness: the purchase of Nijinsky and his recognition of the fabulous Northern Dancer bloodline.

Charles Engelhard, an enormously rich American, was a racehorse owner on the grandest scale. He was Old Money Establishment: schooled at St Paul's and Princeton, and member of the Brook Club in Manhattan and Bucks in London. He had four trainers in England and one each in France, the USA and South Africa, where one of his two giant corporations had platinum interests. He was also an honorary member of England's Jockey Club. Vincent had first met him at the Saratoga sales in summer 1964, and after Engelhard had visited Ballydoyle later that year was sent two horses, both of whom ran unplaced in the 1966 Derby: Right Noble (who, ridden by Lester Piggott, started joint favourite) and Grey Moss. In 1968 he asked Vincent to fly up to Canada to look at a yearling owned by a Canadian tycoon of comparable wealth and power,

E. P. (Eddie) Taylor, based at Windfields Farm near Toronto.

'Charlie Engelhard,' explains Vincent, 'had had a lot of success with Ribot horses around that time. He wanted me to see a Ribot yearling at Eddie Taylor's farm in Toronto. I thought, "My God, it's a long way to go to see one horse! But we'd better do it!" I saw the horse by Ribot and I didn't like him a whole lot. In fact, he had a crooked foreleg. Then I thought I'd better see what else they'd got. I saw this other horse and he really filled my eye.

'I went from there to Saratoga – it was August and the Saratoga season was just beginning. There I met Charlie who was also staying with Jimmy Brady. I said I didn't advise Charlie to have the Ribot colt, but that I did see a horse in Canada by Northern Dancer out of Flaming Page that I thought he should buy. He would be in the sales in Canada the following month.'

The colt came from only the second crop of Northern Dancer, still unproven as a sire. There was nothing then to suggest this was going to be the greatest sire of his day and a huge influence on thoroughbred breeding. Mr Engelhard said he'd send one of his men to bid for the yearling at the Canadian sales. Vincent was anxious. 'His man was entirely inexperienced where the buying of horses was concerned,' he fretted. 'So I was worried he might make some slip-up and I'd lose the horse. But we got him anyhow. He cost Can$84,000, a Canadian record, against Sir Ivor, who cost US$42,000.'

Nijinsky was always 'treated as something special', as O'Brien himself puts it. 'When I got him over from Canada we found he wouldn't eat his oats. We were puzzled and worried as it went on for some days. I called up the manager of

Windfields Farm where he'd been bred. He told me the horse had never been offered oats, and had been fed nuts. It never struck me that a horse might have been used to eating nuts instead of oats, so I said, "Please get some of those nuts over straight away!" But the very day they arrived the horse started to eat oats. All was well.

'He had to be specially trained and needed good handling and patience to get him right. He would always be worked alone before the other horses. He got impatient if he was kept waiting. Early on as a two-year-old, he was in two minds about the whole thing. If I hadn't had really first-class horsemen to ride him I don't believe that we ever could have succeeded with him. Also, I think if he had been trained on public training grounds like Newmarket or the Curragh he could easily have gone the wrong way.'

So in the first months of winter work Vincent O'Brien had to sit down to compose a difficult letter to Nijinsky's owner, Charles Engelhard. This, after all, was the yearling Vincent had picked in preference to the one Mr Engelhard, a valued patron, had asked him to examine, moreover the one who had cost most at the sales. Vincent wrote, 'I am somewhat concerned about Nijinsky's temperament and that he is inclined to resent getting on with his work. My best boys are riding him and we can only hope he will go the right way.'

And after that things began to improve. Nijinsky went to the Curragh and worked out of the stalls there; he was no trouble entering the starting stalls at home and everything went right. 'I was only following the other horses,' says Johnny Brabston, 'but I knew he was some horse.' When Liam Ward came down to ride work, he confirmed Johnny's words about

Nijinsky. 'Between February and May [1969] we all thought here that if he goes the right way he'd be a good horse.'

Things went brilliantly. 'If it were not for two very capable work riders, Johnny Brabston and Danny O'Sullivan,' O'Brien repeats fairly, 'Nijinsky could have easily been spoiled. They had the strength to handle him and the patience not to knock him about.' Once he was on the gallops there were no difficulties, provided he was allowed to get on his way. 'For a horse of his size,' Vincent says with a trace of amusement, 'he came up to a race' – a regular O'Brien phrase – 'surprisingly quickly.'

He won the Erne Stakes on the Curragh at the start of July so easily that, as the lads recall, 'after that first race all Ireland was talking of him'. Word had flown about even before that, for he started odds-on. He never started odds-against until he contested the Epsom Derby halfway through his three-year-old career. Between 12 July and 27 September he won four successive races on Ireland's Curragh including the top two-year-old events, the Railway, the Anglesey and the Beresford Stakes. 'In his races he never sweated,' say the lads, 'he'd pull up dry!' Vincent adds, with less hyperbole, 'Well, as he progressed through a race he sweated less.'

With these four Irish victories behind him, Nijinsky crossed to Newmarket for the Dewhurst Stakes. This, too, he won in such style that he was made favourite for the following year's Classics, and was rated top of the Free Handicap. The difficult, high-mettled horse of whom O'Brien had so nearly despaired nine months earlier had won all his five starts in the space of a mere thirteen weeks. At the end of his two-year-old career Nijinsky was now worth a fortune, and the $84,000 paid for him was a bargain.

The weather on Nijinsky's return from Newmarket after the Dewhurst was bland, but 'that October was golden, it was like summer,' the lads remember. 'The Boss decided to relax Nijinsky by turning him out in the small paddock with his lead horse, My Passion.' The thought of the most valuable colt in Ireland and Britain turned out in a field might bring shivers of dread to some horse people, but the staff at Ballydoyle had developed a calm philosophy about the riches in their care. 'If you went through the list of horses here and thought what we'd got, you'd never sleep at night,' said Gerry Gallagher, the travelling head man. Someone else chips in: 'The Boss turning him out worked wonders. 'Twas like goin' to the Bahamas for a holiday for him. And, d'you know, he never reared again afterwards. He was ridden every day and no problems.'

The spring of 1970 soon came, and the hot winter favourite for the Guineas was in tremendous form. Johnny Brabston rode him in all his home work. 'He looked great in the spring and his early work was terrific.' His prep race for the 2,000 Guineas was the race named after another famous graduate of Ballydoyle; Nijinsky won his sixth race from six starts by taking the Gladness Stakes at the Curragh. The horse went to Newmarket protected by great security. O'Brien hired his own private detective to aid the official guards on The Links stables, as the colt was a prime target for nobbling. Estimates on race day were that, if he won, he would cost bookmakers £500,000 (about £7.5 million in 2005). To keep their future liabilities down, the colt, 3–1 at the season's start, was shortened by the bookmakers to prohibitive odds on: he started 7–4 on favourite for the Guineas. Timeform's *Racehorses of 1970* recognized something quite exceptional: 'In the paddock he outclassed his rivals as seldom a Classic field can have been outclassed before.' And it was not only his quality: in size and scope he also towered over them.

On Guineas morning, 29 April, the *Sporting Life* headline below its one-shilling cover price read in black capital letters three quarters of an inch high, 'Who's Going To Be Second to Nijinsky?' 'He will start the hottest favourite,' wrote Man on the Spot, 'since Colombo landed the odds of 7–2 on back in 1934.' Piggott was quoted by Our Man in Paris: 'The colt is at least 8lb better than Sir Ivor when he won in 1968.' Nijinsky easily won the 2,000 Guineas, by two and a half lengths.

Nijinsky's final preparation for the Derby took place neither at Ballydoyle nor Epsom, but at Sandown Park. With the onset of some coughing at Ballydoyle, Vincent had rushed Nijinsky across to empty, quiet Sandown Park, arriving on the Friday night five days before the race. On the Saturday, he trotted on the course. On Sunday, he worked at half-speed (meaning a good swinging gallop) the reverse way along the back stretch, back to the stables. On Monday, he did the same but a bit quicker, and that afternoon he was moved over to Epsom. On Tuesday morning, his training was in accordance with O'Brien's established pre-Derby pattern: working uphill for four furlongs from the one-and-a-half-mile Derby start. After this, Nijinsky walked down Tattenham Hill with his working partner, Ribotprince, and then they both hacked – 'just lobbing' – along the straight, under the grandstands, towards the winning post and the racecourse stables.

So far so good. And so soon after that a fearful fright. Nijinsky, back in the racecourse stables, was rubbed down. 'The Boss,' say the lads, 'was there watching. Then we noticed the horse starting to paw. He went on pawing and got down in the box and started to sweat.' The symptoms were the sinister precursors of colic. Because a horse is unable to vomit, he cannot, like a man or a dog, get rid of indigestible substances via his mouth, so gas can build up in the stomach and intestines. The guts start to blow up, and under pressure can twist round in the confined space, like a squeezed-in long balloon. The gas, under increasing heat and pressure, continues to expand, piercing the animal with terrible pain. Finally, the twisted gut can rupture, and the horse may die.

Colic had struck Nijinsky the day before the Derby. He was, his lads knew, always slightly prone to a touch of colic. The sweating increased, but it was, the boys remember, a very hot day. Gerry, the travelling head lad, rang the Epsom trainer, Irishman 'Boggy' Whelan, to ask him for the name of a local vet. 'I said something needed checking on the horse's passport! We didn't want anyone to know what was happening.' Vincent comments, 'Boggy Whelan was so helpful to the Ballydoyle horses over many years, and he used to saddle for me if I couldn't be there.' Vincent also telephoned the faithful Bob Griffin over in Ireland, asking him to fly over with all speed. Bob heard Vincent's concise report of the symptoms and said it sounded as if the horse 'had at least got a slight twinge of colic'. He said to Vincent, 'Even if I came over, I couldn't treat the horse. We couldn't give him any medication the day before the race.' Normal veterinary treatment for colitis is the injection of a drug which relaxes the muscles and the intestines which are in spasm. The painful gas can then escape. But Nijinsky was within twenty-nine hours of the race. The local vet confirmed Bob's telephoned diagnosis, and although Ballydoyle's regular vet Demi O'Byrne was promptly flown from Ballydoyle to Epsom, all anyone could do was hope and wait and pray that it passed.

The crisis lasted for about one and a half hours, which for the O'Brien camp seemed infinitely longer. Then the horse became easier. The lads walked across the course to the wood behind the start to gather some grass for Nijinsky. They mixed this with a little soda bicarbonate and some bran, and anxiously proffered it. Tensely, they waited to see if the horse was still feeling queasy and would reject it. Nijinsky ate the little meal. 'He was restful. We stayed watching. The Boss was there all day. And by the evening the horse was as fresh as ever.'

The crisis had passed. Few people knew of the threat to Nijinsky. Even the bookmakers' notorious spy service failed. If word of Nijinsky's attack had leaked out, panic would have struck the betting market. As a result of his interrogation by the Stewards after Larkspur's Derby, O'Brien had no inclination to issue further public bulletins about his horses' health, which might afterwards have seemed misleading.

Nijinsky started favourite for the Derby at 11–8 – the first time in his career he had started at odds-against. Gyr, stoutly bred in the USA and strongly fancied at 100–30, set sail for home on the fast ground two furlongs out. Piggott had merely to shake up Nijinsky and show him the whip. The colt moved into top gear, went past Gyr and won comfortably by two and a half lengths. The time of the race nearly equalled Mahmoud's record in May 1936 at 2m 33.8s, clocked by handheld watches and so regarded as suspect: Nijinsky registered 2m 34.68s. The next time the record was threatened was twelve years later, when Nijinsky's son Golden Fleece took a sixth Epsom Derby home to Ballydoyle. His electronically timed figure was 2m 34.27s.

After Nijinsky's victory, the Engelhards and the O'Briens were taken, as is customary, up to the royal box. But in the excitement of the race, the very stout Mr Engelhard's braces had broken. He was thus presented to the Queen Mother clutching his grey top hat and his stick while keeping up his trousers as best he could with his elbows. 'Oh, Mr Engelhard,' said the Queen Mother with her customary thoughtfulness as the owner in his hour of glory went forward to shake hands, 'do let me take your hat. You seem to be having some difficulty. Can I hold something?' Mr Engelhard shook hands, elbows still holding up his trousers. He said afterwards to Jacqueline, 'If I'd moved my arms, my trousers would have fallen down!'

* * *

Nijinsky's next race was the Irish Derby, and for that he was ridden by Liam Ward. The popularity of the horse and his Irish jockey drew buzzing attention at the Curragh. During the lengthy preliminaries he showed, for the first time on a racecourse, the keyed-up characteristics that had marked his work at home: he sweated up, and he was noticeably upset. But there was no repeat of Sir Ivor's defeat.

The rain hosed down, and in it, after the race, stood Charlie Engelhard with the presentation silver chalice. In the leaden downpour he murmured to Jacqueline O'Brien, pointing at the water in the silver chalice, 'Any minute now this will turn into wine.' Later, when pressed by journalists about how many horses he owned and their cost in keep, he said happily, 'I can tell you one thing – all my horses will eat tonight!'

No problems beset Nijinsky between his ninth successive victory and his return to England to attempt his toughest battle yet in Ascot's King George VI and Queen Elizabeth Stakes on 25 July. It would be the great horse's fifth race in sixteen weeks – proof positive of his magnificent constitution, the delicate timing of O'Brien's training, and the work of the staff with a horse who could, in lesser hands, have turned into a nervous wreck.

His task was formidable. He was the only three-year-old in a field which included two previous Derby winners (English and Italian), the winners of the previous year's French Oaks and the Washington International, and the current holder of the Coronation Cup. But Piggott rode him with supreme confidence. He simply sauntered to the front one furlong out and coasted home, hard-held, from the 1969 Derby winner Blakeney. It was the performance of a horse outstanding not just in his year, but in the experience of generations of racegoers.

But fate had another blow to deal the golden colt. Within a week of his return to Ballydoyle, Nijinsky was struck down by a particularly virulent form of ringworm. 'So much of his hair fell out that he was bald over most of his body,' Vincent reports. 'Of course, there was no way we could put a saddle on him. The most we could do was to lead him out and to lunge him a little.' Then Charlie Engelhard's racing manager David McCall got in touch with O'Brien: 'Charlie would get the greatest pleasure if we could win the Triple Crown with Nijinsky. Do you think, Vincent, you could get him ready in time for the St Leger?'

It was a difficult request. Nijinsky's final grand goal was the Prix de l'Arc de Triomphe. The St Leger, over a quarter of a mile further and run a month earlier, was not the ideal prep race. It says much for the greatness of the horse as well as, sadly, the diminishing standard of the St Leger that Britain's fifth and oldest Classic could be considered merely a 'prep race' for a contest abroad. In the American marketplace, the St Leger is of little importance. To win one may even condemn a horse for lacking one-and-a-quarter-mile speed. In the States, racing men rate only three European races at the top: Epsom's Derby, Ascot's King George VI and Queen Elizabeth Stakes, and Longchamp's Prix de l'Arc de Triomphe. O'Brien adds, 'And the Irish Derby, making four.'

No horse had won the three colts' Classics since Bahram in 1935. Still, O'Brien reasoned, the horse did need one prep race before the Prix de l'Arc de Triomphe, there was nothing else very suitable, and there did not seem much in the race. But time was short. The horse's work had been severely held up by the ringworm. 'Even in late August,' the lads report, 'you could not ride him for ten minutes or he'd bleed.' With little breathing space, the horse 'worked patchy' before going over to Doncaster, the lads recall, but he won the race. 'The opposition may not have been strong,' says Vincent, 'but they certainly set out to make it a test of stamina. He won, but I would say he wouldn't have pulled out any more. Furthermore, he lost 29lb in weight coming back from the St Leger.' The inference is stark: a fit horse loses very little after a race. Up to the St Leger, Nijinsky had gone through his unbeaten career of eleven victories without losing condition. With hindsight, Vincent would say, 'The Leger would not have helped his preparation for the Prix de l'Arc de Triomphe.' But Nijinsky had won the Triple Crown for his popular owner, the first horse to do so for thirty-five years.

Before the Prix de l'Arc de Triomphe, Vincent gave his

customary instructions to Lester. He told him that Nijinsky's coat was coming better every day. 'The horse is working as well as ever.' Then he said, 'The records show that the winner of the Prix de l'Arc de Triomphe invariably holds a prominent position throughout the race. You *must* lie up. Few horses further back than fourth turning into the straight go on to win the Prix de l'Arc de Triomphe.' Vincent subsequently and sadly said, 'So I made those suggestions about riding the horse, that he might not want to be too far out of his ground, turning into the straight – principally because of beaten horses coming back on him. Lester's exact reply to me was, "I don't care if there are one hundred horses in front of me!"'

'Lester had him well behind,' Vincent recounts. 'In fact, he was fourth from last with half a mile to go. And he wasn't getting an opening . . . Still he wasn't getting any opening . . . and he kept edging out, and out, and out. Meanwhile, Yves Saint-Martin, on the inside, was making the best of his way home. He knew his horse Sassafras would get the trip. Lester hit Nijinsky once and the horse ran further left.' The recollection after nearly thirty-five years still makes O'Brien feel wretched. The defeat aches today because Vincent believes it was no fault of Nijinsky's. It hurt initially because it was so desperately close that while the photograph was being developed, Vincent went on hoping. 'I was a good way before the winning post, watching. Everybody around me said the horse had won. I had my doubts, but I hung on to the hope that maybe he had.' Then came one of his characteristic understatements: 'This made things a little tougher to take . . .'

Five months after the race Vincent stated unequivocally to American turf writer Leon Rasmussen, 'I sincerely believe that the run Lester asked Nijinsky to make was over too long a distance, that in the Prix de l'Arc de Triomphe it was an impossibility. The horse had shown Lester such tremendous speed in all his races that he felt he could pick them up whenever he wanted. Once again, Longchamp is different and the horse's health was probably below par . . .' Nijinsky beat Gyr, who finished fourth, by a greater distance than he'd beaten him in the Derby; and he doubled the distance by which he had beaten Blakeney in Ascot's King George VI and Queen Elizabeth Stakes. Compared with the running of those two races he did not run below form. Indeed, he improved on it. But the race was lost.

'Of course, Nijinsky wouldn't have gone for the Champion Stakes if he'd won the Prix de l'Arc de Triomphe,' says Vincent crisply, 'but he seemed all right after the race. The trip hadn't caused him to lose much weight. The opposition seemed weak. It looked as if he had little to beat. And we desperately wanted to let him finish his career on a high note.' Until Longchamp, it had seemed certain that Nijinsky would go right through his racing days unbeaten. 'He looked perfectly well in the paddock at Newmarket,' Vincent remembers, 'but as soon as he started to leave it and go on to the course he began, for the first time, to crack under the attentions of the photographers and all his admirers and the cheering for him which broke out in the parade.' The lads recall, 'He reared up for the first time since he was a two-year-old. He was terribly uptight.' And Vincent says that after the race Noel Murless, who was to English racing what Vincent was to Irish racing, told him, 'I was standing by the gate as they went out onto the course and I saw that Nijinsky was actually trembling. I said to the groundsman who was standing with me, "That horse can't win in the state he's in." ' Nijinsky was beaten by Lorenzaccio, who made all the running. The crowd had milled round their hero even down at the start. 'I saw on the film afterwards that he was a sorry sight,' Vincent says. 'It was a sad day. Really dreadful.' No other race so openly and for so long upset O'Brien.

Nijinsky was retired to stud and went to join Sir Ivor at Bull Hancock's lovely farm Claiborne, set above its lake outside Paris, Kentucky. Vigorous efforts had been made to raise a syndicate from England, Ireland and France to keep the great horse in Europe, but Charlie Engelhard was determined to have him home in America where his own mares could visit him. The horse was syndicated for US$5.5 million and the Engelhard family retained ten shares in him.

How does Vincent compare Nijinsky with his other great horses? 'I would have to rate him first or second. Him or Sir Ivor. For brilliance, Nijinsky. For toughness, Sir Ivor. And Golden Fleece, for he was never tested.' As for those other greats, Ribot and Sea Bird II, Vincent remarks quietly, 'It has to be remembered that Ribot, over three seasons, only left his homeland on three occasions, and Sea Bird only once. At three years old, Nijinsky ran eight times against Sea Bird's five. All but two of Nijinsky's three-year-old races were outside Ireland. He faced international competition at Newmarket, Epsom, Ascot, Doncaster, Longchamp and Newmarket again, with the Irish Derby thrown in. All in one season.' Vincent's case for Nijinsky rests there.

Lester Piggott added his views. 'Nijinsky, Sir Ivor and The Minstrel . . .' he began. 'I've always thought Sir Ivor my favourite. Had a terrific turn of speed. And he was a very sensible horse. And Nijinsky? On his day the most brilliant horse I've ever ridden, on a few days in summertime. The worst times, I s'pose, were when he got beaten in the Prix de l'Arc de Triomphe. And beaten again in the Champion Stakes. Such a public build-up. Such a let-down. Hard to believe really.'

Of Nijinsky's desperately close defeat in the Prix de l'Arc de Triomphe, Liam Ward comments, 'Lester was always convinced you could lie out of your ground in the Prix de l'Arc de Triomphe, but Nijinsky was probably just past his best coming up to this race. The Leger took the edge off him. Vincent was such a perfectionist. He left no stone unturned, which was why he was such a good trainer. He had the best method: always to keep the horses fresh so that you were never riding tired horses. They were always pulling hard at the end of the gallop.

'The really surprising thing is how few horses Vincent had at that time: probably forty to forty-five only at the time of Nijinsky. And what's more, Vincent was even then thinking of cutting back,' Liam Ward emphasizes.

Nijinsky was a champion sire of 156 individual Stakes winners, a world record at the time. They include the Epsom Derby winners Golden Fleece, Shahrastini and Lammtarra, and the Breeders' Cup winners Royal Academy, Dancing Spree and Ferdinand. His best sons at stud included the leading sires Caerleon and Royal Academy, while his daughters have produced multiple Group 1 winners.

CHAPTER 13

HOW THE BOSS TRAINED

'So-called meanness in a horse is rare'

S ome secrets of Vincent's successes can be told by two men who worked for him at crucial stages during Ballydoyle's history. Both Michael Kauntze and John Gosden were assistants to Vincent at times when some of his best horses were in training. They were able to observe the Boss in action, both in private and in public, on the racecourse, in the yard, in the office and – very often – in the winner's enclosure.

When Kauntze, formerly an assistant to two trainers in England, joined Vincent in 1967, Dermot had just retired to set up his successful stud farm at Derrygrath, Cahir. Sir Ivor, after his great year, was still in the yard waiting to go to stud. 'Very soon after I got there, Vincent – whom I called the Boss, of course – put his head through the window of his office and called out to me, "Michael, I'm going away for six weeks. Just keep Sir Ivor ticking over." And shut the window. I thought, "This great Derby winner . . . just keep him ticking over . . . the Boss away for six weeks." I was terrified. Suppose something happened!' John Gosden, now a successful trainer in his own right in both the US and Britain, served two golden years as assistant to Vincent in 1976 and 1977. He went on to win the Derby with Benny the Dip in 1997. 'We had the best horses then in every distance,' he remembers. He speaks of The Minstrel, Alleged, Artaius and Be My Guest.

Gosden and Kauntze did not overlap at Ballydoyle, but they did encounter each other once during 1970, the year of Nijinsky. When Nijinsky succumbed to as bad an infestation of ringworm as anyone could remember, Vincent, who had heard of a New York veterinarian who might have a cure for this dread complaint, arranged for some medicine to be brought over. Gosden, then nineteen, had a holiday job working on tracks at Belmont and Saratoga in New York State and escorting horses to and from the States and Europe. He collected the elixir in New York and handed it over to Kauntze, running across in the rain at Shannon airport. The ringworm infection cleared up just in time for Nijinsky to be trained, albeit with great difficulty, to win the St Leger, and so claim the Triple Crown of the English Classics.

Kauntze and Gosden are of the same mind about the experience of working for Vincent. 'Vincent under pressure never shouted, scarcely raised his voice even,' says Kauntze, 'and hardly ever swore. But you could tell by the look of him striding about that he was angry.' Gosden agrees. 'Vincent was so very on the ball. At times he got very, very tense, with a steely quality, like a taut spring. He was worse when a horse had won a big race than when he'd been beaten! Then he was easier to talk to. Plans had to be rebuilt. You could talk about it. After The Minstrel had won the King George VI at Ascot and was about to be syndicated it was like walking on eggshells at Ballydoyle.'

Recalling the daily routine, Kauntze says, 'We started at eight a.m. and the horses pulled out at 8.30. When I was there, we had fifty to sixty horses.' Some of the staff stood out in Kauntze's mind as being truly exceptional. The five members he picks out are Maurice O'Callaghan, the head man; Danny O'Sullivan, Vincent Rossiter and Johnny Brabston, the top work riders; and Willie Fogarty, the farm manager. Willy spent forty years at Ballydoyle and, no matter what Vincent proposed, he never said no. He immediately shifted all the farm men into the project (including the gardener) and it would be done, whatever the cost. Rossiter's consuming and only interest was horses. He stayed with Vincent for over thirty years and was one of his most valued work riders. He had an uncanny ability to judge pace – an essential skill for a good work rider. 'The Boss was quite tough on his horses,' adds Kauntze. 'Only seven furlongs was the most they'd work at home. But, my God! They worked. It took a tough horse. The two-year-olds wouldn't work until April or May. They'd work on the lawn gallops, three and a half furlongs maximum.'

Gosden recalls how Vincent organized his horses' work. 'He used numbers for speeds. He'd say, "Do a six" – which meant half-speed – "and quicken." He was always honing off that speed. That was the discipline when they went into fast work. Maximum distance seven furlongs. "Everything must have speed," he'd say. Yes, they had to be tough. If a horse wouldn't stand the preparation, they wouldn't become hardened athletes. It was the Ultimate Academy.' John Magnier often came over to watch work when he became not only part of the family but also Vincent's business partner. 'John would stand there, very strongly focused, listening and watching,' says Gosden. 'Robert Sangster came over three or four times a year. Until Magnier and Robert came along, though, Vincent was thinking of cutting right back, making the stables really just a small family-and-friends affair, perhaps twenty-five to thirty horses. Then with John Magnier and Robert Sangster coming in he ended up with sixty plus!'

'Our horses went out in two lots of twenty-five each.' Vincent comments. 'They walked and trotted for half an hour, then did a canter of about four furlongs. Depending on the horses' programmes, they would then do either a second canter or half-speed work of about five furlongs, or faster work. From the time they left their stables until they returned they were out about an hour and a half in all.

'My horses never worked fast more than twice a week. Even in their fast work they were always under restraint; they never worked flat out, nor was the whip ever used on them at home. Every lad was made to carry, but not necessarily use, a stick as colts need to know who is the master. I would be very annoyed to see any boy without one.

'I never worked a horse over a longer trip than the one he would eventually race over. In fact none of my Derby horses, racing over one and a half miles, were worked over more than a mile. I never designed gallops to copy racecourses. I always felt a horse in top condition could cope with local variations. After work the horses were hand-walked and then given a pick of grass for about twenty minutes. The lads used to have a smoke and talk about the work. The horses got a quick rub-down and each one was groomed for half an hour in the afternoons.

'I liked about five or six weeks to break my yearlings, and for quite a while afterwards they were ridden along the roads around the farm, walking and trotting. They then began cantering in circles, right and left. They later started working over stretches of about two furlongs, distances increasing as they progressed. We broke all the yearlings ourselves.'

Throughout his career, Vincent put the needs of the horse before the wishes of the owner. Detailed care and attention made him prosper as a trainer. 'My firm belief is that a horse with classic possibilities shouldn't be over-raced at two. He needs to peak in his three-year-old career when he will run over longer distances. At two, he shouldn't run before June or July at the earliest and not have more than four or five races. I've always felt one of the biggest dangers in running such a horse at two is that he will be competing with fast, earlier-maturing animals who are apt to take him off his feet. In a tight finish there is a grave possibility that he'll get too hard a race. I know very well how hard it is for trainers who are under pressure from owners to get their horses running. But I am certain that patience is rewarded in the end.'

And Vincent's understanding went far deeper than that. 'So-called meanness or ungenerousness in a horse is rare. These terms are very often wrongly applied to unfortunate horses whose courage has been impaired. I tried never to increase my demands on a horse until I was satisfied that he was thriving and enjoying what he was doing. If a horse is asked too much too soon he'll often turn in on himself and dislike racing. Courage is something a horse either has or has not, but it develops from physical strength, well-being and a settled nervous system. All the time in the world doesn't make a moderate horse tops, but it does get the best out of each horse.'

Ballydoyle was the stage, and all who worked there played their vital part on it. The *esprit de corps* at Ballydoyle was high because of the top-class winners produced there. And the Boss was a huge success. He could do no wrong. If he told you to do something you thought odd, he'd probably turn out to be right. Vincent all his life engendered loyalty from his staff. He demanded the strictest standards and was lightning-quick to criticize, spot faults and reprimand errors. He did, however, pay top wages, and his horses' winnings provided rich bonuses. 'We'd follow the Boss over a cliff,' said one employee, 'and land runnin'.'

'I liked my stable jockey to get to know the horses and ride work regularly,' Vincent says. 'I always encouraged my horses to be relaxed and happy in their work at home. In that way I found that they could produce a greater effort in a race. I never allowed a horse to be pushed to his limit at home. I always felt he would produce that bit extra on a racecourse, challenged by different surroundings, crowds, colours, music, loudspeakers, and the general excitement. With the jumpers, my schooling fences were at least twelve inches lower than the regulation jumps at the racetracks. The horses were never asked to jump higher than that at home. Even my three Grand National winners never jumped a higher fence before going to Liverpool where the obstacles were the stiffest and highest in the world. In a race a horse is much more wound up and alert and usually makes more effort, and concentrates more than at home. If you build a Grand National fence at home the risk is that a horse might dig in his toes approaching it and his courage might suffer.' Jacqueline remembers, 'Early Mist was our first Grand National runner, and Vincent realized a week before the race that the horse had never seen a water jump. And the one at Liverpool was very wide.' Vincent spread some lime on the far side of a small schooling fence and popped Early Mist over it to make him stretch. It worked – he won.

'With about fifty horses,' Vincent continues, 'I had a staff of forty-five, of whom thirty looked after the horses and the yard and ten worked on the gallops and the farm. Each stable lad looked after two horses and most of the lads rode the horses out in the mornings. There were three work riders, and horses did their work in pairs or in threes.' Vincent was particularly accurate in assessing horses from this home work; he did not have to run them on a racecourse to find out their form. Jacqueline is still amazed at his uncanny instinct for being able to assess work, spotting strengths and weaknesses that others didn't see. 'I remember particularly one morning when John McShain was over from America, Courts Appeal was to set off in front, and Ballymoss, a couple of lengths behind, would pass him and extend the lead in the final furlong. Courts Appeal stretched the lead and finished far in front, but Vincent was not disappointed. But John McShain was very anxious.'

John Gosden remembers, 'When Lester Piggott came along and came over to ride work there were appalling work mornings. Of course, Lester always wanted to try horses – see how good they really were. There was this morning before The Minstrel ran in the 2,000 Guineas. The two lead horses were Artaius [one of the first Keeneland purchases] and Be My Guest. Lester's instructions were, "Stay with the lead horse." Well, he deliberately got left. He was hardly in sight when the other two came round the bend. Then he deliberately went wide round the bend. And then' – and Gosden's voice rises in astonishment – 'he picked up his stick and gave The Minstrel a crack! The horse literally flew. Vincent got down off the stand in a rage and went back to the house and refused to speak to Lester. Then he banned Lester from riding work for some weeks. After that he let him come over. It was a wet morning, and he made Lester ride six two-year-olds, just trotting down and cantering slowly back! One after the other! No, Lester was not a happy bunny.'

Recalling the run-up to Nijinsky's Derby, Kauntze illustrates Vincent's quick-thinking at a time of crisis. 'About ten days before the Derby, two or three horses in the yard began to cough. Suddenly Vincent slid back the window in his office and called out to me, "We must get those two horses Nijinsky and Riboprince out of the yard."' Kauntze replied, 'Where to, boss? When?' Vincent said, 'Tonight.' Vincent had swiftly arranged that the two horses should lodge in the stables of empty Sandown racecourse. He had also persuaded the management and ground staff on the course not to breathe a word about their secret Irish visitors. 'We got on a Bristol Freighter at Shannon – the two horses and four of us – and flew to Gatwick. We arrived at six a.m. at Sandown. And the four of us arranged to keep watch over the horses in pairs day and night. Vincent used to stay for Epsom at the RAC Country Club nearby. On the Sunday morning at 3.30 Vincent suddenly appeared at the Sandown stables, and luckily for us found us awake and on watch. He said simply to me, "I couldn't sleep, Michael."' Next day there was another swift move. Sandown's clerk of the course told them that they were holding a blood-stock sale at the course. The horses for sale would be arriving at seven a.m., 'so we loaded up Nijinsky and Riboprince and took them across to the racecourse stables at Epsom to wait for the Derby two days later. And there, of course, we had the fright of Nijinsky going down with colic.'

Both of these two future trainers also admired Vincent's skill in attracting American owners. Kauntze was newly arrived at the stables when Vincent made one of his regular trips to the United States. 'The Boss was off to America to collect some more owners over there,' he says, enthusiastically describing as 'a real gent' one of his favourites, Jimmy Cox Brady. Vincent was attracting size-able dollar investments into the Irish racing economy to a level never experienced before. Vincent's owners came over to see their horses, watch them race, and to go on holidays, shooting and fishing in Ireland, England and Scotland. They freely spent their highly desirable dollars. 'Nobody opened up international bloodstock trade as Vincent did,' agrees John Gosden. 'Those Keeneland July Sales were virtually his fiefdom. He knew – probably still knows – all the bloodlines, both sides of the pedigree. Didn't matter how good-looking a horse was, if he wasn't bred right he wouldn't bother looking at him.' John gives a telling description of Vincent's almost magical skill in selecting horses: 'He took his time. He'd look and look. He could get inside their heads.

'When he was in Lexington,' Gosden continues, 'we'd call him daily from Ballydoyle at a certain time and go through the entire work list with him. Everything was covered in detail. Back at Ballydoyle a string of typed notes would fly through the sliding window into my office from his: what sort of a bit a horse was to wear, checking the ground where horses were to work . . .' Vincent handled the owners as delicately as he handled the horses, but he is clear about certain principles. He hated running two of his horses against each other, for example. 'I always tried to avoid running my good horses against each other, to keep good horses unbeaten for as long as possible. If they had to meet, one would be beaten, so obviously I always tried to ensure they had separate programmes.'

The trainer who had to juggle picking the right race for each of his horses with pleasing his owners allows himself a thin smile. 'After all, it is only fair to the owners that they should not clash because the owner who hadn't the retained jockey on his horse would complain. My aim is to avoid horses clashing.' This was a particular problem with American owners, who were totally unaccustomed to the system of retained jockeys.

One of Vincent's guiding principles was 'Know your horse and have plenty of patience with him. Keep him happy at all times.' To judge whether his horses were happy, Vincent would walk quietly around the boxes late at night. 'If a horse loses condition in work or is not eating to my satisfaction or is in any way unsettled, it shows all is not well. This was a signal to go easy, and I would give him a rest, even just walking out, and then start off slowly all over again.

'I used only oats, not nuts. We got samples of oats from Ireland, Canada and Australia and chose the best we could find, storing them over a period if we found a particularly good lot. In the beginning I fed five times a day – two dry feeds and three slightly damp – and we gave mash on Saturdays only. Later at Ballydoyle we fed three times a day. At first the head man would go round with a barrow and put the feed in each horse's pot, but I wanted feed for each horse made up separately in a bucket according to the horse's needs. Then the lad would collect the bucket and give it to the horses he looked after. Grass meal was used to the exclusion of bran as it has more food value. Eggs, stout and skimmed milk powder were also given, especially to horses coming up to a race, as were vitamins and mineral mixtures when required. Stout was stopped several days before a race.'

Race days were very fraught, and none of the family could ask Vincent what he thought might win; his answer would be a curt, 'Read the paper.' It was the family's nanny who was rather good at picking winners, so Jacqueline, when people at a race meeting whispered 'Does he give the horse a chance today?', would pass on Nanny's final selection. To balance the tension of those race days, there were more leisurely moments too. Vincent loved being outdoors at Ballydoyle, particularly with the children, and took delight in small rustic things such as finding the first mushrooms in the fields, collecting early blackberries, or during hay-making helping to make the stooks. Vincent adds with a smile, 'Taking tea with meat and jam sandwiches out to the farm men. Tea never tasted so good.'

'He was so innovative,' David remembers with the eye of an expert. 'He continually researched the latest feeding theories and planted lucerne and comfrey at Ballydoyle to add to the feed. He was always looking for ways to improve the training set-up, to keep the horses settled and relaxed or to cut down risks. He built the first all-weather gallop in Ireland. He installed screens at the start of the gallops so that horses waiting were not upset by others jumping off. He padded all the stable walls with rubber to avoid injuries.' Methods that are routine now.

Vincent also reflects on one of the changes he brought to training. 'I suppose I was one of the first to weigh horses regularly, and every Friday afternoon at Ballydoyle we had a session where all the senior people were present. The horses were weighed and then we looked carefully at each one standing. It gave us an opportunity to see how the horse had muscled up, and to gauge his general well-being. It seemed easier to assess the horse when out of his box. We all enjoyed this part of the routine, and the staff had a good opportunity to give their opinions.' Kauntze recalls one particular weigh day. 'One horse was three kilos down on his usual best racing weight – we'd check with the Weight Book twice a week. Vincent was puzzled by this weight loss. I said, "He did an enormous dropping just before he came out to be weighed, Boss."' Kauntze chuckles. 'It *was* enormous. Guess what Vincent asked next. "Did you weigh it?" '

CHAPTER 14

ROBERTO

'I was told he'd said he had overslept'

One of Vincent's more famous American owners was John Galbreath, owner of Roberto, bred by him at his attractive Darby Dan Farm outside Lexington in one of the prettiest parts of Kentucky's Bluegrass. Galbreath owned a massive construction business in Pittsburgh, Ohio, as well as the Pittsburgh Pirates, one of America's most successful baseball teams. On the roster was Roberto Clemente, after whom Galbreath named his most famous horse.

Vincent met Galbreath during the August season at Saratoga in the late 1960s. It has been said of Saratoga that part of its charm is that it represents, to those to whom racing is a way of life, something to which they can return. Its ways are old-fashioned, and after eleven months of new-fashioned ways it is very restful. 'At Saratoga,' Vincent remembers, 'John Galbreath asked me if I would train for him. A year or so later he asked me would I look at his yearlings during the Keeneland Sales. His yearlings were based either at Columbus, Ohio or close to Keeneland, at Darby Dan Farm.' One of the yearlings offered to Vincent was Roberto, by the good American sire Hail to Reason. Vincent was not impressed. 'Not one of the best-looking yearlings. And like a lot of Hail to Reasons, he didn't have the best of knees.'

Michael Kauntze was Vincent's assistant at Ballydoyle at the time, and his admiration of Roberto was and remains ecstatic. He praises his marvellous movement and his toughness. He puts him right up there with Nijinsky, but stresses, 'He was the most brilliant – *on his day*. If Nijinsky could have met Roberto in the Derby, which would have won? It would entirely depend on what humour Roberto was in. Nijinsky had a fiery temper, but Roberto had a bad temper. When we were practising him in the starting stalls here he wasn't afraid of them, he had a go at them! He attacked them!' Work rider Johnny Brabston concurs. 'Very temperamental in the stalls. Not so much frightened as objecting to them. He didn't like being shut in, so every evening through February and March I used to lead him out and walk through them.' Kauntze put his money where his faith lay: 'I had four months of my salary on Roberto when he won the Derby [in 1972].'

Vincent took particular care of the colt's forelegs and had no trouble with Roberto's doubtful knees in his first season in 1971. 'He proved a very good two-year-old. He won his first three races in Ireland.' He was the top-rated Irish two-year-old and was talked of in the press as another Sir Ivor or Nijinsky.

Then he went to Longchamp for the Grand Criterium. Here the French starter subjected him to the normal stalls test. 'He came out all right the first time,' Brabston, who rode him, reports, 'but the starter wanted him to do it again. The Boss was watching. He wasn't too happy about this. The second

time Roberto reared up, fell back and slipped coming out.' The
French starter thereupon insisted he try again. O'Brien
instantly intervened. 'The Boss was a bit angered,' says
Brabston, putting it mildly, for a slap-up argument erupted,
exacerbated because neither French starter nor Irish trainer
could speak the other's tongue. O'Brien's firmness was
justified, though. He came out of the argument as decisively as
Roberto came out of the stalls in the race. He was dropped in
just behind the leaders by Piggott, but before the straight he
lost ground, and then ran on again to finish fourth. Ballydoyle
was sharply disappointed, and William Hill, then the most
powerful bookmaker around – and, as he complained, a
grievous sufferer from winning bets on Vincent's horses –
announced, 'Roberto is no Derby horse!'

The Grand Criterium that year was about as hot as any ever
run, and the first four home that day at Longchamp included
the following summer's winners of the Irish, French and
English Derbys. Hindsight would reveal that all Roberto's bad
races were run on right-handed tracks. He always tended to
hang to the left even when galloping at home, in spite of being
fitted with a special bit. He disliked going right-handed,
although, as when winning the Derby and the Benson &
Hedges at York, he also drifted right in a race on left-hand
tracks. This is likely to have been caused by the discomfort in
his knees when at full stretch under pressure. If so, this would
make his strange character understandable.

'Over that winter,' Johnny Brabston remembers, 'he got
very strong. We let him forget about the stalls. He was about
the only one in the yard with real Classic potential that winter.
He was always a wonderful mover.'

His prep race for the English 2,000 Guineas was on April Fools' Day at Phoenix Park. Vincent says, 'It rained a great deal and I had grave misgivings about running him. But I finally decided to run, because there wasn't much choice for a prep race, and because I thought that, as it had rained so much, the ground would be sloppy, not holding.' Vincent was still worried about Roberto's knees, and the going at Phoenix Park did not suit the horse at all. 'He won all right, but after the race all was not one hundred per cent with him in front,' says Vincent. 'Bob Griffin expressed his opinion that Roberto was lucky to get away with it. He told me the horse would not want to run on that sort of ground ever again.'

The force of Bob Griffin's opinion here is important. The fact that Roberto's forelegs, particularly his knees, had been seriously threatened by sticky ground was never forgotten by his trainer. The following year, O'Brien was criticized in the press, by the public and by racing's establishment, for refusing to risk him on soft ground in the Eclipse at right-handed Sandown, and again in the Benson & Hedges at York. He stood fast. He lost some popularity. But Roberto retired to stud having had three seasons racing without breaking down on the track. He had not been risked, and this, when it came to retirement to stud, proved of immense benefit to his owners.

Spring came foul and wet in England too. Dermot O'Brien accompanied Roberto to Newmarket a week ahead of the 2,000 Guineas. 'I walked miles over the gallops trying to find a suitable piece of ground to work him on. It rained, and it bloody well rained! In the end Tom Jones [then a leading Newmarket trainer of both jumpers and the flat] gave us a bit of ground.' Even the horse's Australian jockey, Bill 'Weary

Willie' Williamson, was depressed by the difficulties. 'He was not,' says Dermot, 'coming up with much enthusiasm.' The brothers conferred. Vincent urged Dermot to try to cheer Williamson up. 'It was a difficult task,' says Dermot. 'But one day it must have worked, for next morning the horse dropped a couple of points in the ante-post market. So the word must have got about!'

Roberto started the Guineas second favourite. High Top was the favourite, owned by radio and TV tycoon Sir Jules Thorn and trained by Bernard van Cutsem. The favourite bowled along in front. Roberto, however, was kept at the back of the field, and Johnny Brabston remembers Weary Willie saying as he came in, 'I'd have won the race if I'd known the horse better. I hung too far out.' Roberto had to work his way through the ruck, en-countering some scrimmaging on his way forward. He emerged from the field in second place only a furlong from the post. High Top seemed to be coasting home, but Roberto kept on accelerat-ing, drew closer and closer, and got to High Top's girth on the line. He could certainly have been better ridden, but he had showed he was tough and resolute, and that he stayed. He seemed to be an excellent Derby hope, and was on offer after the Guineas at an attractive 8–1. Bookmakers had heard wrongly that in Boucher, O'Brien had a better horse at home.

All went well with Roberto between the Guineas and the Derby, but injury befell his probable partner. Ten days before the Derby Wearie Willie had a bad fall at Kempton. He hurt his shoulder painfully, and was unable to ride. T. P. Burns explains, 'The horse crossed his legs and gave him the mother and father of a fall. He might have been weeks off.' A fall on the flat, though far rarer than a fall when jumping, often does more damage as it is quite unexpected. The jockey is sitting perched up his horse's neck, and when he hits the ground the shock is greater. Furthermore, the flat-race jockey is usually more fragile, lighter and older than his jumping brothers. Vincent remembers this as a difficult time and states that 'Bill Williamson would without question have ridden the colt, had he not fallen and hurt himself.'

It was plain that if Williamson was doubtful then the owner wanted another jockey, and John Galbreath began pressing O'Brien for news. The decision on whether to replace your jockey before a major race on the grounds of possible in-capacity derived from injury is about the cruellest choice a trainer has to make. If the jockey is not 100 per cent in the race and the horse accordingly fails to win, you have let down owner, breeder and stable staff; if, on the other hand, the trainer obeys his owner's wishes and replaces the jockey, what will be his feelings if the poor man proves himself fit enough to ride, or even win, other races that day?

Williamson had to be physically fit enough to ride a tough, lazy horse in an exacting Classic on an eccentric course. Vincent then discovered that Williamson had gone for treat-ment to that good friend of jockeys, cricketers and other sportsmen Bill Tucker, who ran his clinic in Park Street, Mayfair. 'Tucker told me,' says Vincent, 'that we could really only tell if the shoulder was completely right when Bill Williamson got back and rode a horse. Tucker passed him fit to ride on Monday to test the shoulder. I was glad to hear that Williamson was going to ride work for an Epsom trainer on Tuesday morning, the day before the Derby. I felt we could leave the decision until Tuesday, when we would see how his shoulder was after he had ridden out at Epsom.' So the choice was left to the last day before the Derby, when Vincent heard some astonishing news. 'Apparently Williamson hadn't turned up to ride work at Epsom,' Vincent says. 'I was told he'd said he had overslept! In any case, it didn't look very good. John Galbreath was now very angry. He asked me to get Williamson to meet us both at Claridge's. But when I arrived I found Williamson already there. John Galbreath told Williamson that he had considerable experience of athletes' injuries as the owner of the Pittsburgh Pirates, and in his opinion Williamson could not be one hundred per cent fit. He said he wanted Piggott [who was booked to ride Manitoulin, Mrs Galbreath's horse] to ride Roberto, but that Williamson would get the same prize money as Piggott got if the horse won – £6,373 would be the jockey's reward.'

O'Brien takes full responsibility for the change of jockey, which brought upon him a critical fusillade. The decision was ruthless, but perfectly fair, and the offer was generous. Bill Williamson took the pronouncement stoically. 'No,' says Vincent, 'he'd never get livid, he was not that kind of character. It was unfortunate for his own sake that he had not turned up to ride work as arranged on that Tuesday morning.' The British racing press, however, tore into O'Brien, Galbreath and Piggott, accusing them of unsporting behaviour. The public seized on the press reports, and at Epsom the crowd burst into prolonged applause when Williamson rode two winners there on Derby Day.

'Lester rode a great race on Roberto,' says Vincent. 'He did nothing wrong. Lester told me afterwards that the horse wasn't doing much for him, that he should have won much more easily . . . And apparently Roberto's mother was like that. It wasn't every day she would do her best.' The views of some at Ballydoyle concurred, that Roberto should have won by further, that he ran below his best form. Of course, the gentle touch can sometimes win, when hammering will turn an unwilling horse into a resentful one. In the twenty-minute wait for the photo finish to be deciphered the O'Briens had to endure further public harassment. Two large and formidable ladies of the Turf, who may well be identified by senior citizens, bitterly incensed by O'Brien's deposing of Williamson, made their views known to him like trumpets before a battle. One felt powerfully enough about it to threaten the smaller Vincent with her umbrella. Her accomplice in the onslaught 'was a hefty lady', says Vincent, 'who had about me too! And she's never spoken to me since!'

Would Williamson have proved strong enough that day to prevail on Roberto in that desperate short-head struggle over Rheingold? Piggott then was outstandingly the strongest English jockey riding. Would a weaker jockey have succeeded? Press comments were divided between hearty admiration of Piggott's strength and genius, and dismay at the severity with which he had hammered Roberto home. In the latter case, they were misled by the sight of Piggott's fearsome, flailing whip. Nor were the critics aware of Roberto's toughness. Vincent and Johnny Brabston could independently declare that after the race 'there was not a mark on the horse. And he was squealing for his food that evening and ate up every oat.' With Vincent, John Galbreath had rightly gone down to the stables too to check on his winner. Brabston concluded, 'Roberto was so full of himself on our way back that he went nearly berserk when he got on the grass at Gatwick airport.'

In the meantime, Roberto went home to Ireland, worked well, and then ran deplorably in the Irish Derby. Timeform 'knew' this was due to the 'hiding' it saw Roberto receive in the English Derby. Students of other form books can see now that all Roberto's bad races were run on right-hand tracks. Vincent O'Brien adds his own informed comment, which illustrates the intriguing character of this horse. 'Johnny Roe, my retained stable jockey in Ireland, came in for the ride in the Irish Sweeps Derby. He rode the horse out every day between Epsom and the Curragh and he was so careful with him that the horse got wise to him. So he arrived at the Curragh in a very relaxed state of mind and never ran a race at all.' What fools horses can make of people.

After the Irish Derby, Roberto was given a break and then prepared for the Benson & Hedges Gold Cup. Piggott decided to ride Rheingold, who had been to France to win the Grand Prix de Saint Cloud. John Galbreath decided that he would fly over the top-class American jockey, Panamanian-born Braulio Baeza, whose performances in the States Galbreath admired but of whom hardly a soul on the British circuit had ever heard. Britons' view of American racing was more insular then than it is today. British racegoers now recognize the vast scope of American racing and the skill and immense experience of their jockeys, many of whom are greatly superior to the general run of ours. All of them possess clocks in their heads and most have five times the actual race-riding experience of their British counterparts. When the engagement of the mysterious Baeza was announced, some sniggering was heard in corners of the Turf's establishment. Atlases were consulted to discover Panama, where, it was believed, this strange little fellow with the odd name had been riding.

Not that any jockey could seriously hope to overcome the so far undefeated darling of the people, Mr and Mrs John Hislop's Brigadier Gerard, who had won fifteen consecutive races. The formidable Mrs Hislop observed Gerry Gallagher leading Roberto out onto the course to work on the morning of the race. 'At least we don't have to lead our horse,' she sneered. Gerry quietly replied, 'I'm not letting this fellow go till three o'clock this afternoon!'

O'Brien gave Baeza an extremely thorough briefing on Roberto's previous runnings, his preferences, his weaknesses and his strengths. 'Then I said, "But I leave it to you how you ride him."' Now, in America, there is no dawdling. Races on identically flat, left-handed circuits are run at an exceptionally strong pace throughout. Winners usually come from the leading bunch. Front runners often prevail. Quick starts are universal: in front, the fleet-footed fling the muck back onto the slow. Dirt, gritty-dry or mucky-wet, in a horse's and jockey's face is most unpleasant. Sure enough, Baeza shot Roberto out of the stalls at York like a bullet. Crouching low, American style, he kept him flying ahead. Before the horses entered the straight everything behind was off the bit and struggling, with the single exception of the unconquered Brigadier. Roberto kept on galloping at such speed that even the supreme (until then) Brigadier Gerard could not get within a length of him. Had not the Brigadier so easily won the 2,000 Guineas the previous year? Two furlongs out, Joe Mercer's whip hand flashed up on the four-year-old. Another furlong of vain pursuit and the seemingly unconquerable hero was finally beaten. Brigadier Gerard dropped away and Roberto scorched home and broke York's course record.

It was an electric performance. It was also in a different league to any race Roberto had run before, or would run after. The ground, though officially good, was riding fast, and York is left-handed – two things Roberto needed. The distance of the Benson & Hedges, one mile two and a half furlongs, may really have been his best distance; one and a half miles, except around easy Epsom, may have been too far. Vincent nods, and adds, 'Also the dead-level track, rather than the ups and down of Epsom, probably suited him better because of his knees.' Most important of all, especially with a colt who had run lazily in the Irish Derby, perhaps 'conning' his jockey, was the startling change of riding styles. The dash of a new man on top came as a shock to Roberto. He ran as if galvanized, prompting racecourse rumours about Baeza's rather lengthy whip with, some said, a battery hidden in the jockey's breeches and a wire running up his sleeve; others said the whip itself concealed battery and button. O'Brien plainly says, 'Complete nonsense.' He is most complimentary about Baeza's riding at York. 'He rode a beautiful race. I remember Noel Murless saying afterwards, "Some of the English jockeys had better open their eyes and take another look at Baeza. He certainly knows how to ride!"'

Two disappointments closed Roberto's three-year-old season. His prep race for the Prix de l'Arc de Triomphe was the Prix Niel. Hard to Beat, the French Derby winner, beat Roberto a length, and this time Baeza had not shot out of the gate. He'd simply followed Hard to Beat and had never looked like catching him.

For a prep race, though, that was not too bad. Tough as he was, a hard battle before the major target could have come too close.

For the Prix de l'Arc de Triomphe, the ground was surprisingly firm. So too was O'Brien's condemnation of Baeza's tactics. 'He thought he knew how to ride Longchamp after the Prix Niel. There was no question of having a discussion, of taking advice! He had it all figured out. He'd pop him off in front and make all.' Another top-class American jockey was also riding in the race, this time with a French-sounding name: Lafitt Pincay was riding O'Brien's Boucher, winner of the St Leger. He, too, decided to jump off and go. 'They went so fast,' says Vincent, still cross about it, 'that they did the first five furlongs in the same time it took to run the big French sprint, the Prix de l'Abbaye, that day. And they covered the first mile quicker than in the one-mile Prix du Moulin, also on the same day!' Both horses weakened, but Roberto was the first home. He finished seventh, with Hard to Beat eighth, so the form of the two Longchamp races was close enough. San-San was the first filly to win in nineteen years. Some critics were quick to say that the Prix de l'Arc de Triomphe further emphasized how extraordinary had been Roberto's 'bee-sting' victory at York. Vincent quietly replies, 'But, after all, he had won the Derby, beating Rheingold who went on to win the Prix de l'Arc de Triomphe.'

John Galbreath, having bred the horse, wanted him back on his Darby Dan Farm in Kentucky, but he decided to keep the colt in training for a four-year-old campaign in 1973. This was a move against the tide of three-year-olds being whisked away as soon as they had done enough to value themselves highly, before they could depreciate. After all, with a courageously won Epsom Derby plus a vividly won Benson & Hedges,

Roberto had done enough to recommend himself highly to American breeders.

'He won the Coronation Cup at Epsom,' says Vincent, 'and he very nearly broke the course record.' In fact, his time was faster than any Derby winner since Mahmoud in 1936. But from then on almost everything went wrong. 'John Galbreath's son Dan and his wife Liz came over from America to watch the horse run in the Eclipse,' says Vincent. That year it was run at Kempton, because Sandown was being rebuilt. Thunderstorms soaked the ground. O'Brien decided it was too soft to risk Roberto and withdrew the horse on the morning of the race. 'I went to Kempton and acquainted the Stewards of my presence there,' he reports, 'in case they wished to talk to me. I wasn't bound to do this as the ground had changed overnight, so I was entitled to withdraw the horse. John Hislop, one of the acting Stewards, had some words to say about this, and I proposed that we should both go out and inspect the ground.' Hislop, a true sportsman, held that a good horse should be able to run on any ground. There ensued a vignette which could have been clipped from a French comedy: two senior pillars of racing hopping about in argument on Kempton's turf – O'Brien says 'John Hislop was pretty sharp with me' – using their feet on the pocked ground to demonstrate their opposing cases. 'Hislop would press sods back to show how level it was. I'd dig my heel into the holes to make them bigger!' Roberto did not run. The Galbreaths had again come 3,500 miles for nothing. Jacqueline says, 'I was able to get two Centre Court Wimbledon tickets so they could watch the tennis final, which was some little consolation. They were keen tennis players.'

Then Roberto ran badly in the King George VI and Queen

Elizabeth Stakes. Vincent also withdrew him from the Benson & Hedges at York because the ground was terrible again, and then he pulled a ligament at home and was retired. Back at Darby Dan Farm Roberto turned out to be a successful stallion, particularly as a sire of sires: his famous sons include Kris S, Red Ransom and Dynaformer, all carrying on the Hail to Reason line. Dynaformer was the sire of the brilliant 2006 Kentucky Derby winner Barbaro who after six straight wins had to be put down a few weeks later after an accident in the Preakness.

The Galbreaths accepted their costly disappointment with their enriching triumphs. They 'confirmed their interest in Ireland' Jacqueline reports, 'by coming for many years to shoot at Birr Castle, the home of Lord Rose'. The shoot was efficiently run by Vincent's former jockey Liam Ward, a crack shot. Vincent took them snipe shooting on the little Galway bogs. John Galbreath, a very experienced shot said, 'It's the most darn difficult bird ever. I only raised my gun out of politeness to my host'.

Much else was about to be raised by Americans in the horse world, not so much out of politeness to the invaders but out of admiration: the Triumvirate of Sangster, O'Brien and Magnier were about to spend millions of dollars at Keeneland Sales, Kentucky, and to take back to Ireland some wonderful horses.

CHAPTER 15

THE SYNDICATE

'Find the very best trainer'

V incent O'Brien, and his family before him, had known the Magnier family well, socially and through horses, for several generations. Both were old Cork families. The Magniers had been in the horse business since the early nineteenth century. When Vincent's father died in 1943 and all the horses had to be sold, the only one remaining in the yard was Oversway, Vincent's first winner, leased from Michael Magnier, John's grandfather.

The Magniers' Grange Stud near Fermoy was famous in the 1950s in Britain and Ireland for having stood the illustrious Cottage, the pre-eminent National Hunt sire of at least two decades, and sire of Cottage Rake, who first made Vincent's name in both islands. During the post-war years almost every steeplechaser on offer in Ireland was said to be either by Cottage or related to him. Young John Magnier was running the 300-acre Grange Stud in the 1970s for his mother Evie, a lady of great style who had been widowed young. She had been matron of honour at Vincent and Jacqueline's wedding. In 1973 John bought and founded the 200-acre Castlehyde Stud nearby. The two studs together stood just three stallions. By 1975, thirteen stallions were standing, including Green God, Deep Diver, Deep Run and Sun Prince.

Vincent had already set up an American syndicate with Bull Hancock in Kentucky. It ended sadly on Hancock's premature death, but the concept had taken root in Vincent's mind. In partnership with Tim Vigors, Vincent owned the Coolmore Stud, beautifully positioned at the foot of Slievenamon, just down the road from Ballydoyle. Tim, the former Battle of Britain pilot, had established a business in Oxfordshire selling Piper aircraft, but had reverted to the bloodstock business. He loved hunting, racing, breeding and dealing. Tim had moved to Coolmore in 1968, converting the place which his father had owned since 1945 into a very attractive stud farm. 'I was very much in the stud business before John and Robert came along,' Vincent stresses. 'In 1973 I bought two-thirds of Coolmore, the family home of Tim Vigors. He needed money to settle a divorce case and did not want to continue managing the stud.'

In 1972 Coolmore stood two stallions, King Emperor and Gala Performance. It had plans for three more – Thatch, Home Guard and Rheingold, who had been bought for a million pounds after winning the Prix de l'Arc de Triomphe and who was ready to move in the following season. 'As Tim did not want to continue living in Ireland,' Vincent says, 'we looked for a manager and I decided to approach John Magnier to manage Coolmore. In my opinion he had exceptional ability and was the most capable young man in Europe for the job. Later, we talked about amalgamating his studs in Fermoy with ours. A condition of the deal was that John would live at

Coolmore. He loved Grange and did not want to move, but he finally agreed to do so.' It helped, of course, that John was engaged to Vincent's glamorous daughter Sue. The stud farms of Coolmore and Castlehyde were amalgamated into a three-way partnership. The first link of the Triumvirate was forged.

John Magnier, born in 1948, has made Coolmore, with operations in America and in Australia, one of the top thoroughbred breeding complexes in the world. Intense, focused, brilliantly able and tough, mind clicking like a computer, he has always looked older than his years. He lives his life at a tremendous rate, far more the modern tycoon than any normal Irish horseman – pacing about, giving instructions on his mobile, and discussing different businesses and financial enterprises across the world while still organizing the continuing expansion of the Coolmore stud empire.

In 1971, at Haydock races, Magnier had met and become friendly with quietly spoken Robert Sangster, the heir-in-waiting of his family firm Vernons Pools. Robert Sangster would earn international renown in racing and breeding. His name became famous, his racing friends were legion and his generosity immense, but he sadly died from cancer in April 2004, a grievous loss to the thoroughbred world. Sangster's family business Vernons Pools was locally based and was sponsoring the Vernons Sprint Cup, Haydock's most important flat race of the year. The fancied winner was Green God, which John had purchased just before the race as a potential stallion for one of his expanding stud farms. John explained to Robert the economics of breeding and what a good stallion might earn.

Robert was already involved in racing in a considerable way. He had horses under both rules, but mainly for the flat with Eric Cousins at Sandy Brow in Shropshire. Robert and his first wife Christine lived at Swettenham Hall in Cheshire. There Robert had set up a 200-acre stud with fifteen resident brood mares. He sold the progeny at the Newmarket December Sales and at Deauville, and was generally successful in a minor way. Robert's father, who did not discourage the racing activities of his only son, could see that Robert was capable of making a success in the thoroughbred industry. He recognized there could be money in breeding. As his vast collection of horses expanded, Robert showed a remarkable grasp of the whole bloodstock field. He knew the breeding of all his animals, where they were located in his global empire, their pedigrees and their future plans.

At the time that he met John Magnier, Sangster had approached the then Lord Derby for some advice about racing. John Derby, a man of great charm, came from the same part of England as the Sangsters but from a very different background – the earldom went back to 1485. Vincent had trained for his younger brother Hugh Stanley whose horse Alberoni had won the Irish National and the Galway Plate. Early in his career, Hugh was considered to be a bit of a black sheep and was encouraged by the family to go out to New Zealand and Australia. He told Vincent, 'I took the precaution of writing to the Mayor of Auckland to say that I would be arriving and that I was Lord Derby's brother.' Hugh was delighted to be met by a band on the quay, and was given a magnificent reception.

The affable Lord Derby asked Robert Sangster to lunch at his splendid home, Knowsley. They talked of racing and

Robert's horses. Robert reported afterwards, 'I told him I wanted to get into racing in a big way. He said, "My advice is, find the very best trainer and be prepared to spend a million pounds."' Some years later Lord Derby confirmed that this was precisely the counsel he had given 'Young Sangster', adding with mournful sincerity and a deep sigh, 'If only I had followed my own advice myself . . .'

For Sangster, the advice was like seeing an avenue of traffic lights stretching into the distance on an empty road, and all of them suddenly becoming green. Through his new friend John Magnier, who was so encouraging, he could surely get access to Vincent O'Brien, who certainly seemed 'the very best trainer'. He recalled that he and Magnier had discussed at Haydock the difficulties of getting good stallions at fair prices. The case of Green God, who had won the Vernons Sprint in 1971, was an example. His owner David Robinson, the TV tycoon and philanthropist who employed three trainers, could market as stallions his good winners at high prices, yielding him large profits. It would be much better, surely, John Magnier decided, to get into that market early, to produce highly desirable and therefore big-earning stallions. But the horses first must win top races, preferably Classics. That meant having them picked by a known, consummate judge and trained by an expert. Was there anyone better than Vincent O'Brien, his neighbour, partner in the Coolmore group of studs, and now his father-in-law?

Of course, very big funds would be needed. American prices had so far excluded European buyers. High prize money in bookmaker-free America meant horses could be far bigger earners on the track, so they cost more. Now, here, keen as mustard to invest, was the Vernons Pool's heir Robert Sangster, likeable with a nice, dry wit and wry smile, lavishly hospitable and an admirer of Vincent O'Brien, to whom he had been introduced at Keeneland several years earlier.

Magnier brought Sangster to discuss these ideas with O'Brien, and the purpose of the syndicate fell neatly and swiftly into place. Here was the brilliant picker, trainer and expert on bloodlines; here was the man who would become the cleverest in the breeding business; and here was an Englishman with a lot of money to invest in this exciting partnership. A difference in character suited them all the more. Vincent disliked publicity and distrusted the press. John Magnier is a private man who rarely gives interviews. Robert Sangster, on the contrary, was only too happy to promote the virtues of racehorses, stallions, mares, foals and yearlings in which the partnership had money invested and would want to market profitably. Neither Vincent nor John, then, wanted horses to run in their names. Robert enjoyed it. Therefore Robert, who sometimes owned only 40 per cent of the many exciting winners he enjoyed, could run them in his colours, talk about 'my' horse and 'our' plans, and give the racing press and TV interviewers bundles of helpful quotes. From a marketing point of view he did a very important job for the three of them, one neither of the other two partners wanted to undertake.

Vincent was delighted with the project. It was, after all, he who had done so much already to advertise the virtues of American bloodlines. He had himself been part of the brief syndicate with Bull Hancock. He already knew and admired the power and efficiency of Keeneland Sales under its welcoming president Ted Bassett in Kentucky. Vincent also, though this fact was little advertised, had considerable experience of breeding. The Ballydoyle Stud was established in 1952 and within a couple of years had bred Chamier, the Irish Derby winner. Vincent bought and ran Longfield Stud, Cashel, and stood stallions such as Hugh Lupus, Chamier and the good American sprinter Polly's Jet. During the 1970s he set up Lyonstown Stud near Rosegreen, Ballydoyle's closest village. The Honour Board proudly pinned to the wall outside the yard's entrance names the animals bred there, including Sadler's Wells, El Gran Senor, El Prado, Glenstal, King's Lake, Dr Devious and many others, right on the doorstep of Ballydoyle under Vincent's watchful eye and careful planning.

The great patrons of the Turf in the past – landed aristocrats in England, hugely rich industrialists in Britain and America – had never had to look at breeding in this businesslike way. They owned stud farms and sometimes produced a good horse which became a stallion, sending their own mares to the horse, swapping nominations (or 'seasons' as they are called in the USA) with friends. The new idea the syndicate brought to racing was the concept of 'buying to make stallions' in a commercial way. Previously, horses were sold to America with no thought for the future of bloodstock. The biggest movement of good stallions and top-class mares to America in those days was exactly what Vincent and Magnier decided to reverse. Europe's best blood was no longer going to go to the USA; it was going to come back.

'I like American horses,' Vincent observes. 'They can race more than ours; they are stabled at the track; they're taken from stables to racecourse – no long travelling involved. But because they are raced more often the horses must be tough to stand up to it; they've got to be genuine and game. They also have to be very sound because of the type of dirt surface on which they race. This is really hard on horses' legs. I think American trainers and vets are tremendous experts to keep the horses on the go like they do.

'We would try to turn the tide,' Vincent continues. 'We would organize a syndicate to buy yearlings which I would train, and from which we could make our own stallions. We also looked at buying very well-bred fillies for racing and then breeding.'

Although Vincent previously had bought horses primarily to win races and establish their futures as stallions for the benefit of the owners, at this stage in his career he was, through Coolmore, already involved in partnerships in stallions which he had successfully trained. He had learned from 'Uncle Jack' Mulcahy that he must always insist on a piece of the action. If the new scheme worked he would be part of a far bigger action. Horses selected and trained by him to win Classic races could be syndicated for millions of dollars and still bring in a large income from nominations. With Robert Sangster's money to bolster the initial investments, Vincent had considerably more power to do what he desired: buy more good horses to win great races and produce top stallions for the bloodstock industry.

On his retirement, Vincent was asked what he considered to be his best achievement. He replied, 'I would feel satisfaction in having done my bit for the Irish bloodstock industry, and for Ireland.'

CHAPTER 16

ROYAL ASCOT 1975

'Like old times, Vincent!'

Vincent always said he really loved Ascot, but not for its peripheral fripperies – the clothes, the gossip, the crowds, watching the royal procession, meeting people or spotting celebrities. He was always sprucely turned out himself, and favoured a dove-grey morning tailcoat rather than the more popular black one. But he was a man who shunned crowds and chatter. What he loved at Ascot was the quality of its racing and the fact that he so often triumphed there. And he had an astonishing Royal Ascot in 1975: seven winners from eight runners, and these wins came from only fifteen horses of three years and over in training at Ballydoyle.

On the first day of that Ascot meeting Vincent won the Queen Anne Stakes with Imperial March, owned by Walter Mullady of Chicago, and the biggest prize of the day with Gallina, bought for £165,000 at Keeneland. Lester Piggott, who had first ridden for Vincent when the great mare Gladness won the 1958 Gold Cup, rode Gallina, the very easy winner of the Ribbesdale Stakes for Simon Fraser of the famous old Scots family the Lovats. The jockey on Imperial March was Gianfranco Dettori, father of the later Ascot superstar, champion jockey Frankie. His father had been recommended to Vincent by Lester, when Vincent asked him who could 'do' 7st 10lb. Jacqueline O'Brien's knowledge of Italian was called upon to make her the interpreter for Vincent's instructions to Gianfranco, and for his report afterwards. Gianfranco had been champion in Italy six times.

Vincent had intended a third runner on that first day of Royal Ascot, which he believed would be his banker of the meeting. But Hail the Pirates got cast in his box on the Monday night and couldn't run in the Prince of Wales Stakes. The form of that race and Vincent's confidence suggested strongly that had he run, Vincent would have landed a treble. As it was, a man in the crowd shouted out to Vincent as Gallina came into the winner's enclosure, 'Like old times, Vincent!' 'Yes indeed,' Vincent replied, pleased at this recall of his domination of the jumping game.

On the next day, up came another O'Brien double, making it four winners from four runners. 'Four Leprechauns On Overtime For Vincent!' shouted the *Sporting Life* headline. Lester brought Gay Fandango home ahead of the Queen's Joking Apart, and Vincent generously admitted that the royal filly's difficulties in running had helped his victory. Gay Fandango was owned by Alan Clore, who lived in France and was the son of the rich English property developer Sir Charles Clore. In the Queen's Vase, Vincent's aptly named Blood Royal just got home, ridden by Lester again, for Mrs George F. Getty II, another of Vincent's wealthy American owners.

Gold Cup Thursday brought Vincent's fifth winner from

five successive runners – a new Ascot record. This winner, Swingtime, like all the others, was American-bred – public proof of Vincent's trend-setting American strategy. Vincent got Willie Carson up to sit on Swingtime's back to get a feel of her at six o'clock that summer morning. The filly won the Cork and Orrery Stakes in the afternoon for Vincent's close friend and long-time supporter 'Uncle Jack' Mulcahy.

The last day brought Vincent's sixth winner in that tricky six-furlong handicap the Wokingham. This was Boone's Cabin, named after the ancestor of Derby winner Sir Ivor's charming breeder, Alice Chandler. The colt was the first race-horse owned by Robert Sangster to be trained by Vincent and ridden by Lester, who carried a record ten stone to victory. Boone's Cabin was a five-year-old full horse and had been at Ballydoyle for practically all his life, winning a few useful, if not important, races. Robert kept suggesting to Vincent that to save training fees and raise some capital the horse should be sold as a stallion to some small country. Vincent's patience excelled itself. 'I don't think we should get rid of him just yet,' he kept repeating. This was the subject of cheerful joking by Robert. Vincent's patience finally paid off with this astonishing dividend in the Wokingham. The horse Robert had wanted to sell for so long carried the heaviest burden in the Wokingham since Trappist won in 1878. Boone's Cabin was one of the first of the stallions to be flown to Australia for southern hemisphere covering. He was due to come back to continue his duties in England but injured himself and had to miss the plane.

As if his extraordinary six wins at Royal Ascot was insufficient, Vincent provided a seventh winner as a tailpiece on the Saturday, Ascot Heath Day, when Mrs Haefner's Guillaume Tell, ridden once more by Lester Piggott, won the Churchill Stakes. The eighth horse, Sir Penfro, ran only because he was being returned to his English owner, Jim Philips of Dalham Stud, Newmarket, who said he would like to have a runner at the meeting.

A large picture frame, modestly headed 'Royal Ascot 1975', now hangs in Vincent's bow-windowed study overlooking a lake in Co. Kildare. It contains seven neatly captioned photographs of this memorable seven-winner Ascot meeting. Vincent was so justifiably proud of this glorious week that he insisted on moving a much-loved still-life to make way for this Ascot collage. He can glance at it to his left as he watches his regular racing on television.

Nijinsky (Lester Piggott), struck down with colic the day before, beats French ace Gyr comfortably to win the 1970 Derby in near record time.

Nijinsky's Derby, 1970. Susan, Jane and Elizabeth were allowed out from Woldingham Convent for the occasion.

ABOVE: *The family Christmas card for 1968. From left to right: Liz, Jane, Vincent, Sue, David, Jacqueline and Charles, with Sir Ivor.*

Sir Ivor winning the 1968 Epsom Derby in spectacular style.

ABOVE: *Lester Piggott drives Roberto home to beat Rheingold a short head in the 1972 Epsom Derby.*

BELOW: *Constructing by hand the new all-weather Ballydoyle gallop in the 1960s, probably the first ever to be laid down. The plastic was porous.*

ABOVE: *Alan Clore's Gay Fandango (Lester Piggott) beats the Queen's Joking Apart to win the 1975 Jersey Stakes in Vincent's memorable Ascot meeting.*

BELOW: *The founding trio of the famous syndicate. From left to right: John Magnier, his wife Sue (Vincent's daughter), Vincent and Robert Sangster.*

OPPOSITE: *The Queen discussed with Vincent the race named after her parents.*

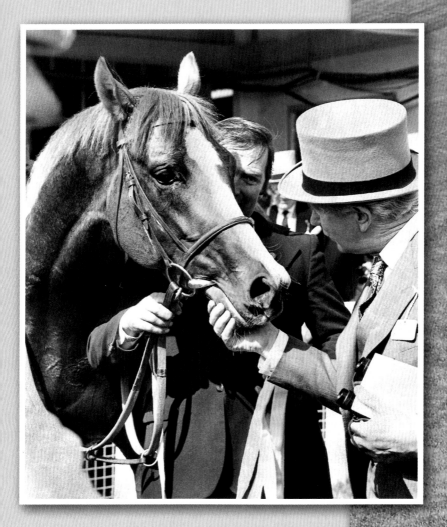

ABOVE: *A tough man in a tough profession. But look at his tenderness with The Minstrel after the Derby.*

OPPOSITE: *Lester gives The Minstrel a marvellous ride to beat Hot Grove for the Derby. Others thought him too severe.*

ABOVE: *Alleged wins his first Prix de l'Arc de Triomphe.*

TOP LEFT: *In the presidential box: Valery Giscard d'Estaing and his wife talk to Lester, Susan Sangster, Vincent and Robert Sangster.*

LEFT: *Alleged striding out on the sawdust gallop at Ballydoyle.*

CHAPTER 17

THE MINSTREL

'They don't have to be big to be good'

Vincent O'Brien was about thirty years ahead of his European competitors in his discovery of Keeneland. In the 1960s Vincent could have said that 70 per cent of his owners were American; by 1980 he could declare that 'seventy or seventy-five per cent of the horses in my yard are American-bred'. The syndicate swooped down on the Keeneland Sales and began to bring back to Britain and Ireland many of the bloodlines lost to America. A number of very rich individuals joined Sangster, Magnier and O'Brien to provide the necessary funds. These rich men realized that racing profitability lay not in European prize money but in the shrewd buying of the best yearlings, to make them into Classic winners under 'the best trainer in Europe', and then stand them as world-class sires.

The fringe members of the syndicate changed over the years, but they included Simon Fraser, the Scottish laird; Stavros Niarchos, the Greek shipping owner; Alan Clore; Jack Mulcahy; Danny Schwartz, a construction engineer; Charles St

George, a London insurance broker; and Jean-Pierre Binet, a Parisian and owner of Dickens Hill, second in the English and Irish Derbys of 1979, trained by Mick O'Toole.

No successful army ever advances without careful and expert reconnaissance. In the case of the select raids on the sales led by Vincent O'Brien the reconnaissance was conducted by Tom Cooper, who was a director of the Irish branch of the old and trusted British Bloodstock Agency. He had a great 'eye for a horse' and was a good selector of yearlings. Cooper had led Vincent to look at Larkspur. 'Certainly Larkspur would have been the first sale I was involved with. After that, at Newmarket during the sales, Vincent used to kindly take me round when he was looking at the yearlings. He used to do this when everyone had gone racing and there was peace and quiet round the sales rings and paddocks. It was just on a friendship basis more than anything else. And from those Newmarket days it just developed into the present teamwork. The objective is to buy a horse with a pedigree that will make him a desirable stallion if his racecourse performance is good enough.' Then he points out the next best markets. 'If he's not good enough for here or Europe he can still be a very valuable asset to stud farms all over the world, from Argentina to Japan to Australia.

'Before the yearlings go to the sales,' Cooper continues, 'I try to see them on the farms in the early mornings, when they're turned out, to see how they move cantering in the paddocks.' Those first few strides, the first quick turn, and changing legs reveal the animal's action and his athletic balance and thrust. One of Vincent's vivid yardsticks lingers: 'A good horse should move like a male ballet dancer.' Both

Nijinskys – four-legged and two-legged – confirm the simile. Tom would begin by eliminating those that would not do. How easy this sounds, but how painful – and it frequently happens – when a yearling rejected by a bloodstock agent or trainer goes on to win big races for someone else. On those Tom liked he recorded brief descriptions. 'I bring a Dictaphone with me and take notes on all I like. When I come back to Ireland I send a copy to Vincent and a copy to Robert Sangster,' Tom explained at the peak of the syndicate's successes. 'I just hope it helps them when Vincent's having a good look at them at the actual sale. That's his role. Vincent makes the final decision. He is a great judge.'

The party would arrive at Blue Grass Field, the Lexington airport where Arab 737s squatted just across the main road from Keeneland's sales pavilion, the encampment of stabling and vendors' dainty little refreshment stands. All this lies behind the excellent racecourse, where even the buildings and stands are painted a subdued rural green. For decades in this totally profit-for-charities organization no running commentary was heard; Keeneland assumed that its racegoers were all experts who could read races without noisy aids.

Bob Griffin, whose association with O'Brien lasted forty years, was going round too, checking possible yearlings for defects. 'I examine everything,' said Bob, 'to see that there are no conditions likely to cause lameness. And eyes and heart, of course – heart is very important.' He would lean over, stethoscope plugged into his ears, and place it on a yearling's heart. He would listen to the beat, then look up over the horse's withers at O'Brien with his famous nod and smile and add, 'Wish mine were as good!' Conversely, he sometimes had to murmur to Vincent, 'I wouldn't touch that.' Between them they tried not to allow any tiny defects to escape notice. But in the misty areas of tiny doubts, heads came together; there were *sotto voce* discussions as Sangster and the rest of the syndicate waited upon the decision of the maestro. 'I wouldn't quite like those knees . . . on the other hand he is a very good mover . . .' Conformation is gone over. Snatches of conversation escape from the earnest group of millionaires seeking their next investments in fragile, four-legged creatures who may never run fast enough to cover their costs. 'Probably the best pedigree in the catalogue . . . He's a good-looking colt . . . Quite a big horse, or will be. He's got a lot to like about him. Walks well . . . Fractionally overshot of his mouth, but I think it's more he puts his lip out – makes it look worse than it is . . . This one's quite nice, not very big. He looks a sharp individual. I can see him coming early to hand . . .' A particular yearling is crossed out as a reject, marked as a possible, or specially selected to join a short-list of a dozen. Out of this, the syndicate will finally pick about half. On these they will spend around $10 million in a babble of hectic minutes, interspersed with the yelps of the team of bid-spotters and, from the high podium, the coaxing southern drawl of the auctioneers.

The syndicate was ably assisted by Demi O'Byrne. With Bob Griffin, he looked after all the great O'Brien horses of the 1970s and 1980s. After the episode of the Epsom colic, whenever Nijinsky travelled Demi was with him. He is now a world-renowned judge of all types of bloodstock and principal adviser for Michael Tabor, who is a partner of John Magnier, and an important owner at Ballydoyle and Coolmore.

Demi acknowledges that 'I owe so much of my knowledge

to Vincent, who in the 1960s had advised me to select a perfect individual and keep the image in my head, measuring all others against it. Vincent suggested then that I look at Valoris. He urged me to consider pedigree, quality and scope in a yearling.' Some two decades later, Vincent remarked to Jacqueline, 'If you want a good picture of a horse as a model, go look at Caerleon.'

The Ballydoyle team at Keeneland kept reappraising one small chestnut colt in the long lines of barns decked out in vendors' colours and emblazoned with breeding boards. There stood O'Brien in his short-sleeved shirt and straw hat, catalogue in hand, sunglasses in his top left pocket, immaculate in the sweating humidity, trying to foresee the small colt's future. He cannot remember how many times he had this colt out, or how many minutes he spent looking at him. While Vincent examines him, his earnest advisers stand back in silence, protecting the small, dapper figure in front who, like a footballer about to take a vital penalty, stands and stares. It is as if Vincent can see not only into the yearling's heart and lungs but into his brain, into his character, and thus, by definition, into his future. It is magical, almost mystical to watch. The hard-bitten professionals who comprise his team realize this. They stand back in mute concentration, heads inclined, their backs forming a semi-circle, a shield against any intrusions. It takes some patience to stand and watch. Some younger members of the team wonder if it will ever finish, and when they will get into the shade with a drink.

Now Vincent is gazing again at another colt's head. 'In a colt I think it's vital that he shouldn't have a feminine head,' he says. 'He must have a masculine head to stand up to the rigours not only of the training but of all the things a prospective top horse has to go through – travelling, strange surroundings, crowds on big days and so forth. A horse with great ability who will not try is a real heartache, and sometimes this trait is visible in the head of the yearling, or in its behaviour as it goes in and out of the stable, indeed as it acts in and out of the box.'

The responsibility resting on O'Brien was awesome. The feeling that he might finally pick yearlings all of whom would fail abysmally was always present. No-one in racing is infallible. The loss of Vincent's investment stake, even though he was by now a rich man, would hurt him far less than the dent his reputation would suffer. No expert dare lose that. Yet each year, the magic touch continued. His ability to see deeper than most into a yearling's frame and mind remained.

As the hour of the sale approaches, the debate continues. Vincent O'Brien carefully, quietly sums up. Of one 'possible', beautifully bred: 'The one with conformation problems is the Nijinsky . . .' Of another one, on the small side: 'He's a very late foal, born 20 May. You've got to take that into account . . .' Of another: 'He looks backward. Nothing like the majority of colts we've seen here.' Of another: 'He doesn't have the best of forelegs. If he was bred any other way, I wouldn't consider him.' And of another, showing the length of vision required: 'I think you'd want to count him out as a two-year-old and not do too much with him next year, hoping he'd develop, given extra time. That's the only consideration on which I would agree to have him.' If Vincent did not want him, he wasn't bought.

At any auction, regular dealers have personal signs recognized by the auctioneer to disguise their interest. The syndicate were somewhat slicker. Tom Cooper would be told to bid boldly up to, say, $300,000, then shake his head and walk away. Robert Sangster might not be seated with Vincent in the theatrical slopes of the arena at all. He could be lurking at the back of the auctioneer's lofty rostrum where yet another 'spotter' waited. These are Keeneland employees, yapping like terriers in front of the aisles, relaying bids back to the big men on the rostrum. Bids could thus be advanced invisibly. The bidding, no-bidding devices of the O'Brien team seemed to some observers a trifle overdone. Vincent took no notice. He needed time to assess the different yearlings on the ever-shrinking short-list of likely targets. Robert Sangster was the newest and least experienced of the syndicate, as he frequently admitted, but with his quick business mind he learned swiftly. For him, the bidding positions and signals were a vivid slice of this new, top-level dramatic play into which he had now plunged headlong.

The purpose was plain. If the supreme Vincent O'Brien, backed by his expert team and plentiful money, were interested in Lot 123 (or Hip No. 123 as Americans put it), this could be seen as an obvious lead to a likely winner. But, of course, if O'Brien and Co. really liked the animal, to outbid them one would need deep pockets. 'The biggest problem besetting the bloodstock industry at the moment,' Vincent used to say, 'is that we must pay cash at the sales for a yearling. But few stallions are paid for with instant cash. They are sold on terms covering four or five years. There's a long gap between buying the yearling and getting your money back, even if he turns out very good!'

When the group first assaulted Keeneland it was bliss for

the breeders. As Keeneland's president for many years, Ted Bassett would regularly remark, with warm admiration, that American bloodstock sales had never before seen anything like the power and drive of the syndicate.

Some people have an eye for a horse; most do not. Some top trainers, expert at conditioning their charges, at knowing the form and placing them well, often have no eye at all. They rely on agents. In Vincent's case he was doubly blessed: he could pick horses as well as train them. Who can nominate anyone more adept in both vital spheres of the racing game? What was more, he was already an authority on the American pedigrees. John Magnier still has such respect for his father-in-law that he humbly refers to him as 'MV'. He points out, 'MV must be one of the best judges in the world. I mean, the records show he's bought so many horses and he's turned down so many others. I'm trying to learn why.'

It seemed very unlikely that the syndicate's plan would immediately pay dividends. But they struck oil at once. From their first crop of yearlings came the Derby winner The Minstrel, the Eclipse winner Artaius, and Be My Guest, bought at Goffs in Ireland. The double Prix de l'Arc de Triomphe winner Alleged, purchased in California, joined the group as a two-year-old. The fact that that first year was a great success meant that the group could go back with confidence. It was like winning in the casino early in the evening and playing for the rest of the night with casino money. Courage comes more easily. John Magnier recalled, thirty years on, that while they were spending hundreds of thousands of dollars at Keeneland they had to borrow £30,000 from the Agricultural Credit Corporation to fund the purchase of cattle at home.

The Minstrel's attraction for Vincent O'Brien, on paper, was plain. He was not only by the same sire, Northern Dancer, as Nijinsky, but his dam Fleur was the daughter of Nijinsky's dam, Flaming Page, and thus Nijinsky's half-sister. The chestnut had been bred by the same man too, Canadian millionaire E. P. Taylor. Eddie Taylor started off with a brewing business inherited from his grandfather and over the years as well as expanding the brewery operations he gained control over many of Canada's biggest and best known companies from farm machinery to grocery stores. His own thoroughbred breeding program began in 1936 and accelerated rapidly in the early 1950s.

He consolidated Canadian racing by closing unprofitable courses and became such an important figure in Canadian racing and breeding that Milt Dunnell of the *Toronto Daily Star* said 'the last time he was not man of the year in Canadian Thoroughbred Racing was the year before he came in'.

Northern Dancer, foaled in 1961, was bred by Taylor at his Windfields stud farm outside Toronto. The colt, described as 'a bit of a boyo' as a yearling, was sent to the sales but failed to make his small Can$25,000 reserve; he came back to be broken in the big Canadian barns which shielded the Taylor youngsters from the fierce bites of winter. The small, butty colt started racing, naturally, in Canada, winning five from seven starts. He first ran in the USA at the New York track Aqueduct. He was trained by the famous South American trainer and fabled Latin charmer Horatio Luro. Northern Dancer remains the greatest star of Canadian racing. Rejected at public auction as a yearling, he was syndicated for US$2.4 million and stood at Windfields Stud in Maryland. His stud career lasted until

1987, and at the height of his fame, to send one mare to him cost around US$1 million – at which rate he was pleasurably earning about $50 million a year.

The fact that the chestnut The Minstrel in no way resembled the mighty Nijinsky would have put off most buyers. You have had a brilliant Northern Dancer who is big and bay. Here is his small relation, a chestnut with, as Vincent says, 'an awful lot of white about him'. You could expect that if one was good, the other, so different, would not be. The Minstrel at home, in training and on the racecourse was quite different from Nijinsky. Where Nijinsky was highly strung, difficult, temperamental and had brilliant speed, The Minstrel was tough, brave, sound and possessed stamina. They shared one symptom of a good Northern Dancer: they both had a tendency to sweat at the racecourse.

It was subsequently suggested that Vincent's doubts were primarily about the colt's colour. His chestnut colour was good, hard, even fierce, not the suspect 'washy' colour which few horsemen like. The amount of white about him would have made some horsemen 'go home without him', for the ancient rhyme runs:

> *One leg buy,*
> *Two try,*
> *Three doubt,*
> *Four come home without.*

The reason for this may simply be that horses' legs devoid of pigment are prone to more infections of the skin. In any event, the colour did not deter Vincent.

'I remember,' reflects Vincent, 'when I bought him as a yearling I was definitely concerned about his size, not his colour. I remember going back to his box more than once to have a look at him again to see if I could make myself feel any easier about it. He was small. He grew in the end. He was just short of 15.3, which was big enough. But this Northern Dancer breed is something new in the racehorse world: they don't have to be big to be good.' Picking winners does not just require a 'good eye for a horse', but a complete understanding of bloodlines. Vincent was far from infallible, of course. Many horses he bought did not prosper. But it is the number of top-class winners he picked and trained which is outstanding. Even the morning after he had bought The Minstrel for just over $200,000 O'Brien was back looking at the colt again. 'Did we or did we not make a good buy? He was small and compact, but with not much scope. Yet I'd say he was one of the toughest horses I've ever trained! He was a very lucky horse and never had any setbacks. However, he didn't have quite the brilliant early career of Sir Ivor or Nijinsky.'

In almost every other stable in Europe, The Minstrel's two-year-old career would have been the subject of rapture. He was unbeaten in his first three races. His racing life began later than most of O'Brien's classic hopefuls, for he did not appear until 8 September 1976. John Gosden, then Vincent's assistant at Ballydoyle, says of The Minstrel, 'No trouble in training except that he'd get worked up before the start of a race. I always led him with the jockey on his back. And you had to be careful not to overdo the training with him. Both as a two-year-old and as a three-year-old, The Minstrel needed time, which was what you would expect of something big and gangly like Alleged.

You would not anticipate a small, compact colt to require age to improve.' But this, like a premier cru wine, was the case with The Minstrel.

The Minstrel won his first race, the Moy Stakes at the Curragh, by an easy five lengths. Unchallenged, he still broke the track record. Fewer than three weeks later he went to Leopardstown and won the Larkspur Stakes – yet another race named after a horse of Vincent's. Three weeks' break and he arrived at Newmarket for the Dewhurst Stakes. 'He did wind up as a two-year-old winning the Dewhurst comfortably by four lengths, but,' O'Brien confirms, 'not as impressively as Nijinsky.' At that stage he was still not receiving rave notices in the British racing press. Timeform was one of the few organs prepared to trumpet out its praise. 'How he comes to receive only 8st 13lb in the two-year-olds Free Handicap,' it boomed, 'we cannot imagine.' Putting its rating where its lips were, it rated The Minstrel exceptionally high with 116 at the end of his first season. It could afford next year to boast about its perspicacity.

The Minstrel escaped ailments and setbacks and through the winter continued to thrive. This would prove the fortunate pattern of his life. He was not only as tough as a middleweight professional boxer, taking a series of hard fights in his stride, but he kept improving his physique. He was that rarity – an easy horse to train. This should not detract from his trainer and his staff who prepared him for his targets and picked them correctly. And nothing can diminish the power of Piggott's riding of the little chestnut. The image shimmers on of the tall, grey-faced man bent over the small, white-faced chestnut, the jockey with his whip held aloft and the battling colt with his head heroically stuck forward.

The Minstrel's first outing as a three-year-old in 1977 proved the point, on his visit to Ascot for the 2,000 Guineas Trial. 'The ground was barely raceable,' says O'Brien, 'so bad they couldn't use the starting stalls, and had to start by flag. He won all right, but most of the opposition never won a race again. The going finished them.' Here was more proof of The Minstrel's courage and of his exceptional ability to act with equal speed and lack of strain on any type of going, hard or soft.

Still unbeaten, The Minstrel went off to Newmarket for the 2,000 Guineas accompanied by Jack Mulcahy's brilliant Cloonlara, who was rated as a two-year-old at ten pounds above The Minstrel. She looked a very good prospect for the 1,000 Guineas. Those were two bad days for the O'Briens. Both horses started hot favourites; both got beaten. The Minstrel was beaten two lengths into third place. In the Irish 2,000 Guineas he was beaten only a short head, but finished in front of Nebbiolo, who had beaten him in the English 2,000 Guineas. Nebbiolo hampered him at a tricky moment at the Curragh, and The Minstrel could not quite beat Pampapaul.

'He was a bit unlucky,' says Vincent. 'Lester thought he would have won. But the question then was whether he'd run in the Derby.' No excuses – on to the next target. Would The Minstrel be ready to do himself justice at Epsom? Should Vincent wait till the Irish Derby, giving the colt more time to recover? 'I had a discussion with Lester that night,' Vincent recalls. 'I could see he'd considered what other likely rides he might have. He was in favour of running him. He said to me, "If you run him, I'll ride him."' 'That,' Dermot O'Brien commented drily, 'was better than any question or answer!'

In the eight weeks between that Ascot bog and the Epsom

Derby, The Minstrel had endured three particularly difficult races. Many English experts expected the small chestnut to appear at Epsom looking like an over-raced rabbit. The racing world knew, however, that he was strongly fancied by his stable. Robert Sangster's principal partners in the horse were Vincent O'Brien, John Magnier and Simon Fraser. There were other partners too, including Alan Clore and David Nagle, John's best friend from Ireland. A week before the Derby, the partners received a bid of $1 million from America for their colt. They firmly refused it, and by so doing enriched themselves jointly after the race by some $4.5 million. The refusal of the bid, and Piggott's selection of The Minstrel, told the world of the confidence at Ballydoyle.

Epsom was set to launch the following week's nationwide Silver Jubilee festivities of Queen Elizabeth II. On Derby Day the course danced with flags and ribbons, red, white and blue, in merry tribute to one of England's most ardent and well-informed racing supporters. Jubilee top hats looking like Union Jacks contrasted with the more formal wear in the Members' Enclosure. On the crowded Downs where an estimated 250,000 people were pouring in, a sad man paced along carrying a sandwich board which waggishly warned, 'Be Sure Your Wins Will Find You Out'.

The French invader Blushing Groom started favourite, though elderly English chauvinists who were convinced that 'Frogs can't ride Epsom' gave him no chance. His jockey, Henri Samani, was thought by them to be vastly inferior to better-known names such as Freddy Head and Yves Saint-Martin, yet Head had always had a hapless time round Epsom. Blushing Groom was beaten, but not through any misjudgement. Like a number of others in a slightly sub-standard Derby field, he failed to stay. Because The Minstrel was inclined to sweat up before a race Vincent was afraid the long parade, noise and general hurdy-gurdy atmosphere would distress him. He plugged the horse's ears with cotton wool so he would not be able to hear clearly, and John Gosden walked down to the start to remove it before the race. The prevention worked. Good trainers overcome psychological problems.

Piggott, *sans pareil* around those extraordinary Downs, soon had The Minstrel exquisitely placed. Only Hot Grove and Blushing Groom had a chance in the straight. It took The Minstrel nearly three furlongs to draw up with Hot Grove, to struggle alongside him under the full force of Piggott, and to get just in front as the winning post loomed. Lester said, 'I won in the final ten yards.' 'He had to run hard to win,' says Vincent. 'He proved himself very game. Lester had to be hard on him. I'd certainly say he needed all Lester's power and skill on him at Epsom that day.'

'The Minstrel's Derby was no foregone conclusion,' Jacqueline states firmly. 'We'd gone to Newmarket hoping for a double Guineas victory from Cloonlara and The Minstrel. Both horses had failed to come up to expectations and the trip home in the small plane from Newmarket was very silent and miserable. We hoped so much things would be different at Epsom. They were! The Minstrel had a hard race but was so very game and genuine. He was a lovely character, kind and gentle in the stable. I remember once explaining this to visitors with my back to him and he leant out and gave me a playful nip on the shoulder-blade. I went to the Derby with a very black, bruised back – my own fault entirely.'

Such a hard race, the grandstand experts decided, would now finish The Minstrel. But not at all. He went home, ate up and flourished to such an extent that O'Brien decided to run him in the Irish Derby three and a half weeks later, the race which had been his alternative to Epsom. He kept in mind, additionally, Ascot's great race in July, to which its famous sponsors De Beers had now added in 1975 the modest word 'Diamond' to 'King George VI and Queen Elizabeth Stakes'.

There was a further complication in Vincent's uncertainty about the Irish Derby. 'The decision whether to run The Minstrel in the Irish Derby was one of the hardest choices I ever had to make,' he says. First he had to decide whether Ascot would come too soon for the horse after the Curragh, but there was an additional complication of some significance. This illustrates a trainer's dilemma when he has more than one star horse with different owners. 'We worked Alleged with The Minstrel after the Epsom Derby and we then knew we'd got an exceptional horse in Alleged,' says Vincent. Bob Fluor, a part-owner of Alleged, had invited all his executives and relations to fly over to the Curragh to watch his colt run in the Irish Derby ridden by Lester. The Fluor Corporation was the tenth largest corporation in the world. The inference is that when the head of such an empire wants a horse to run, run it must, where, when and how he chooses.

Sangster filled in the background to the controversy. 'I could see that Vincent was very edgy all the way through Ascot and between the two Derbys. I knew something was worrying him. It was that he didn't want to run Alleged in the Irish Derby; he didn't feel he'd perform his best on hard ground. He wanted to run The Minstrel. As I owned forty per cent

[Sangster's usual stake] in both horses, and between us the European partners owned seventy per cent, I said, "To hell with it. We'll run The Minstrel." Bob Fluor didn't take this very happily. I think he understood in the end. In fact, I said I would buy him out, valuing Alleged for a million pounds. He sold most of his share, but I think he retained five per cent. So he was still happy when Alleged won the Prix de l'Arc de Triomphe!'

The Irish Derby was The Minstrel's easiest victory of the year, which puts into perspective the difficulty of the others. For although he won by one and a half lengths, he was objected to by the second horse, Lucky Sovereign, who had been well behind him at Epsom. The Minstrel had veered right across the course towards the stands to such an extent that the Stewards inquired into possible interference. He had once again to be driven out to win, and in so doing had hung outwards across the course.

The victory made him favourite for Ascot on 23 July – his sixth contest in sixteen weeks, an intensity of programme which few modern top-class flat racehorses normally stand. But his appearance under the trees at Ascot's sloping paddock drew a hum of admiration. The cynosure of all eyes had actually developed and thickened since Epsom.

O'Brien's view then was that The Minstrel might not be a true mile-and-a-half horse. His form in the Irish Derby and at Ascot contradicts this, allowing for Epsom's eccentricities, but every stop had to be pulled out by Piggott at Ascot. On the minus side, the horse was very slowly away in a field which included five major Classic winners: the only other three-year-old, Crystal Palace, winner of the French Derby, and the four-year-olds Exceller, Crow, Orange Bay and Bruni. On the plus side, Piggott typically stole a smooth run up on the inside turning for home. This time Vincent, so full of praise for Piggott in the English Derby, was more critical. 'Lester struck the front quite early – too soon, I'd say, for the horse. All these American horses are not out-and-out stayers. Coming to the front too early exposed him to the risk of getting beat by an out-and-out stayer.' In Vincent's view, his horse, having hit the front too soon, was stopping at the finish, holding on only through courage (plus Piggott's strength) from Orange Bay, who was fighting back at him all the way to the post. 'He won by the shortest of short heads. Perhaps three inches!'

The Minstrel had now proved himself in a succession of hard battles to be the best middle-distance horse in Europe. His breeder, E. P. Taylor, wanted him back to stand with Northern Dancer at Windfields Farm, so he bought half of him from the owners (Sangster, O'Brien, Magnier and co.), valuing the colt at $9 million. This was forty-five times the price paid after that long and painstaking deliberation at Keeneland that hot July two years earlier.

It was the pattern of the colt's racing to win under pressure, often at the last moment. His retirement came precipitously, and the rush of his departure from Ireland before the season was finished reflected this. The O'Brien intelligence service swiftly got wind of an impending clampdown by the American authorities on the importation of any European horses into America due to a severe outbreak of equine metritis here. The Minstrel, with only hours to spare before the ban came down, was whisked out of Ireland and into the States on the first available air charter. The little chestnut had bravely run all his races under pressure; his departure to return to the land of his birth followed the same bustling pattern.

Although The Minstrel died comparatively early at the age of sixteen of laminitis, a condition of the foot normally associated with children's portly ponies, he had a successful stud career. He has had plenty of good winners of all sorts and distances in a variety of European countries: France, Italy, Ireland, Germany and England, rather more than in America. His best colts to race were L'Emigrant and Palace Music, and he bred some outstanding fillies: Treizieme, Minstrella, Melodist, Musical Bliss and Silver Fling. At the height of his popularity, in the bloodstock boom of the mid-1980s, his stud fee was £185,000.

* * *

Vincent's reactions after winning a big race are well revealed by Denis McCarthy, an old friend and owner of his, and for six years Senior Steward of the Turf Club. McCarthy recalls, 'After The Minstrel had won the Derby at Epsom – I hadn't gone – I happened to be down at Cork the following day and I drove up in the evening. Any time I'm passing Ballydoyle, I would call in to see Vincent.

'So I arrived there about six o'clock and I walked into the house. The front door was open. I walked towards the drawing room at the end of the corridor and I heard a voice saying, "Hello, Denis." I looked round and Vincent was sitting there, quietly working. This I thought was amazing. But it sums up the attitude of the man. He wants to get on with it; he's finished with what happened. He wants to go on and see what he's going to do in the future. There he was then, working at his desk, preparing entries and working out his programme for the rest of the year. In fact, he asked me if I would like to have a look at the horses. We both went round the stables and had a look at the horses quite normally, as if he hadn't won the Derby the day before!'

Denis pondered the secret of Vincent's success. 'There are a lot of things to be considered. He has the greatest dedication to his work. He's capable of very hard work. There's no doubt that he has done that all his life. He is a perfectionist: everything has to be just right. He has ambition. He leaves nothing to chance. He examines everything in detail and makes certain as far as he possibly can that the horse is right for the race in question. This is part of his success.

'I've known him for a number of years. In fact my late father had horses with him and I've had horses with him, and with some success. I see no changes in him at all, and that I think makes him popular. I know the public love to see him and he hasn't lost his head, even with all the success he has had.' Had he any weaknesses? 'I suppose we all have weaknesses. He probably hasn't enjoyed himself enough. Maybe he has worked too hard. Maybe he's too dedicated – if that's a weakness.'

McCarthy points out how much Vincent has done for racing and breeding in Ireland. 'He's brought a lot of American and British owners into this country to run their horses here. And this has certainly set a target for the young trainers who are coming up now. We have some very good young trainers coming through now and I think they are encouraged to go places even further than they might by looking at what Vincent has done. He has, of course, won every race in Britain and Ireland worth winning. Someone said he seems to have won everything but the Boat Race! I have said many times that Vincent would have been as successful in any profession he chose. I think he's really put Irish racing on the map. If you go to America or to the Far East his name is on the lips of all the racing people. All the world would have to admit that Irish racing is now up at the top. Certainly a lot of that is due to what Vincent has done.'

A good illustration of what McCarthy was talking about, and an enduring example of Vincent's influence on the blood-stock world, is that of Be My Guest, picked, trained and placed at Coolmore by him. A life-sized bronze statue of Be My Guest stands outside Goffs Sales Ring at Kill. There is another at Coolmore. And both with good reason. This good-looking chestnut is worthy of celebration in both places. He briefly broke the European record price as a yearling at Goffs, though the son of Northern Dancer out of America's top filly What a Treat had been foaled in the USA. Vincent outbid Stavros Niarchos for him at 127,000 guineas. In so doing he was ful-filling the first step of the syndicate's plans. Here was an American-bred horse, yet bought in Ireland, owned by Mrs Diana Manning, the sister of Raymond Guest, to be trained by Vincent and then retired to stud at Coolmore. There, exactly as intended, he would become the huge empire's foundation stallion of the Northern Dancer line.

It was Be My Guest's misfortune to be born in the same year as Derby winner The Minstrel, Prix de l'Arc de Triomphe double winner Alleged, the ace miler Artaius and Godswalk, all trained by Vincent and all officially rated above Be My Guest. There was a true *embarras de richesses* at Ballydoyle in those years. Indeed, Be My Guest ran at Epsom behind The Minstrel. But he won the Blue Riband Trial Stakes there, and the Waterford Crystal Mile at Goodwood, and another Group 3.

'Be My Guest,' Vincent said in the 1980s, 'is one of those horses that is proving a better sire than a racehorse. He has a top-class pedigree, and to head the European sires' list, with only his two first crops to race for him, must be a record. He is one of the horses that proves Northern Dancer's unbelievable strength as a sire of sires.' He started off as champion first season sire in 1987, and the very next year he was Coolmore's first champion sire of Great Britain and Ireland. His first three-year-old crop yielded five Group winners, including David O'Brien's Derby-winning Assert and the very good Classic filly On the House. His fees started modestly at 5,000 guineas and then shot up to 75,000 guineas. He was soon covering nearly a hundred mares. Be My Guest firmly established the aims of the syndicate. They had found, made and could go on very profitably selling most of the nominations but as well improving their own mares with their own very successful stallion.

CHAPTER 18

ALLEGED

'I must say he surprised me'

There was never such a thing as a 'Vincent O'Brien type'. His winners came in all sizes, colours, shapes and characters. Nijinsky and The Minstrel, though so closely related, were different in almost every aspect, save for their ability to win Classics – and even that they did differently. Dapper little Larkspur could not have looked more different from the imposing Golden Fleece, who had the build of a Cheltenham Gold Cup favourite. But both won their Derbys, Vincent's first and last Classic triumphs at Epsom.

Alleged, whose career overlapped The Minstrel's, was a totally different type to the small, tough chestnut with so much white about him that his critics called him 'flashy'. He was even acquired differently because, although Alleged was part of the syndicate's first year, he was bought not as a yearling, not at Keeneland, Kentucky, and not by Vincent. O'Brien remembers that the colt was at Keeneland Sales as a yearling, 'and I must have seen him. With the pedigree he had, he was a horse I would have looked at. But I don't remember him!

Apparently he wasn't well presented and was very immature at the time.'

Alleged's sire, Hoist the Flag, was saved for stud by the skill of American veterinary science and surgery. Having won five of his first six races, he fractured a hind pastern when being wound up for the Kentucky Derby. He might easily have been destroyed on the spot, but he underwent a major operation in which a piece of his hipbone was cut out and transplanted as a bone graft into the broken pastern. The Hoist the Flag yearling son failed to reach his $40,000 reserve and was not sold in the ring. Vincent picks up the story: 'A chap from California bought him from the breeder June McKnight for something below $40,000. He turned out to be Monty Roberts, the man who became famous for the way he used to break in young and difficult horses. Roberts planned to resell the two-year-old. I wasn't there, but Robert Sangster and Billy McDonald were, and they bought the horse.'

For this sale for horses-in-training, the two-year-olds on offer were given strong work on the track. It would certainly be exceptional for any potentially top horse in Europe. Nothing of any consequence is doing much more than quiet canters at Newmarket in January. Yet in the red dawns over Los Angeles, the backward two-year-old Alleged was being whizzed round the dirt track of Hollywood Park and being asked to find some speed. Handled by the expert 'breaker' and dealer Monty Roberts, he was produced at the sales in very good condition.

Robert Sangster attended the sales with his friend Billy McDonald. McDonald was a car salesman from Belfast who by repute specialized in Rolls Royces. 'I actually bought Alleged myself,' Robert Sangster reflects, with both modesty and surprise, 'at the two-year-old in-training sale in California. In the ring he made $165,000 and I was offered a profit of $25,000 by Hoss Inman, a Texan in a ten-gallon hat. I said to Billy McDonald, "Let's take the twenty-five thousand dollars; we have done very well out of the sale," but Billy, being typically Irish, asked for $225,000. Mr Inman said, "No. You can keep your horse." So, but for Billy, you probably would never have heard of Alleged again.' Ulsterman Billy McDonald was forever proud of the role he played, and the number plate of his car in California henceforth read 'Alleged'.

Robert's partner in this deal was the millionaire industrialist Bob Fluor. 'Alleged was going to be trained out in California by Tom Pratt,' says Sangster. 'I went up and saw the horse a week later and thought he'd best be trained by Vincent in Ireland. So I recommended he be sent across to Vincent. And after that, he only lost one race in his whole career.' The advice Sangster had taken in California was that Alleged's knees might well not stand up to the extra strain of racing on dirt out there. They had already had to be blistered. The horse was in full training to such an extent that he was doing 'time trials' on the track. His knees did not appreciate this. Ironically, it was the ability of American horses to stand their tougher racing conditions that was one of the earliest attractions for O'Brien.

When Alleged arrived at Ballydoyle he was greeted by the staff without much enthusiasm for the bargain. No-one there thought a world-beater had come to join them. The best they could say was that he was 'moderate'. Even with the benefit of hindsight, the staff were frank. 'Very scrawny; looked terrible,' said one. 'Never carried much condition,' opined another. Farm manager Willie Fogarty declared, 'He was weak and backward. He never carried what we call the "Ballydoyle condition". He was very slack over his loins.' Vincent disagreed. 'He was a nice horse, who needed time.' And T. P. Burns gave his opinion when the two-year-old arrived: 'I saw no objections to him. I thought he'd be all right.' They all agreed that Alleged had a very good head and outlook. This was one aspect found in almost every O'Brien horse over nearly fifty years. Although there were many different types, they all gave you the same bold, handsome look from head and eyes and ears. As mankind judges one another, so the wise judge of horses picks them by the look they give. The perfectly made equine machine is no good without that invisible motor of courage and the will to win.

Alleged did not prove to be a favourite in the yard. Jacqueline O'Brien remembers, 'The boys said he was not an easy horse in the box. He was often cross, like his great-grandfather Ribot.' John Gosden says, 'He was kind, but if you were silly enough to bend over in his box he'd have a go at you. He was a masculine horse, aggressive in the stable. He had a wonderful head, strong and powerful, very broad between the eyes. He was not nasty. He was straightforward. He meant business. But he was marvellously relaxed on the racecourse.'

The sun nearly always shines in California. Even in January the horses start working on the tracks at six a.m. because by eleven, when the last of a trainer's six or seven 'sets' has finished, the weather is as warm as an English July. Alleged certainly felt the cold when he arrived at Ballydoyle in 1976, for the sun scarcely shines on Ireland in February. 'He was a little slow in conditioning,' Vincent recalls. 'I suppose the change of climate had something to do with it. So I gave him most of the year and brought him along only in the autumn. He did no serious work before August. I just got him up to a run right at the end of the season – actually in the first week of November. He won at the Curragh, and you'd like the way he won: he was going away at the end, very nicely. He was never a very robust horse in training – which was just as well, as he was that bit lighter on his legs. The stock of his sire, Hoist the Flag, give a lot of trouble with their legs – knees and joints usually. It's a question of bone structure.'

In the spring of Alleged's three-year-old season, 1977, the staff recall him working 'really well'. They were the more disappointed, therefore, when, as they put it, 'he just scraped home in his first race, the Ballydoyle Stakes at Leopardstown, towards the end of April'. O'Brien says, 'He didn't show me a great deal early on, and I didn't press him. He only just won that first race and there was nothing very exciting about the way he won it. So I talked myself out of pressing on with him. I decided to give him a little bit more time and a chance to improve.'

Like all else in life, training is about timing. But the trainer of good flat horses is locked into an inflexible racing calendar. Where a jumping man with a top-class chaser may have three or four cracks at steeplechasing's single Classic, the Cheltenham Gold Cup, the man on the flat has only three dates for his three-year-old Classic colt. It is no good a Derby hopeful only getting ready in July. In Alleged's case O'Brien had long ago abandoned any notion of early successes. The Epsom Derby was never on his schedule. 'I didn't run him again until the Royal Whip at the Curragh in the middle of May, and then he was only one of three to run from Ballydoyle. Tommy Murphy rode Meneval, a four-year-old. Alleged was ridden by Peadar Matthews, one of our work riders. Valinsky was ridden by Lester as he had won very impressively as a two-year-old.' Against these two stable companions, Alleged started the complete outsider at 33–1. Vincent goes on, 'Valinsky struck the front as they came into the straight and looked as though he'd win. Then Alleged cruised up to him and beat him quite comfortably. Then I realized he was a pretty nice horse. We knew we had a good horse.' The lads remember the day clearly. 'The crowds were dumbfounded!'

It was, however, the year of The Minstrel. So came the decision, resented by Alleged's American co-owner Bob Fluor, that Alleged would not go for the Irish Derby. O'Brien's decision was affected by four factors: Alleged still needed time; he did not want hard ground; The Minstrel had recovered so quickly from Epsom that he could win the Irish Derby; and, twinkling ahead, lay the lure of the Prix de l'Arc de Triomphe for Alleged. 'I took my time with him,' Vincent goes on, 'and I didn't run him between the Gallinule Stakes at the Curragh on 28 May, which he won easily by a length, and York in August – a gap of nearly three months.'

The race chosen was the Great Voltigeur Stakes, which produced a very strong field, including horses such as Hot Grove, Lucky Sovereign and Classic Example, who had been placed behind The Minstrel in the English and Irish Derbys. These were left gasping when Alleged accelerated dramatically three furlongs from home and won by eight lengths, with complete disdain for his pursuers. 'I must say,' Vincent comments, 'he surprised me. He just simply trotted up!' Though 1977 had already been enriched by the victories of The Minstrel in his two Derbys and in Ascot's 'Diamond' Stakes, Timeform pronounced that Alleged's Voltigeur victory 'changed the face of European racing for the year' – it was as dramatic as that.

O'Brien was more occupied in mapping out a programme than polishing the panegyrics. 'Then he was in the Prix de l'Arc de Triomphe, and I thought, "August to the first week in October. He needs a race in between." There wasn't really any suitable prep race for him except the Leger. And I really wasn't keen to run him in the Leger before the Prix de l'Arc de Triomphe. I always think it's a bad prep for the Prix de l'Arc de Triomphe for a three-year-old, to run him over a mile and three quarters. It's almost like two miles, because it's a big galloping course. But anyhow, there wasn't any other race to run him in.'

Horses are not alone in remembering places and races. Nijinsky's race for the St Leger, giving him the Triple Crown, had been hard won, and contributed to his defeat in the Prix de l'Arc de Triomphe. Such thoughts loomed large in O'Brien's mind as he weighed the pros and cons. Even the same phrases used for Nijinsky's St Leger came up again for Alleged. 'I thought, "Well, the opposition doesn't look too strong. He doesn't seem to have all that to beat." I thought that I'd take a chance. I thought he'd probably have an easy race. But it didn't work out quite like that.'

To most stables, the presence of the Queen's Oaks-winning filly Dunfermline, accompanied by her pacemaker Gregarious, would prove at least a threat in the St Leger. Pat Eddery on Classic Example could be dangerous. But Alleged, ridden by Lester Piggott in the colours of Mr Fluor, started at 4–7; Dunfermline, ridden by the engaging Willie Carson, was a 10–1 chance. The Queen would dearly have loved to be at Doncaster to see her homebred Classic-winning filly run, but she was up at Balmoral on what is supposed to be her Scottish holiday, but it is the custom for her to invite the current prime minister and spouse to spend a weekend there, so Mr Jim Callaghan was staying to discuss affairs of state. Duty, as usual, came first, ahead of the Queen's special pleasure.

The glorious day she missed was one of sadness and frustration for the O'Brien raiders. Their horse had been hot favourite for the St Leger since York. 'There was great confidence here,' the lads recall. 'But I must say,' Vincent comments critically, 'Lester rode an extraordinary race on him. The Queen's filly had her pacemaker. He set a good pace, a strong pace. And Lester quite early moved up second and had Dunfermline behind him! And when the filly's pacemaker was finished with, Lester went on with Alleged. Well, he looked as if he was going to win, but just inside the last furlong, the filly came on. She just outstayed him, and duly she got up to beat him. What was he thinking about? I don't know . . .' And Vincent shakes his head.

His younger son Charles, now a trainer himself in Ireland, was then a ten-year-old schoolboy, and he went to Doncaster with his father. He remembers, 'This was probably the only time ever the Boss lost his cool on a racecourse, using some sharp language to Lester outside the weighing room – to the interest of the bystanders! Lester was totally unmoved and just shrugged his shoulders.' The Ballydoyle staff declared robustly and sardonically, 'Well, Dunfermline had two pacemakers that day, didn't she? Her own and Alleged! If Alleged had been held up, he'd never have been beat. Never.' They remember, however, that 'he came out of the Leger very well – he'd just been kept ticking over between the Voltigeur and the Leger'. But T. P. Burns comments, 'He grew peevish. You wouldn't want to be in the stable with him!'

That St Leger would prove to be Alleged's solitary defeat in three years and ten races. Bob Fluor sold most of his share in Alleged to Robert Sangster, but kept 5 per cent. David O'Brien remembers flying with Bob from California to Paris to enjoy Vincent's second Prix de l'Arc de Triomphe victory. 'Lester rode a wonderful race on the horse,' says Vincent. 'Having a chat with Lester beforehand, he said he didn't think they'd go a great pace, which turned out to be correct. Lester thought that because it was a pretty open race a lot of the jockeys would think they had a chance. Therefore they wouldn't go crazy. He was right. So Lester lay pretty close to the pace. Coming down the hill he was second, and when they started to turn for home he took up the running and went on from there.' The lads still have the impression that 'he made all the running. And we were disappointed to see him leading that early, for the Prix de l'Arc de Triomphe is not a race you would want to be making it all in!' Their early fears were swiftly confounded. Alleged quickened so brilliantly that nothing else could match him. He came home an easy one-and-a-half-lengths winner from the top-class New Zealand horse Balmerino, who had been sent to England to campaign that year. Alleged was the first three-year-old to win the Prix de l'Arc de Triomphe since San San in 1972, five years earlier.

'The horse won really well,' Vincent sums up, 'and then we decided to keep him on, train him as a four-year-old and aim him at the Prix de l'Arc de Triomphe again.' That one sentence covers weeks of discussions, of heart-searching financial calculations and prognostications of what 1978 should bring. It was extremely tempting to retire him then and capitalize him at several million dollars as a stallion. He had easily won Europe's greatest race. His Voltigeur victory had drawn rave notices. Backward though he'd been, he had been sufficiently advanced to win as a two-year-old. All these things would count richly with breeders.

O'Brien came under pressure from his co-owners to take the enormous profit which awaited them. He had cost only $165,000. The Minstrel had been syndicated for $9 million; Alleged would make as much. There, dangling like great sacks of gold, jangled a profit of well over $8 million. And a race-horse can go wrong any time. Surely it was better to sell while he was sound and safe and victorious? In straight money-talk the deal was obvious: Alleged's age meant he could not win a Classic. Therefore, unless he could win a second Prix de l'Arc de Triomphe or Ascot's King George VI and Queen Elizabeth Diamond Stakes, he could hardly enhance his value by staying in training as a four-year-old. The actuarial odds against winning two Prix de l'Arc de Triomphes were enormous. You had to go back more than twenty years to the supreme Ribot in 1955 and 1956 to find the last dual winner.

O'Brien quietly, unsurprisingly, had his way. He pointed out that Alleged had done very little racing in his life – 'he was a fresh horse'. He reminded his partners that, though a second Prix de l'Arc de Triomphe would be his supreme objective, there were a number of attractive, important and rich races to be picked up on the way. Provided that the ground did not turn too firm next summer, there was the King George VI and Queen Elizabeth Diamond Stakes. If The Minstrel had won it, so could Alleged. There was also the Eclipse at Sandown, and the Benson & Hedges at York. Earlier, the Coronation Cup at

Epsom and Ascot's Hardwicke Stakes were possibilities, though winning either would not significantly enhance his stud value. While Alleged's future was debated by his shareholders, there was no doubt at all in the minds of the staff working at Ballydoyle. 'We all knew he'd stay in training as a four-year-old!'

But once again, as it nearly always is with horses, 'man proposes; God disposes'. Although Alleged did quite well over the winter – 'he never looked that great,' said the lads, 'he always had a dull coat' – things began to go wrong in the spring and summer of 1978. The ground grew firm. He again ran in and won the Royal Whip on the Curragh, but the race jarred his knees. 'He was short in his action,' the lads remember. 'He had to be rested, and we treated his knees.' Dave Walsh, the blacksmith, recalls, 'The horse was also lame behind and not in his foot' – a typical blacksmith's diagnosis. Then, Alleged went down with a virus that plagued O'Brien's stable that summer. 'He got it pretty heavily,' says Vincent, 'and we had to be prepared to sit back with him and wait, and give him plenty of time to get over it.'

The weeks fled past. All those tempting prizes which had been Alleged's targets the previous autumn were being lost. The muttering began. Had it not proved a disastrous decision to keep him in training? He had, by the end of August, won only one race in Ireland. Had he gone to stud in Kentucky he would have earned more than a million dollars already. 'We had to wait,' says Vincent calmly, 'and it was September before I got him up to a race again. There was nothing available in Ireland or England, so I had to send him to France.' He flew from Shannon to Paris to run at Longchamp in the Prix du Prince d'Orange. The lads report that he flew alone, without a lead horse. 'He didn't need friends.'

After nearly a year with only one race, the expectations were that Alleged would be in urgent need of this race. 'Actually,' says O'Brien, 'he broke the track record for that race and distance, which was quite something after not having had a run since May.' The turn of phrase is significantly unusual for the modest and reticent O'Brien. Winning this race was a great feat of training. Yet it was only the final stepping-stone to a sort of immortality among the racehorses of the world.

Alleged flew back to Shannon. Twelve days later he was back in France to attempt the principal purpose of that season, his second Prix de l'Arc de Triomphe. To the delays in his train-ing was now added a further change. In 1977, the ground had ridden fast. Piggott had then foxed the opposition by keeping him at half throttle near the front before suddenly losing them with a surge of speed that could only be unleashed on fast turf. This time, it rained for two days. The going turned soft – too soft, some thought, for Alleged's speed. And on this ground, too, another doubt was aired: might Piggott keep Alleged too far back, as he had done with Nijinsky and Park Top?

But all turned out as smooth as silk. 'Lester rode a some-what similar race,' says Vincent, 'not quite as prominent as he'd been the year before, but still not too far off the pace. The horse had a very clear run and, again, when he hit the straight he was quickly in front. There was nothing to catch him from there home.' Since the Great War only five horses had won two Prix de l'Arc de Triomphes: Ksar in 1921 and 1922; then the strange Motrico, who came up from France's south-west to win it in 1930 as a five-year-old and then in 1932 as a seven-year-old; Corrida at four and five in 1936 and 1937; Tantième at three and four in 1950 and 1951; and, of course, Ribot a few years after that.

Five years later, T. P. Burns was sitting in his office on a chill winter's afternoon, overlooking the stable yard at Ballydoyle. A smile warmed his face in contemplation of that great day at Longchamp. He summed it up simply. 'It was a case of mission accomplished. Robert Sangster, as usual, generously hosted a celebration party at Régines. Vincent, equally typically, wanted to have a quiet evening. He went to bed and to sleep at seven, woke at eleven, and dined alone at Fouquet's on the Champs Elysées, while at Régines the effervescent Mrs Susan Sangster, known to her friends as "the Sheila", was aptly dancing to "Waltzing Matilda" on the top of the table.'

Robert Sangster, in the July after that famous victory, stood shirt-sleeved among the sale barns at Keeneland and put the business aspect of the operation. 'After the second Prix de l'Arc de Triomphe, we syndicated Alleged here in Kentucky for roughly $13 million. This may seem an unbelievable figure, but in fact it's quite simple. It's based on his earning capacity in that the horse stands at $80,000 and he can cover forty mares. So he earns $3.2 million a year. And a horse is normally valued on a four-year purchase of his earnings.'

Vincent, too, kept his share of the horse, meaning that he could either use his nominations to send a mare or two of his own to the stallion, or sell his nominations for a year. Up to that time it was accepted practice to syndicate a stallion into forty shares or thereabouts. This conserved his labours on the one hand, and on the other maintained the value of his stock.

In the 1980s bigger books became the norm due to advances in veterinary techniques which enabled stallions less wastefully to cover up to four times more mares. Studs extended the stallions' workload and earnings capacity. Covering larger books of mares with a lower fee enabled breeders to use stallions which otherwise they could not have afforded.

But the business was going to explode in another way, predominantly led by John Magnier, Vincent and Robert Sangster, who owned large stud farms in Australia. The trick was to keep the stallions working all year round. Instead of just late January to June in the northern hemisphere, they then continued their not unpleasant labours in the southern half of the world. The Coolmore group's base in Australia, plus greatly improved air transport, made year-round mating commonplace. The stallions seemed to flourish with the new regime and benefited from their spell in the sun. Changing stallions from one hemisphere to another for part of their season was started by the syndicate and is now a widespread practise.

CHAPTER 19

STORM BIRD

'The Invisible Horse'

When Lester Piggott left to work in England, in 1981, Vincent was delighted to take on Pat Eddery. 'I knew Pat's maternal grandfather, who was one of the top jockeys riding in Ireland from the 1920s to the 1940s,' he says. 'Jack Moylan used to ride for my father and then he rode for me when I started to train at Churchtown – in fact he came from Churchtown.' Jack Moylan and Pat's father, Jimmy, were both Irish champion jockeys. Remarkably Jack, riding Slide On, and Jimmy on Good Morning dead-heated for the Irish 2,000 Guineas at the Curragh in 1944.

Pat Eddery had won the Derby on Grundy and the Oaks on Polygamy, and was champion jockey in Britain from 1974 to 1977 (and again in 1986, 1988 and 1989). By the time popular Pat retired in November 2003 after thirty-six years in the saddle he had been champion jockey eleven times; unusually for any jockey, he was champion in two countries, for he won the Irish title in 1982, his second year at Ballydoyle. The start of Pat Eddery's O'Brien connection in 1981 should have meant the continuation of the career of the brilliant Storm Bird, ridden by him to win the Dewhurst in 1980. Unfortunately, this did not happen.

This mysterious colt had cost the syndicate $1 million at Keeneland. Particularly good-looking, he was Canadian-bred, being by Northern Dancer, the sire so loved and so promoted by Vincent, and out of the winner of the Canadian Oaks, South Ocean. The similarities in his breeding with both Nijinsky and The Minstrel – though he physically resembled neither and was halfway between them in size – must have made everyone else at Keeneland that hot July evening sure that the syndicate would buy him, provided Vincent liked him as an individual. No matter what bidding deceptions and merry pranks Robert Sangster had played to disguise their interest, they had to go to the million to get him.

As a two-year-old Champion, Storm Bird looked a tremendous bargain. The colt was unbeaten in all his five races, progressing in the customary O'Brien style as he proved himself ready for stronger tests. He started with easy victories in Ireland, then in the Group 2 National Stakes, giving weight away all round to a good field and ridden by Tommy Murphy, he spurted away, winning easily. Storm Bird's final test as a two-year-old was the Dewhurst Stakes at autumnal Newmarket, a race favoured by Vincent if he thought he had a Classic horse for the following year. Piggott and he had already won it five times. Seven furlongs on the straight Rowley Mile course is the ideal test for the following spring's 2,000 Guineas. His rider this time was Pat Eddery. The opposition included two winners of the hottest races in England and in France, To-Agori-Mou and Miswaki respectively. To-Agori-Mou and Storm Bird left the field trailing, and Vincent's colt, in a driving finish, won courageously. At that instant Vincent, Robert, Pat and the syndicate were all dreaming of a glorious Classic year in 1981.

Then everything went horribly wrong. The winter favourite for both the 2,000 Guineas and the Derby – his breeding strongly suggested he would stay one and a half miles at Epsom – suffered a macabre assault in the New Year. The night attack could have leapt from the pages of one of the numerous racing thrillers currently in vogue. A former employee of Vincent's, who, it seemed, bore some mysterious grudge, got into the hapless Storm Bird's box in the dark with a hefty pair of scissors and hacked away at the poor colt's mane, forelock and tail. The animal may have been surprised, but was not physically wounded.

The assailant was brought to trial in Clonmel and severely cautioned. During the trial, evidence was given as to the colt's likely value: it revealed that the $1 million yearling was now insured for $15 million. As favourite for the first two English Classics, this was a fair valuation for 1981, when bloodstock prices were becoming, with hindsight, ridiculous. It is a top-of-the-range example of the soaring market at the time. The Minstrel, bustled off to stud in the USA ahead of the equine metritis ban, had been valued, on his 50 per cent sale back to E. P. Taylor at Windfields, at $9 million. That was only three and a half years earlier, and he had won not just the Epsom Derby, but the Irish Derby and the King George VI and Queen Elizabeth Diamond Stakes. Yet Storm Bird was now valued at nearly twice that figure. It was not surprising that some anxious onlookers of the changing racing scene were certain that stallion valuations were going crazy. The crash which always follows inflated booms was coming soon.

Rumours about Storm Bird reverberated around the turf's gossipy world. Only the basic facts leaked out of Ballydoyle. The bookmakers, particularly the wily Ladbrokes, normally have agents close to, or moles inside, big racing stables. Little was heard from any spy. It was officially announced that, mercifully, there seemed to be nothing physically wrong with the colt. His first race was to be in early April in the race named after Gladness.

Because of the criticism and the ridicule in some quarters about Storm Bird's three-year-old non-career in 1981, it is worth reflecting that the syndicate, and particularly Robert Sangster, had believed at Christmas time that they were sitting on an asset worth at least $15 million. Just as with a board of directors in a private company worth an enormous sum at face value based on past performance, it was important to maintain that value, even to enhance it. The asset was subsequently going to be sold or part-sold, and it was necessary for its sale price to be high to fund other acquisitions – and there had been some expensive failures whose value had plunged. In these circumstances, the senior partners in a private company are disinclined to advise possible future buyers – in a racehorse's case, studs and other syndicates – that anything is other than rosy with the 'asset'. Where millions are at stake on the ability and soundness of potential stallions, it is not surprising that well-bred good horses who miss engagements are not declared to have strained ligaments or tendons disclosing physical weakness. Stone bruises and strained muscles are more often given as the causes of temporary lay-offs while the situation is being assessed.

The racing world awaited Storm Bird's first run as a three-year-old with curiosity and lively anticipation. Punters held hopeful vouchers for ante-post wagers on the 2,000 Guineas, the Derby or both. Many more than these brave, far-seeing, or more often foolhardy souls were the millions who followed racing for fun and were delighted as much by the arrival, presence and performance of a truly top-class horse as by a winning bet.

Storm Bird certainly had seemed this. But just before he was due to have his first run of the year in the Gladness Stakes, Ballydoyle pronounced him a non-runner: he was lame of his off-hind leg. It was not suggested that he had trodden on a stone; nor was it suggested that there was anything serious about the lameness. There were doubts at home about his mental attitude. He cannot have been showing any zest at Ballydoyle, so he was taken – a regular training ploy – to gallop on a racecourse to increase his enthusiasm. He worked badly at Naas racecourse. Worse was to come. Before the 2,000 Guineas Vincent had to report that Storm Bird was coughing and could not run. The season went on without him. Entries were made for Storm Bird, but he did not run. This caused anxiety and anguish at Ballydoyle, and in the syndicate, and especially in Sangster. Observers in England with nothing to lose, and spiked perhaps by envy of the syndicate's great early successes, began to mock the whole sad process of engagements being made and plans announced, followed every time by cancellations.

There was, however, an able understudy in King's Lake, a Nijinsky colt out of Fish Bar, the dam of the brilliant filly Cloonlara. King's Lake, ridden by Pat Eddery, was the

Ballydoyle representative in the Irish 2,000 Guineas. He won the race, beating the English 2,000 Guineas winner To-Agori-Mou by a neck. But the Stewards decided that King's Lake had caused interference to the runner-up and reversed the placings. After he heard the verdict, Vincent – who had not been called to the Stewards' inquiry – went out onto the road behind the stands and walked up and down, agitated, before returning to the Stewards Room to do what he'd never done before: he appealed against the verdict. He was extremely upset as he believed his horse, on the rails, had veered outwards only marginally, while To-Agori-Mou had come in considerably towards him. The racegoers at the Curragh, united in their belief that an injustice had been done, found their views confirmed by Timeform, which wrote, 'We lay no claim to infallibility, but in our view the film of the last two furlongs of the Irish 2,000 Guineas was misinterpreted by the local Stewards.' The appeal, two weeks later, attended by top lawyers and lasting over seven hours, overturned the Stewards' decision. King's Lake kept the Guineas.

The battle between the two great horses continued. To-Agori-Mou beat King's Lake in the St James Palace Stakes at Royal Ascot by a similar margin, and Greville Starkey raised two fingers to the crowd as he crossed the line. Pat Eddery wrote that Starkey 'raised his fingers in what may have been a victory sign to the crowd or may have been something more unpleasant directed at me'. However, the positions were reversed at Goodwood's Sussex Stakes when King's Lake showed excellent acceleration to win by a head. King's Lake went on to win the Irish Champion Stakes.

Meanwhile, the Derby came and went without Storm Bird,

the winter favourite. It was won with immense ease by the Aga Khan's odds-on but doomed Shergar. The Irish Derby was also missed. Last year's wonder colt still could not run. Nor did he appear at Royal Ascot. The press continued to poke fun at 'The Invisible Horse', whose case was not considered remotely amusing by those involved with him. Then, at Keeneland's July sales, Robert Sangster received a call which changed the whole picture.

Robert, Vincent and John Magnier were at breakfast in their usual hotel, the Hyatt in Lexington, when George Harris, a well-known bloodstock agent (in fact more a dealer in stallion shares and nominations), asked them in the course of sales chat what value they had in mind for Storm Bird. The figure of $15 million, given in the court case as the colt's insurance value, was repeated. Later that day Harris, who ran his dealing business in New York City, came back to say he had a client who would pay that sum. If the three were astonished or delighted, they gave no sign of it. Vincent had always been a highly successful poker player and had brought off fabled wagers on his horses. John Magnier is inscrutable; Sangster was a cool, shrewd businessman. Moreover, Harris had been told that the $15 million was simply a starting figure. This did not deter the bold agent, although it had already been revealed that the Aga Khan's easy Derby winner Shergar had been syndicated at a value of $10 million (it had been the Aga's wish to stand him in Ireland at a sensible price for the benefit of local breeders). But Storm Bird, still to run that year, was being priced at something in excess of $15 million. Certainly his Dewhurst form was well confirmed. But why had he not run as a three-year-old?

When discussions resumed, Sangster, O'Brien and Magnier resolved to ask for $28 million ($24 million as a minimum). The bidders were Dr William Lockridge, a well-known breeder and vet who owned Ashford Stud, a very grand stud farm near Versailles, Kentucky, with his partner Robert Hefner II, who came from Oklahoma and was reputedly hugely wealthy in the oil and gas business. This was the stuff of life to Robert Sangster. Deals in bloodstock were how the shrewd and circumspect Magnier was making his name. Vincent had founded his fortunes by bringing off long-plotted gambles on his horses, in those distant Churchtown days.

An astounding deal was done. The syndicate would sell three quarters of Storm Bird for $21 million, valuing at $28 million the colt for which they had paid an unusually high $1 million only two years earlier. He was going to stand at Ashford. The remaining quarter was kept by the syndicate. Great indeed was the relief of the trio.

The money was to be paid to them in instalments – the customary method of closing big bloodstock deals. Only one third of the agreed $21 million had been paid before the natural gas market, in which Hefner's companies were deeply involved, slipped, plunged and crashed. Lockridge found that, as a partner with Hefner in Ashford, he too was now entangled in deep debt. In short, the stud farm and some of the shares in Storm Bird and the stallion's management finally had to be handed over to the syndicate in part payment of the debt incurred by the amazing Storm Bird sale and purchase.

Later, towards the close of the story, there would be a further, happier connection with O'Brien and Sangster as Bill

Lockridge was the breeder, among a number of successful horses, of a filly called Crimson Saint. She would prove to be the dam of Royal Academy, the last great winner in the O'Brien story.

But before then, and before the crash of Hefner's fortune and the forced transfer of the Ashford property, there was still Storm Bird's last and so far unused racing season to start and to complete. It was done in one race, and in France. Lockridge had vetted Storm Bird himself and found nothing amiss. The enormous and complicated deal had been settled, but the huge debts incurred by Hefner, dragging his partner Lockridge down with them, were piled up, awaiting clearance. The horse's new owners would therefore very much like to see their expensive purchase run. So far Storm Bird's non-appearances had perversely and quite illogically increased his value.

It would be pleasant to conclude this tale of early brilliance followed by almost an entire season of absence with an account of a final dazzling victory. Indeed, in August it was reported that Storm Bird would be targeted at October's Prix de l'Arc de Triomphe. There were reports too of a good gallop Storm Bird had done with King's Lake. Vincent selected his prep race to be over the course at Longchamp in the Prix du Prince d'Orange, which Alleged had won as his preliminary before his second Prix de l'Arc de Triomphe. There were nine runners, and Storm Bird could only finish in front of just two of them. It was a sad end to the colt's racing career.

Could his second, far longer career as a stallion redeem the balance and justify his expense? It certainly could. Storm Bird stood at the huge fee, to begin with, of $175,000. He made an excellent start and has been one of the most successful stallions in American racing history. Storm Bird enjoyed a long career standing at Ashford in Kentucky, which of course had fallen into the hands of the syndicate in part settlement of the debts incurred by Hefner, and thus Lockridge. It has been developed extensively and is the American arm of the Coolmore Stud complex. Storm Bird went on covering mares until the end of the 1999 season, when he was retired. In the winter of 2004 he was struck with a severe bout of colic and was put down. By his death he had sired sixty-two individual Stakes winners, including the top-class filly Indian Skimmer, Bluebird, Prince of Birds, Mukaddamah and Balanchine – one of only two fillies to win the Irish Derby in the twentieth century. Storm Bird additionally proved a great sire of brood mares. His son Storm Cat continued to be a prodigiously successful sire and had up to the end of 2004 sired 129 Stakes winners.

CHAPTER 20

GOLDEN FLEECE

'Like a male ballet dancer'

n the year 1980, when Storm Bird ended his scintillating two-year-old career by winning a particularly strong Dewhurst Stakes at Newmarket, a larger, outstanding-looking Nijinsky yearling was bought at Keeneland. The bitter disappointments of Storm Bird's three-year-old season left the syndicate of O'Brien, Sangster and Magnier with something new to relish, to plan and hope for, with the exciting purchase of Golden Fleece.

In those early 1980s it must have seemed to the syndicate as if this golden roll was sweeping on for ever. What amazed racing's experts then, and a quarter of a century later, was how relatively few Vincent O'Brien's numbers were. He was buying big, but the number of horses in training was small. Not for him the 150 horse power, even 200 horse power establishments later prevailing; forty to high fifties remained O'Brien's average-size stable. Many horsemen today cannot believe that any man can give full attention to 150 horses. Yes, he can depute to assistants and head lads, but . . .

The syndicate wasn't interested in just buying horses: they also found time to buy the Phoenix Park racecourse, the attractive track on the north side of Dublin which was on the verge of financial collapse. The members of the syndicate, including Stavros Niarchos and Danny Schwartz, together with Vincent, Robert and John, were partners in this huge enterprise. The stands were rebuilt and refurbished, the parade ring was placed in front of the stands, and the track, which included a new six-furlong straight, was improved. Sadly, after ten years the racecourse, on the unfashionable north side of Dublin, was closed again through lack of public support. The Coolmore-sponsored Phoenix Champion Stakes was one of the Group 1 Irish races started here by Vincent. It moved to Leopardstown, and has since become one of the highest-rated races in the world for three-year-olds and upwards.

Golden Fleece was purchased in 1980 at $775,000, which put him in the top ten most expensive yearlings of that year. One of his rivals would be Assert, trained by Vincent's son David, who had seen the colt as a yearling at Moyglare Stud in Ireland. He was to be sold at the Goffs Sales in Paris, and David went there to buy him. The vet David employed turned the colt down for general unsoundness, but David decided to recommend Robert Sangster to buy him anyway. The yearling made about £16,000, which, as things turned out, proved an amazing bargain for the winner of two Derbys.

Not everybody was enchanted by Golden Fleece when they saw him as a yearling. Harry Thomson 'Tom' Jones, trainer at Newmarket of more than a hundred horses, had the finance available to buy an expensive colt or two for the Maktoum brothers. But he did not want to spend Maktoum money on

ABOVE: *The O'Briens' 1983 Christmas card starring El Gran Senor,
Jamie and David Myerscough and Sean McClory, three of
their seventeen grandchildren.*

BELOW: *The lovable, unlucky Storm Bird has a word in the ear of young
Sean McClory, Liz's son.*

ABOVE: *Secreto, trained just across the gallops from Vincent and driven along by Christy Roche, gets home four inches ahead of El Gran Senor and Pat Eddery.*

TOP LEFT: *David O'Brien with Secreto after narrowly beating his father's El Gran Senor in the Epsom Derby.*

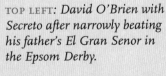

LEFT: *Vincent and Golden Fleece, his sixth and final Derby winner, who tragically died of cancer soon afterwards.*

OPPOSITE TOP: *John Magnier and Robert Sangster at Newmarket sales considering purchases.*

BELOW LEFT: *Royal Academy and a beaming John Reid are led in by Christy Ryan after winning Newmarket's July Cup.*

BELOW RIGHT: *Vincent and Charles under pressure to find a top colt at Keeneland. Royal Academy proved the answer.*

ABOVE: *Sadler's Wells, champion sire of Great Britain and Ireland for fourteen years, breaking High Flyer's record of thirteen consecutive championships in 1798 that had stood for 200 years. Sadler's Wells is the outstanding successor to Northern Dancer.*

OPPOSITE: *Lester with Vincent on the Ballydoyle gallops after a work morning. There was never any great need for verbal communication between these two maestros.*

RIGHT: *Receiving his Doctorate of Science from the Chancellor of Ulster University, Rabbi Julia Neuberger. He also has a Doctorate, from the National University of Ireland.*

OPPOSITE: *In the elegant drawing room at Ballydoyle: Vincent considers a racing book, with Goldie the Labrador.*

ABOVE: *Jacqueline leads in Royal Academy and Lester after their astonishing Breeders' Cup victory.*

*Vincent's last winner at the Ascot he loved. The old duo reunited,
as a smiling Lester Piggott on College Chapel is led in after winning the
1993 Cork and Orrery, Vincent's fifth winner of that race. This
was the last victory of these two maestros and it was felt they gave
a virtuoso performance.*

this Nijinsky yearling. 'Didn't like him at all! Thought him a great big boat of a horse,' he remarked cheerfully later, watching Touching Wood, the double Classic winner he bought instead, being exercised at stud at Newmarket. Two years later, Touching Wood was overwhelmed in the Epsom Derby by that whirlwind run of Golden Fleece which so nearly clipped the old course record. Touching Wood still proved very well bought at the same sales for Maktoum Al Maktoum, for, after his Derby second to Golden Fleece, he won the St Leger in the fastest time since the Triple Crown winner Bahram back in 1935. And then he won the Irish St Leger too.

Just as Tom Jones had looked at Golden Fleece and turned away, so must O'Brien and his team of experts have looked at Touching Wood, for the latter was by O'Brien's Derby winner Roberto out of a mare by Vaguely Noble. Golden Fleece, the Nijinsky colt, was also out of a Vaguely Noble mare, but a better-bred one.

In the days of the July Sales the team usually flew into Lexington on the Wednesday before the sales began on Monday. Then, at Keeneland, they worked eight to ten hours a day, inspecting from Thursday to Sunday as the yearlings arrived. Vincent would start to go quietly through his shortened list of 'possibles', looking first at heads, eyes and ears to give him the first impression of character. Vincent says himself, 'I feel I get better each year from experience, but I'm always a learner. I never think the moment's arrived when I think I know all there is to know.' Meanwhile, the syndicate would be polishing their deceptive bidding tactics. 'People can tell what we're likely to be after,' Sangster said, 'but they don't know the final selection. Most consignors have probably got twelve animals in the sale. We may only look at six, then narrow it down to three. But we'll probably put a couple of "fourth ones" in to have them vetted. We'll probably bring those out more often than the ones we're really interested in, just so we don't alert the vendor as to which is our selection.'

After such labours, feints and crafty bidding, Golden Fleece made his $775,000 and came over, a glorious-looking yearling, to Ballydoyle. His reception was markedly different from that given by the staff to Alleged. 'Big strong colt,' they say. T. P. Burns thought him 'a top "store type"', meaning that TP thought Golden Fleece had the size and strength as well as the quality to make it as a top-class steeplechaser. Certainly from the moment of his purchase in July 1980 he particularly pleased the eye of racing enthusiasts who love the jumping game. He was big, but balanced; weighty, but quick in action – 'like a male ballet dancer', as O'Brien once described the correct athleticism of a jumper.

As part of his preparation for his first two-year-old race, at Leopardstown in September 1981, Golden Fleece went twice to the Curragh with some stable companions to work after racing. He travelled up without difficulty, worked very satis-factorily, and then as calmly returned home. There were no signs of anxiety in the horsebox. Ridden by Pat Eddery, he won his one-mile maiden race so commandingly that his name was being buzzed all round Ireland. Once again he completed the long haul from Tipperary up to Leopardstown and back calmly. No-one except Vincent O'Brien's eldest son David knew how much Golden Fleece had beaten that day. The runner-up was the two-year-old Assert, one of David's first horses in training. David's yard was on the far side of the Ballydoyle gallops. He used these before his father's string came out. Father and son were discreet competitors.

David had made a remarkably successful start as a trainer. Having finished his studies early in accountancy in Dublin, he came home to assist his father – a demanding task, as Michael Kauntze, John Gosden and T. P. Burns had all discovered before him. It could be said that David could not have failed to be a brilliant trainer. It was in his breeding, and in his training. He had, after all, studied from a very early age and then officially assisted the greatest European trainer of the last three centuries. Even so, the speed with which he hit the heights was extraordinary. It was so extraordinary that there were some in the gossipy world of racing who surmised and then whispered, 'Young David is really in a satellite yard of his father's. Vincent will be doing all the training of those horses too.' This, as became obvious within the year, was total nonsense. David had a burning ambition to prove himself; Vincent preserved the attitude of a proud but competitive father. In the case of the two good colts, he longed for David to succeed but not, he hoped, at his expense.

Young David kept his cards very close to his chest. This became very important when Assert, the same age as Golden Fleece and bought so inexpensively in France, sharply improved on his first run behind Golden Fleece at Leopardstown. He went on to win the Beresford Stakes at the Curragh very easily. David thought so highly of him that he then sent him across to run in the William Hill Futurity at Doncaster. He got bumped and a little jostled in the race, lost his action a quarter of a mile from home, and finished eighth. David was very disappointed with the run at Doncaster, but well pleased with the progress the horse was making. By the spring of 1982 Assert seemed to him something quite out of the ordinary. He was to prove so nearly the equal of Golden Fleece that only one pound would separate them at the end of that year.

Assert had been one of a flock of two-year-old winners produced by David in his first season. Now, as their three-year-old seasons opened, it would be difficult to prevent him meeting Golden Fleece. They were each owned principally by Robert Sangster; if he had owned all of both the situation might have been easier. As it was, he gave David carte blanche to plot Assert's programme without regard to Golden Fleece. Neither father nor son ever had any reason to complain about Sangster's interference in running plans, although he had millions invested in his shares of horses. Neither trainer would discuss with the other plans for their Classic hopes – for Golden Fleece and Assert were certainly that.

The plan for Golden Fleece, after Leopardstown in 1981, was for him to run in the Larkspur Stakes. To this end he was taken over to Thomastown Castle, the nearby stud and training quarters of Tommy Stack, who rode Red Rum in his third record-breaking victory in the Grand National. Thomastown had been built into a high-class training establishment during the 1970s by Phonsie O'Brien. Using Thomastown from time to time gave the Ballydoyle horses a change of scene, and practice in travelling, working, loading and unloading – all helpful rehearsals for race days proper. No trainer worth his fee runs a valuable newcomer without a dummy run.

Gerry Gallagher, the travelling head man, took Golden Fleece over to Thomastown. 'He had only normal space in the box,'

Gerry explains, 'then, on our way back, he suddenly got into a panic. It was fear of being shut in, for he was such a big horse. He broke out sweating and kicked and kicked against the back of the box. He was covered white with sweat, and there were cuts inside both his hind-legs from where he'd kicked himself.' The colt had suffered a bad bout of claustrophobia. Horses connect things and places with feelings; the next sight of the horsebox with its ramp down might again spur panic. If this fear could not be conquered, the colt would not be able to travel, and few race-horses outside Newmarket and the Curragh can be led from their stables to a racecourse. There was certainly no question of this being possible down in the mountain-ringed countryside of remote Tipperary.

Under Vincent's very capable and caring long-serving assistants Brian Molony and Dhruba Selvaratnam, the long process of rehabilitation began. To restore Golden Fleece's confidence he would be taken out in the horsebox with the partitions removed so that he had double room. He would go out twice every week all winter long, from October to April. He was driven first a little way and then unloaded. Then further. By such patient small steps, he completed the full stride to recovery. But it had been a very anxious winter. And there loomed doubts about whether he could ever be taken to England.

The same dislike of being shut in affected Golden Fleece in the starting stalls, so he was also made to practise in them twice weekly throughout that winter. All the time he was watched particularly for any further signs of that tense temperament shown by his sire Nijinsky, which might have been inherited by his big bay son. In the hour of triumph that

June, O'Brien immediately told the press what they must have guessed. But he wanted it definitely recorded 'how much I owe to the care and patience of my staff'.

Golden Fleece's first prep race for the 1982 Derby was only the second of his career, and at the start of the season he was a 25–1 shot for the Derby. He won the Ballymoss Stakes at the Curragh in mid-April with such ludicrous ease that more than one professional English observer of that year's racing was positive he had witnessed a wonder horse, and recommended him for the Derby to his Sunday newspaper's readers. The horse certainly had brilliant speed. Not since his sire, Nijinsky, had there been, even in O'Brien's yard, a horse bred to stay one and a half miles and yet possessed of such astonishing acceleration. Some doubt had to exist in the trainer's mind. He said that spring, 'When a horse is as fast as this, you would have to wonder whether he will really stay.' And he added, using for him singular emphasis, 'And he has such speed!'

Golden Fleece's next race brought him and Assert together on the same course, Leopardstown, where they had met the previous autumn. Once again the big bay won with derisory ease, with Pat Eddery 'sitting against him', as if on the training ground, where O'Brien might have told him, 'Just go steady. Don't let him off the bit.' Eddery said of his sauntering victory in the Derby Trial at Leopardstown, 'He was so free! They put two pacemakers in for him. But I still couldn't hold him. I shouted to Vincent Rossiter to go on, but he couldn't go any faster!'

It was a spectacular performance for any judge of horse-flesh. But some form-book students looked at the race sceptically. Golden Fleece's nearest pursuer was David

O'Brien's Assert, who was making his first appearance of the season and seemed to the cynics to be enjoying an unarduous outing. To this Vincent replies, 'I thought Assert put up an excellent performance to finish second to Golden Fleece, beaten two and a half lengths. Golden Fleece was being eased inside the last furlong. Before this, Assert had been making ground. His jockey rightly did not give him a hard race when he saw he had no hope of catching the winner.' Third was another Ballydoyle horse, Lords, a just-over-the-million-dollar purchase running in the colours the Californian tycoon Danny Schwartz, a member of the syndicate. Not every million-dollar yearling they bought automatically succeeded. As Vincent points out, 'It's no good just talking about the big prices we finally get for some. Remember the others. We never anticipated that each horse would be able to cover his cost; our hope was that the ones that turned out well would carry the others.' But Lords easily won his next race – a big field of maidens.

Schwartz had a good share in one great horse, Vincent's Royal Ascot winner Solinus, who ran in the American's name and colours. Solinus swept the board in the sprint races of 1977 and 1978, winning eight of his ten races including the Coventry Stakes, the King's Stand Stakes, the William Hill July Cup and the William Hill Sprint Championship. He won a trio of races which had not been achieved since Abernant a quarter of a century earlier. But, like some other big punters in the flexible syndicate, including the Greek ship-owning billionaire Stavros Niarchos, Schwartz decided to quit in the end, after a good run. He had became a loyal friend of the O'Briens and Sangster. He was an essential provider of what the syndicate

urgently needed as the Arab raids strengthened at Keeneland
– namely, his liquid capital. He frequently said, 'We need a
royally bred colt to win the Derby or something similar every
single year. Or we'll go bust.' He spoke the chilling truth. But
he knew his trainer well. 'Vincent had a strange communication with horses. It seemed when he looked a horse
in his eye he knew what it was thinking. Vincent always
felt a horse's eyes were extremely important when judging
one.'

After Leopardstown's Nijinsky Stakes in early May, which
was to be Golden Fleece's last run before the Epsom Derby,
and the penultimate race of his life, sceptics who had not
witnessed Golden Fleece in action were less impressed by his
form than those who had watched him in Ireland. These had
no sooner returned to England with glowing reports than
mishaps began to befall their hero.

Pat Eddery had reported after riding him at home, 'Golden
Fleece was a highly strung horse; he didn't like patting on the
neck or being fussed with. Riding out, if he did anything silly
you wouldn't want to give him a slap, or he wouldn't go well.
You had to coax him along. He was a horse you had to watch
all the time. You couldn't ride him with a long rein or you'd be
on the floor! Very quick at spinning round, he was. For a big
horse he was very sharp. He was a real man!' 'At the time of
the Irish 1,000 Guineas,' says T. P. Burns ruefully, 'Golden
Fleece whipped round and dropped me on the gallops at
home.' His leap and twist must have been great to decant that
former top jockey on the flat and over hurdles. The fall off
Golden Fleece painfully broke poor TP's ankle. Golden Fleece
then got loose on the gallops. Nothing is more alarming. At

Newmarket, until they railed most of the roadsides, horses were sometimes killed. A loose horse, alarmed or excited by flapping stirrup leathers and irons acting like a jockey's kicking heels, and bewildered by trailing reins, can often slip over or crash into fences, breaking a leg. Golden Fleece returned safely to the yard at Ballydoyle. He had no roads to cross. He had not travelled a tenth of the distance wildly traversed by the 1981 Derby winner Shergar, who got more than five miles down roads around Newmarket before being caught, unharmed, by a nimble milkman in an astonished village.

Then, only ten days before the Derby, Golden Fleece's off-hind hock swelled up. 'He was not quite sound,' O'Brien stresses, 'and we suspected a small spavin. Bob Griffin moved in once more.' Such a mishap so close to the Classic put the colt's contention in doubt. David O'Brien had already been considering whether to take on his father with Assert, and Robert Sangster had given him free rein to do so. Until Golden Fleece's lameness, David had been inclined to go for the French 'Derby', the Prix du Jockey Club, run four days after the Epsom race, and then come back to Ireland for the Irish Derby. This latter race had also been in Vincent's mind for Golden Fleece, if all went well in the English Derby.

Since following Golden Fleece home at Leopardstown, Assert had massacred a good field for the Gallinule Stakes on the Curragh. The fourth horse there, nearly fifteen lengths behind him, had been second the time before to Golden Fleece, beaten only three lengths. Assert was improving quickly enough to put him in the same class as Golden Fleece. 'Nearly in,' cautions Vincent. Assert was a likely Classic winner, if not at Epsom then in France or Ireland. If Golden

Fleece did not recover in time for Epsom, Sangster had a superb deputy in Assert.

Davy Walsh, the Ballydoyle blacksmith who had shod five previous Derby winners, had already been taking precautionary measures with Golden Fleece to help support the massive colt's hindlegs. He had started to shoe him with raised heels behind, which would just tilt the foot a fraction forward, taking a little strain off the hock. 'I made the shoes so that they got deeper towards the back and curled round.' Meanwhile, though they couldn't ride the horse, it was necessary to keep him moving. 'Was he fresh!' TP says. 'He was a very fresh horse anyway!' He was led out twice a day for three days. It was like watching a clock ticking away. 'We were running out of time,' TP remembers grimly. 'Thankfully, on the fourth day, we were on his back again.'

Between then and his departure for Epsom, which would be on the Saturday before Wednesday (2 June), Pat Eddery came over twice to ride the Derby favourite. The lads remember Golden Fleece working on 26 May with his two expensive workmates Lords and Pilgrim; Lords went past Pilgrim, and Pat Eddery on Golden Fleece went past Lords and dropped his hands. Vincent asked Eddery, 'Did he do enough?' The lads recall with glee, 'Lords went out the back door!' 'The second piece of work,' says Vincent, 'was on the Friday with Pilgrim. Golden Fleece drew ten lengths away and Pat was very pleased.' This is a typical understatement by the trainer, who 'did not think it right to show excitement'. Still, internally he must have been thrilled by these performances.

The decision to run at Epsom was made. For a little while, David O'Brien remained uncertain whether to take on Golden

Fleece with Assert. He came under no pressure from either his father or from Robert Sangster. 'He finally decided,' Vincent reports, 'that his colt's action was more suited to a good galloping course – Chantilly rather than Epsom.' Then it was heard that Persepolis, probably the best French one-and-a-half-mile colt, would run at Epsom instead of Chantilly in the Prix du Jockey Club. This would give Golden Fleece a harder task but make the French 'Derby' easier. David decided to go to Chantilly, although no foreign-trained horse had ever won that race on the beautiful French course below the château. Jalmood and Peacetime were, like Persepolis, also fancied to beat Golden Fleece at Epsom. The latter's hold-up had not, it seemed, improved his chances.

There also remained anxiety about Golden Fleece's flight to England. It would be his first experience of air travel. The syndicate's 'Skyvan', built by Short and Harland in Belfast, and used from the airstrip built like a road along the bottom of the Ballydoyle gallops, was not considered large enough. 'He'd not fit in!' said T. P. Burns. The Skyvan had been bought by Robert Sangster's company and converted as recommended by O'Brien to take two horses standing side by side, loaded from the rear. Commuters from New York up to Albany, the airport for Saratoga Springs for many years, used the same box-like, high-wing, reliable aircraft. The snag was its low roof space for a big horse. Vincent decided to charter a CL44 from Shannon to Gatwick. Flying horses to England was very expensive, especially if the horse did not win. Golden Fleece would travel with his equine companion, General Custer. As a precaution against an outbreak of the previous year's panic, Vincent had cotton wool put in Golden Fleece's ears and a hood over his head. The customs officers at Gatwick were alerted so that there would be minimal delay. Gerry reported, 'The customs were waiting for us. They looked after us very well.'

The flight passed without a hitch and the Derby favourite arrived safely in the racecourse stables four days before the race. He had overcome getting loose; he had recovered from his spavin; his trainer seemed dexterously to have caught up the lost days' work. All seemed bright and shining. But now another threat was poised to break out. The colt, at the worst possible moment, was about to cough.

On the Sunday, Golden Fleece walked out twice at Epsom. O'Brien thought the big horse might still be short of exercise. The following day he obtained special permission to work on the course itself, so the horse went to the Derby start and worked over five furlongs at a nice speed. 'Pat rode him,' recalls Vincent, 'from the one-and-a-half-mile gate to the seven-furlong starting gate.' On Tuesday morning, thirty hours before the Derby, Golden Fleece and General Custer went to the start again, worked two furlongs at half-speed and then quickened for the final two furlongs. O'Brien was, as usual, out to watch and listen. As the two horses were pulled up to walk down Tattenham Hill and round Tattenham Corner, Golden Fleece coughed a number of times. This is a dreadful sound for any trainer at any time. It is worse when a good horse does it several times before a major race – each extra cough seems more sinister. But for the favourite on the day before the Epsom Derby . . .

Normally at Epsom the O'Brien horses used to canter quietly on the grandstand side of the course and pull up at the winning post. A group of photographers and racing journalists would be standing there watching. Pat Eddery and Gerry Gallagher, who was riding the lead horse, decided to canter on along the stands' side, as if all was well, and not pull up at the winning post in front of the photographers and journalists. They took the horses on to the stables and Pat got off to let Golden Fleece's lad lead him in. Pat waited anxiously to talk to Vincent, who came hurrying up. They had an urgent, troubled discussion. Bob Griffin was telephoned at once with what seemed like another version of Nijinsky's pre-race drama. But the colt, Bob was told, had no discharge from his nose. More important, he was not running a temperature. He was a little hot, but it was a very hot day. Bob said reassuringly, 'It could be the heat that caused some dehydration and made him cough.' Griffin's calm accuracy was now proverbial at Ballydoyle. It was a question again of crossing fingers and praying. No medication, even had it been allowed by the rules of racing, could have averted the onset of a fever.

Should they now announce to the waiting world what had happened? Suppose he coughed in the morning and couldn't even run? The public backing him that day would all lose their bets. Suppose the horse coughed in the race, ran deplorably, had even to be pulled up? A trainer has to make such knife-edge decisions. The O'Brien camp resolved to make no announcement for the moment but to wait and see what would happen. A man was stationed outside Golden Fleece's box all day 'to listen and report if the colt coughed again'. The horse, to their blessed relief, did not. And in the world outside, no-one caught even a whisper that anything was amiss with the Derby favourite.

Golden Fleece had not impressed everyone who had

watched him in action at Epsom on those two days before the race. This was the first occasion he had set foot in England, and some observers got up early to catch a glimpse of him. Once a reporter with the *Sporting Life*, and now with Channel 4, John McCririck possesses a sharp brain behind a bizarre exterior. He declared on Derby day morning on the front page, 'Watching Golden Fleece in his spin with General Custer, I can't remember seeing a leading Derby contender with a more scratchy action in his faster paces.' To support this unusual view – knowledgeable racing observers always found Golden Fleece a tremendous galloper – he quoted from an unnamed 'local trainer' who said, 'The Irish star lumbered along like a great tank!'

Some tank. Some lumberer. Some observer . . .

To right the balance, three real tipsters buzzed loud for Golden Fleece. Michael O'Hehir, the great Irish commentator, was one of those who had been impressed by Golden Fleece winning the race named after his sire, Nijinsky, at Leopardstown. 'Augur' of the *Sporting Life* made him a confident selection, though referred mysteriously to 'his alleged bad temper' (no-one at Ballydoyle found him bad-tempered). Also in the *Sporting Life*, Dick Whitford said succinctly, 'Any recipe for a potential Derby winner would call for the exact credentials possessed by Golden Fleece.'

None of these gentlemen could know that their selection had started ominously to cough on the eve of the race. Those who quizzed Vincent O'Brien were puzzled that he did not show unbridled optimism. And there was no way of knowing whether the cough might not break out again in the paddock, at the start, during the race. Stress triggers diseases; heat accelerates fever. So O'Brien repeated his assessment of the favourite. The colt had brilliant speed – such brilliant speed – and he just hoped he would stay one and a half miles. 'I'm hopeful,' he repeated again and again to the press, tongues out for something firmer and juicier with which to appease hungry sports editors.

O'Brien was staying as usual in the RAC Country Club nearby, but in the thick of things. The tension also gripped Robert Sangster, who, like his partner Vincent, disguised emotion behind a mask of calm. Robert stayed in the Isle of Man, playing golf most of Tuesday while the crisis brewed on the dreaded sound of a cough. He told a friend he couldn't bear to go to Epsom till the last minute. He did not arrive until the morning of the race. His three sons – Guy, then a stockbroker, Ben and Adam, still at school – came to the races. The two boys had touched trouble at Harrow for betting. Both said they had not even had a pound on Golden Fleece, who had been 33–1 at the start of the year and 25–1 in April. He would start 3–1 with the bookies, with 4–1 paid by the Tote.

As the Epsom Downs course centre is free to enter, no-one really knows how many people came to that Derby Day. Three quarters of a million was a figure bandied about among those in the more exclusive but then quaint and elderly stands. Racegoers included the Queen, Prince Philip and Princess Anne, as well as Joe Gormley, an ardent racing man just retired from the chair of the National Union of Mineworkers. There were also actor Albert Finney, the new American ambassador Henry E. Catto, Joe Louis and actress Britt Ekland. There were two of the famous brothers from Dubai: Sheik Mohammed, who, among his sixty horses in England, owned the much-fancied Derby hope Jalmood; and his seven-years-older brother Maktoum al Maktoum, who was running Touching Wood, the horse Tom Jones had preferred as a Keeneland yearling to Golden Fleece.

In the television perch in the stands, pale, wrinkled, with a light jacket over his colours for another lesser race, was the man who would have ridden Golden Fleece had he continued his links with Ballydoyle. Lester Piggott, the best Derby rider of the century and probably of all time, was without a ride in the race. He would have been on Simply Great for his new stable, Henry Cecil's at Newmarket, but this once promising colt was a late withdrawal, and the housewives of Britain, who made 'Piggott in the Derby' their annual flutter, were saved a loser. Instead, Lester was making comments about the runners to Brough Scott, in front of the TV cameras. Like the fox with the grapes, Piggott was critical of Golden Fleece.

In his old seat in the saddle was his replacement, the thirty-year-old Pat Eddery, whose wife Carolyn had produced their first child, Nicola Jane, on the Saturday Golden Fleece flew over. She watched the race on TV. She saw that, in spite of the sweltering day, Golden Fleece sweated less than many in the paddock. The thunderstorm which drenched the course before racing took the sting out of the firm Epsom turf but left the air as humid as Kentucky, where O'Brien had bought Golden Fleece twenty-two months before. He looked magnificent. He proceeded calmly to the Derby start. In those days, to reach the starting stalls the most valuable horses in Europe progressed along a track which was as scruffy as an old livery stable trail, past broken bottles, cans, orange peel, kids on ponies, and boozing day-trippers.

Pat Eddery reported, 'For the Derby the Boss decided to use a sheepskin noseband.' Expert observers in the press thought this was the first time O'Brien had ever used one in the Derby. 'With this on, he really settled and relaxed, though he was sweating at the start,' said Eddery. Indeed, Golden Fleece entered the starting gate as calmly as a bishop squeezing into his cathedral stall. At 3.38 p.m., three minutes late, when the starter let them go, he sprang off with the leading bunch up that steep, right-turning bend past the wood. With O'Brien doubting his horse's stamina, Eddery had been told to settle him towards the back of the field. He comments, 'It could have helped that he'd had those two mornings' slow cantering from the start, which he'd enjoyed. Golden Fleece helped himself to win the Derby because he relaxed so well.' He settled to such an extent that he was almost last going down Tattenham Hill. There were only three horses behind him at the bottom of the hill as the leaders rushed round Tattenham Corner and swung into the straight.

A sight occurred then which far transcended even that of Shergar's devastating victory the year before. For Golden Fleece, coming from the back of the field, shot through them like a bullet. Once he had sped through the ruck, Eddery moved him leisurely towards the outside. Ahead on the rails galloped Norwick, Peacetime and Silver Hawk, with Touching Wood battling through. Eddery then seemed calmly to pause, as the driver of a Ferrari might glance at old bangers as he swept by. Golden Fleece then unleashed his astonishing acceleration and quickened again; he was suddenly clear and striding home unchallenged. 'He's won the world's greatest race,' said Eddery, still astonished as he rode in, 'and he still has to be extended! The Derby was the first time I could hold him. He's learned to race. He'll have no problems now.' He was longing to ride him in all the big races ahead. 'On the way home, I said to Mum and Terry [Ellis, Pat's brother-in-law and manager], "Think what's to come!"'

On his retirement twenty-one years later, with another Derby won in 1990 on Quest for Fame and four Prix de l'Arc de Triomphes won between 1980 and 1987, Pat Eddery still marvelled about Golden Fleece. 'The only time he switched off and didn't pull was in the Derby. We'd cantered on the course from the start and Vincent put a sheepskin noseband on him. The difference was unbelievable! He came out of the gate and never took hold of his bit! Turning for home I only had two or three behind me. When I pulled out, he just took off. He made up so much ground that at the winning post I took a pull on him. He was brilliant!'

In none of Golden Fleece's four races had he ever been exerted. His speed for the Derby one and a half miles, 2m 34.27s, set the record since electrical timing was introduced in 1964, nearly twenty years earlier. It almost equalled Mahmoud's hand-timed, and so still suspect, record of 2m 33.8s from May 1936.

In the glow of victory, Vincent O'Brien declared that he would have to rank Golden Fleece with Nijinsky and Sir Ivor at the top of the six Epsom Derby winners he had so far trained. By 2005 he had not changed this view. Eighteen months after the race, Pat Eddery remained adamant that the horse was the best he had ridden.

No sooner was the race over than the trainers of the second, third and fourth horses announced that they had no intention of trying to take on this spectacular winner in the Irish Derby. As a result, Golden Fleece was quoted odds-on for that race, which would, without Assert, have proved another cantering conquest for him. So, would Assert take him on? The official assessments for the season's end placed the two colts clear at the top of their trees. In the Free Handicap, Golden Fleece was given 10st followed by Assert at 9st 13lb; next came Awaasif at 9st 7lb and Touching Wood (winner of the two St Legers) on 9st 6lb. The International Classification, compiled jointly by the official handicappers of France, Great Britain and Ireland, gave Golden Fleece 94, Assert 93, level with Green Forest, and Akiyda, winner of the Prix de l'Arc de Triomphe, on 89.

But the Derby was to be Golden Fleece's last race, which allowed Assert a much clearer run to make 1982 the annus mirabilis for the Sangster colours. Four days after Golden Fleece's Derby, Assert won the French Derby and then the Irish Derby at the Curragh by ten lengths, making the rest look rubbish. He was beaten a neck in Ascot's King George VI and Queen Elizabeth Diamond Stakes by Kalaglow, but then cantered home, clearly the easiest winner to date, of the Benson & Hedges Gold Cup at York.

No-one who saw Golden Fleece's double electric spurt to his Derby victory will ever forget it, but, sadly, the slender thread by which the fortunes of even the greatest racehorses tenuously hang began to fray, then snap.

Those dread coughs on the eve of the Derby were not a transient threat. Within ten days of that tremendous race, Golden Fleece went down with a virus. In most cases this will disappear in about ten days; Golden Fleece's cold dragged on for three weeks. Plans for him to run in the Irish Sweeps

Derby were quickly abandoned. And then, when his cold finally dried up and he was eased back into work, his off hind-leg swelled up, just as his near one had done ten days before the Derby. 'By the time that had gone down,' Vincent recalls resignedly, 'it would have taken another six weeks just to get him ready.'

Golden Fleece was therefore retired to stud. His valuation was similar to that of Assert – about $25 million. But, as Robert Sangster, on one of the rare occasions he showed public excitement, burst out after the Derby, 'We're talking about a great horse and a great race! Why spoil it talking about money?' Golden Fleece was retained at Coolmore, where he stood at £100,000 a service.

Only eighteen months after his Derby triumph came the catastrophe. In December 1983, the great horse was struck down with cancer. He had covered only fourteen mares in his second season. A team of American surgeons were flown over to operate on him. The operation seemed successful. Then, in late February 1984, he began to sicken again. He fought for his life with immense courage, but in vain. O'Brien's comment after his sixth Epsom Derby win had been in keeping with his character. He'd declared about Golden Fleece, 'I'm privileged to have been associated with a really great horse.' But before the flat race season of 1984 had begun, this truly brilliant Derby winner, the great glory of 1982, marvellously bred, was dead.

CHAPTER 21

FATHER AND SON

'Losing trainer, winning father'

For David O'Brien, 1982 was a remarkable year. He had landed an unusually difficult double by winning both the French Derby and the Irish Derby with Assert. This was an extraordinary achievement for any twenty-five-year-old, however well bred and well taught for racing. His contemporaries at that age were not long out of universities, looking for jobs, learning a trade or settling onto the bottom rung of jobs in less hazardous professions. David had made his name precociously, and though not yet a public figure, he was talked about and highly thought of in racing's big business circles.

Over in Kentucky at the Keeneland Sales, a very rich bus company owner from Caracas, Venezuela, bought a yearling and sought advice about finding a European trainer. He was already into racing in Venezuela. His fortune had founded a thoroughbred stud there. Señor Luigi Miglietti purchased a colt by the supreme Northern Dancer for $340,000 and chose the yearling himself. The colt's price was remarkably less than the cost of a nomination to his sire. It was below the average price of all the yearlings sold at that Keeneland Sale. Furthermore, he had been on Vincent O'Brien's short-list, before the great man came round to inspect him. Vincent was not the only expert to reject him. The colt had bad front legs.

Señor Miglietti learned that, in view of the colt's forelegs – in the opinion of many he was heavy-topped – it would be better if he were sent to be trained and raced on the less testing turf in Europe. Several experts at the sales put forward the name of David O'Brien. His brilliant start with Assert was fresh in racing people's minds that summer. The O'Brien name itself had a sort of magic, even to the non-English-speaking Miglietti, though the coach company millionaire had never had a horse in training in Europe.

The reasons why the colt, to be called Secreto, had not cost more were precisely those which had caused Señor Miglietti's advisers to recommend he send the colt to Europe: biggish bulk, slightly suspect forelegs. Two of Miglietti's American advisers, Michael Brod and Barry Weisbord, knew David O'Brien well and had seen and greatly admired the splendour of the gallops at Ballydoyle. They described the place enthusiastically. Brod added that David was 'very professional' – a phrase which pleased Luigi Miglietti.

In December the yearling colt, as yet unbroken, arrived at David O'Brien's stables, on the opposite side of Vincent's home and gallops at Ballydoyle. Proximity was further maximized as David, as yet unmarried, was living in the house at Ballydoyle with Vincent and Jacqueline. Both trainers were being as reticent as serious poker players about the hands of good horses each was holding.

David's horses were in his newly built yard, extended and modernized from what was originally an isolation yard for Vincent's newly arrived horses. David was the very essence of a hands-on trainer. He fed all his horses himself, rising at 5.30 a.m. to do a task usually given to the head man in any sizeable stable. He also put the bandages on every horse that needed them. He cheerfully admitted this with pride. Grander trainers might not be able to put on a bandage which neither slips nor constricts.

The good colt in Vincent's yard at that time was El Gran Senor, named after the famous South American trainer the brilliant Horatio Luro, who trained his sire, Northern Dancer. On top of the South American connections there was now another: both Secreto and El Gran Senor were by Northern Dancer. El Gran Senor was full brother to Try My Best, trained by Vincent to be the top two-year-old of 1977 and winner of the Dewhurst. After this Robert Sangster and Vincent bought two-thirds of the dam Sex Appeal from E. P. Taylor, who kept his one-third until the end of 1983. Year after year the mare, for obvious reasons, was sent back to Northern Dancer, the supreme stallion whom Vincent hugely admired and had, for European eyes, discovered and promoted. Sex Appeal's lightning was given every chance of striking more than twice. El Gran Senor's background was an exception to Vincent's general practice then of buying all his yearlings at Keeneland, but the syndicate hoped that they would eventually breed as well as buy their yearlings.

The colt was not only exceedingly handsome, but possessed of such a lovable temperament that he endeared himself to the O'Brien family as well as to all the staff. In the family's

Christmas card of 1983, he relaxes as placidly as an old hunter outside the Ballydoyle front door. He was described the following year as having 'a brow as broad as an intellectual's and an expression as calmly benign as a saint's'. He did have a minor defect, though, which might have dissuaded Vincent O'Brien from buying him at a sale: he had a slight 'parrot mouth'. His upper teeth slightly overshot his lower row, but so unobtrusively as to be invisible until you opened the mouth in his handsome head. The defect can affect a horse's ability to pick grass or hay. Not every trainer is concerned by it, but it certainly can hinder him from masticating his food. Breeders could hold it against a stallion as it is a hereditary defect.

El Gran Senor was unbeaten in all his four starts as a two-year-old in 1983. His three Irish victories before the Dewhurst were all at odds-on and run in five weeks between 3 August and 10 September. He started favourite for the Dewhurst and had a tough battle to overcome the very highly rated Rainbow Quest who, under Pat Eddery, would later win the 1985 Prix de l'Arc de Triomphe. With the Dewhurst victory, the unbeaten 'Senor' was Europe's champion two-year-old, and hopes soared at Ballydoyle for his coming Classic season.

As a three-year-old the Senor beat his stable companion Sadler's Wells in the Gladness Stakes at the Curragh at 1–3, as Sadler's Wells, ridden by George McGrath, would later beat Secreto in the Irish Guineas. The Senor increased his winnings to £100,000 and seemed to be proving far superior to Secreto. The 2,000 Guineas at Newmarket was forecast as 'needing a great deal of winning', and also as 'a clash of giants'. Secreto did not contest the Guineas, but the strong competition included Rainbow Quest.

The start of the Guineas was delayed. Down behind the stalls Pat Eddery slipped off the colt's back, and casting one arm fondly round his neck, leaned nonchalantly back against his shoulder with his legs crossed. The relaxed, affectionate moment illustrated the colt's marvellous nature. It resembled that of a child with a much-loved, gentle pony.

The race was run at a good pace. El Gran Senor was able to execute something which makes a good horse a great one: he could accelerate twice, and make two different challenges. The 'clash of giants' did not materialize. The high-class field fell away behind him as he shot away from Chief Singer, Lear Fan and Rainbow Quest. He won unextended, ears pricked above that handsome head, in nearly two seconds quicker than standard time. Vincent was pressed to evaluate his star. 'Today he was in a class of his own,' he said quietly. As to comparisons with his six previous Derby winners, he added, 'I believe his Guineas performance today is on a level with Nijinsky's and Sir Ivor's.' These were the last two Guineas winners to win the Derby. 'If he wins at Epsom next month he could be the best I've trained.' From Vincent this was praise pitched truly high.

But what about his stamina? Would he get the extra half mile? Might he be a brilliant one-and-a-quarter-mile horse, such as Sir Ivor, whose speed and superior class enabled him to conserve enough stamina to win the mile-and-a-half Derby at Epsom? Vincent pointed out how relaxed in running the Senor was and that he could draw stamina from his dam's sire Buckpasser. He declared, 'Mile-and-a-quarter horses possessed with outstanding speed can win the Derby.' Bookmakers and public concurred. As El Gran Senor sailed past the post at Newmarket he was installed sizzling hot favourite for the

Derby, his next run. Nothing went wrong with him in the interim. Indeed, his work was described as 'phenomenal'. Jacqueline reported, 'I can't ever remember any horse here doing so well.'

In the weeks before the Derby, rain fell spasmodically on Epsom. It fell heavily on the Monday and Tuesday before the race, which was still held on its time-honoured Wednesday. On Tuesday, Vincent took his daughter Sue Magnier with him to face the press and TV cameras outside the old stable block. For once, he did not have the colt worked on the course. He explained, 'He did a good bit of work at home before he left to fly over.' But he had the horse led out for the cameras. The Senor sleepily looked at the excited crowd, strolled amiably around the stable yard, then ambled back into his box. Questions about whether the rain-softened ground would affect him were repeatedly put. Vincent was, as normal, patient and polite. He kept saying that his horse 'acted on any going, but the softer it is, the more it becomes a test of stamina'. But the press wanted Vincent to compare this colt's chances with those of Golden Fleece two years earlier. Then, Vincent had said he was 'hopeful' rather than 'confident', as he knew what the press did not – that Golden Fleece had had a bout of coughing. 'Hopeful' he often used; 'confident' very seldom. Now, with a small smile, he said quietly, 'I'm confident.'

His son David was making careful plans too. He had not wished to share El Gran Senor's hired aircraft from Ireland. He wanted to fly Secreto over one day earlier and to work him round Tattenham Corner on the wet Tuesday morning. Secreto impressed spotters out on the track. David reported, 'He handled the corner well.' David and Christy Roche, his Irish jockey, walked the entire track twice.

The race day crowds around the pre-parade ring jostled to look at Vincent's wonder horse. They were reported to be 'bigger than at any time in the last ten years'. Guarded by Gerry Gallagher, Ballydoyle's well-known travelling head lad, on one side and by Willie Fogarty's son Matt on the other, the Senor, focus of several hundred eyes, behaved immaculately. His tail occasionally flicked, a foot occasionally gave a small stamp. He was even more relaxed on the long parade up the course.

Secreto, too, had been admired. He looked in tremendous shape. He was noted as 'striking'; his 'presence' was praised. David had run him only once as a two-year-old: he won the Tetrarch Stakes at the Curragh very impressively. David had then decided to take on Vincent's and Robert Sangster's top juvenile Sadler's Wells in the Irish 2,000 Guineas. A tremendous race ensued, with Secreto favourite but finishing a close third by a neck and half a length to Sadler's Wells and the French raider Procida. It could be deduced that those dubious legs made him a touch tricky to train. But it was also deduced that if Vincent's Sadler's Wells could beat him, even more so could El Gran Senor.

The American breeders' world believed that El Gran Senor was the natural successor to his father Northern Dancer. So brisk was the competition to get hold of him as a stallion that a syndicate of extremely rich and bold Americans put in an extraordinary bid to Robert Sangster: they offered him $40 million for half of the Senor provided he won the Derby – as now seemed highly likely. In a world of crazy prices, this topped the lot, making the three-year-old colt potentially worth $80 million.

The betting public and the bookmakers believed he would win. Vincent had said he was confident. His 8–11 starting price for the Derby was the shortest for nearly forty years. Jacqueline O'Brien, however, was in two minds. After the race she confessed that she knew to what degree her son David and his Irish jockey, Christy Roche, had been 'planning and thinking and working out how they could test El Gran Senor's stamina'. The presumption was that as the Senor's only weakness was likely to be lack of stamina, then the response must be to test it fully. David did not, however, run a pacemaker. Luckily for him, both Tom Jones and Guy Harwood did run pacemakers for their two fancied runners, Ilium and Alphabatim.

Vincent, with Robert Sangster and son-in-law John Magnier, climbed up the steps below the TV platform in the winner's enclosure. Of only seventeen runners, ten started at 50–1 or longer. Before the 2,000 Guineas, Vincent's orders to Pat Eddery had been simple: 'The longer you wait, the further you will win.' 'But before the Derby,' said Pat, 'the guv'nor didn't give me any more instructions.' The brief words before the Guineas hung around to haunt the day.

Pat, confidently poised midfield, let the Senor improve to follow Claude Monet's progress going down the hill. Al Talaq, Tom Jones's pacemaker, had led from the mile starting post until he had swung round Tattenham Corner and into the daunting straight. At that point an astonishing sight caused a tremendous mumbling hum to rush through the crowd. They had spotted Pat, still behind Claude Monet in fifth place, sitting up and clutching a double handful of reins as if he was simply riding a piece of very steady work at home. His hands looked to be just resting on the Senor's withers as the colt lobbed along, totally unextended. Around him elbows and heels shoved and drove, whips waved and cracked. But he seemed to be just cantering. Someone in the upstairs press box bellowed, 'The favourite wins six lengths – when Pat lets him go!' There were shouts of assenting glee. Eddery was going so easily in the straight that he could casually turn to regard the jockey on his right. This was Christy Roche, always an energetic rider, and now shoving and pushing Secreto along as hard as he could go. Secreto seemed fully extended. Pat said afterwards, 'I thought I had a stone in hand there.'

At that moment Claude Monet choked and stopped so abruptly that Pat had to switch outside him. 'Suddenly I had nothing in front of me.' He had hit the front nearly two furlongs out. But what should a man do left in front too early? Vincent's words before the Guineas had been, 'The longer you wait . . .' Pat decided to conserve doubtful stamina a little longer. He kept a firm hold on the Senor's head. As he did so, Secreto, under Roche's continued, almost frantic driving, loomed up on his outside. Pat said, 'Secreto on the outside was just getting going.' And Christy said afterwards, 'It was the thought of El Gran Senor not staying that kept me going! I was really happy to see that little rise in the ground!'

Indeed, as the two horses reached Epsom's final rise to the post, the whole aspect of the race shattered and a long-drawn-out, horrified moan escaped from the huge crowd. Their favourite, a second ago going with all-conquering ease, was suddenly under pressure. And he was not pulling away. Secreto battled on, gaining, gaining. The two colts, trained by father and son on opposite sides of the same Tipperary gallops, were locked together, heads nodding, necks dipping alternately. They came together. They brushed. They battled on. Up to the very last stride of the one and a half miles it seemed (most of the crowd prayed) that the favourite had just hung on. By inches. He had not. Secreto's muzzle was by luck, as it crossed the line, held a little higher than the Senor's. The distance was four inches after a race of 2,560 yards.

Vincent had lost his last chance, as it would transpire, of a seventh Epsom Derby. He had declared his confidence in winning. He was a partner in the horse as well as being his trainer. Yet he had been beaten in the world's most famous flat race by his own much-loved, recently married son David.

As a dejected Eddery rode back to unsaddle, he bent down to declare to Vincent, 'I have never been going so easy in a race two furlongs out and got beat!' He explained that as they started the final rise – he called it significantly 'the hill' – 'I started to get after my horse. I still thought I'd win. But the horse on the outside kept fighting. He's quite tough, that horse. He just got me on the line.'

The shaken crowd had desperately awaited the result of the photo finish. David, hatless, had jerked his head forward as the horses battled like athletes straining for the tape. When the result was given, he was hugely moved as he went forward to greet his winner – his third Derby in his brief career, and the most famous one. Yet he had defeated his father. The crowd, surprisingly in a way, since the hottest favourite for thirty-seven years had just been beaten, gave David a rousing reception. His mother, Jacqueline, festooned with her usual cameras, hurried into the winner's circle to hug him.

'I'm sorry,' said David.

'For goodness' sake, don't say that!' she exclaimed. 'Dad and I are both just thrilled.' She looked as if she totally meant it, split as she was by pride in her son and sympathy for her husband, who had seemed to love El Gran Senor more than any other horse over the previous thirty years.

Then, astonishingly, came two announcements: first, 'Stewards' Inquiry', then the news that Eddery was objecting to the winner 'for leaning on me'. When Vincent heard this, he was visibly shaken. His head shook. Ten minutes dragged by. Then another announcement: 'Result stands.' There was again an eruption of cheering.

Brough Scott, leading the ITV television coverage, plucked a reluctant Vincent from the throng to interview him. He introduced him with the perfect phrase 'Losing trainer, winning father' – a brilliant off-the-cuff assessment. He pressed Vincent about the loss of those millions of dollars. Wasn't it forty million in the colt's value? Vincent said, looking proudly across at a modestly smiling David, 'The money simply doesn't matter. I'm absolutely thrilled for my son.' And he clearly was. He then emphasized, 'I'm so glad the objection went the way it did.' He had had no idea that Pat would object. 'I'd never have got over it if the race had been taken from my son.' Then David was quizzed by Brough about beating his father. He replied with great force, 'It has nothing to do with beating my father. It was winning the Derby. It's a wonderful day.' Had he fancied his horse? David retorted, 'Well, I wouldn't have brought him over if I didn't give him a good chance on his home work.' And he gave one of his shy, sideways smiles.

The Queen Mother was gazing down on the remarkable family from the royal box with understanding and admiration. She immediately asked the Queen's racing manager, Lord Porchester, to go down with an invitation. Henry Porchester leant over the rails of the winner's enclosure to say, 'Queen Elizabeth' – which is how her circle always referred to that marvellous old lady – 'would like you *all* to come up to the royal box because it's such a *family* affair.'

Compensation to a lesser degree swiftly followed in the Irish Derby. Secreto's owner was engaged in trying to sell half his horse and declined to run. Darshaan, the top-class French winner of the Prix du Jockey Club, the French Derby, wasn't risked on the hard, fast ground. There was no great test of whether El Gran Senor truly stayed one and a half miles, for the pace on the Curragh was slow and he could conserve his brilliant speed to sprint away from Rainbow Quest in the last furlong, as so many had dreamed he would do at Epsom. Did he lose at Epsom because he didn't quite stay? Was he beaten because, left in front so long, he began to dawdle? Was Pat Eddery caught unawares by the long, tremendously vigorous challenge by his Irish rival Christy Roche on Secreto? Pat's answer was always logical and the same: 'If I'd won by four inches, you'd say he stayed!'

Plans for running the Senor in the autumn, and then even as a four-year-old, were abandoned when he had serious trouble in a hoof. He was operated on at Ballydoyle by the top American veterinary surgeon specializing in horses' hooves, but he was not able to repair the injury.

Alas, a far more serious failure was in store. The handsome, brilliant 2,000 Guineas winner proved that he was not half as fertile a stallion as everyone had hoped. In his first and second years, from more than 120 coverings he got only forty-eight mares in foal. He had started his stud career covering at an immense $200,000 a time; within five years his fee had shrunk to $50,000. Although he has produced some good horses, such as Belmez, who won the King George VI and Queen Elizabeth Diamond Stakes, and Rodrigo de Triano, who won the Guineas, the fertility problem meant fewer mares and fewer runners for the stallion. Secreto went to stud at Calumet Farm valued at $40 million. He proved a disappointment as a stallion.

Northern Dancer's legacy of exceptional ability, first discovered by Vincent, was continued not only by Nijinsky and El Gran Senor, but by Storm Bird, Try My Best and, in particular, by the prolific outstanding sire Sadler's Wells. Sadler's Wells was the second foal of Fairy Bridge, the smart filly clever Billy McDonald had seen out in the paddock with a bunch of fillies at Claiborne. He found out from the stud groom that she was the most impressive of the bunch. The syndicate bought her for $40,000 and she was knocked down to Billy at Saratoga Sales in 1976.

Sadlers Wells was a contemporary of El Gran Senor, winning the Irish 2,000 Guineas, the Eclipse and the Irish Champion Stakes. Standing at Coolmore, he has now become the champion of champions as a sire. He has been the champion sire of Great Britain and Ireland for fourteen years, thirteen of them consecutive (Caerleon, also trained by Vincent, was responsible for the break in 1991 when he took over the title with his most famous offspring, Generous). Tony Morris, a world expert on breeding, said of Sadler's Wells, 'He is a phenomenon whose like might not appear for another 200 years.' By 2005, Sadler's Wells had sired over 230 Stakes winners, with his progeny winning nearly every top race in Europe; they have also had great success in America. He has become the outstanding successor to Northern Dancer. His best offspring so far include Montjeu, who won six Group 1 races; Galileo, dual Derby winner; High Chaparral, dual Derby winner and dual Breeders' Cup winner; and Salsabil, one of only two fillies to win the Irish Derby in the twentieth century.

Both Vincent and Sadler's Wells have been acclaimed as the best in several centuries of racing and breeding. It seems fitting that the man from Co. Cork who discovered and made Northern Dancer also made Northern Dancer's son into the record-breaking sire he has been for fourteen astonishing years.

David O'Brien retired from training in 1988, to the astonishment of the racing fraternity. David, unlike his father, a master of delegation, had been determined to do everything himself and this left little time for his wife and young family. He bought a vineyard, Château Vignelaure, in Provence, within sight of Cezanne's Mont Ste Victoire.

David was an extremely good trainer; he is now acclaimed by the critics as one of the leading winemakers in the region. Could Vincent have been as good at growing vines and making wines? 'I think he would,' exclaims David. 'He has a love and understanding of nature and he'd appreciate the cycle of the vine as much as I do. While I was searching for a vineyard my father would often accompany me to look at different properties. I appreciated his help and valued highly his advice – he has a real feeling for things of quality, a vision of their future potential, whether horses or properties.'

CHAPTER 22

ROYAL ACADEMY

'Stop looking, we've found him'

J ust as the rise of the syndicate in the 1970s had seemed such a brilliant and simple idea, so did the conception of Classic Thoroughbreds. But there were fundamental and fatal differences. The syndicate's operations profited mightily for seven or eight rich harvests. Classic Thoroughbreds, with one magical exception, did not profit at all.

The Triumvirate had been a new idea operated by three men with special skills and money, but with a simple aim: to buy yearlings at Keeneland bred to win Classics, to train them well, and then to capitalize them at twenty or thirty times their cost as leading stallions. It was new, even in Kentucky. The three men between them had all the skills. Vincent could pick, train and advise on breeding and bloodlines; John Magnier understood the breeding side's finances and opportunities, as well as bringing into play his knowledge of bloodstock breeding; and Robert Sangster brought enthusiasm, capital and a zest for promotion.

Vitally, their operation had been launched on a bloodstock

market that was healthy and rising quickly, but which was conservative in attitude. Before the syndicate burst upon the scene, stallions were still covering around forty-five mares a year; when the syndicate hit its stride, its stallions were covering double that number of mares each season. They were able to add considerably to those figures by switching stallions between the hemispheres, thereby servicing mares all year round. Any business that suddenly, at little extra cost, quadruples its earnings instantly becomes more profitable. And top-class yearlings were in demand.

The golden bubble of yearling sales ran for a brief ten years. Then, like all bubble investments, it finally burst. The arrival of the enormously rich sheikhs of Dubai drove prices to heady heights in competition with the syndicate. Prices up to $13 million were paid for yearlings. In 1985, to the curiosity and speculation of the racing world, Robert, John, Vincent and their wives were invited by Sheikh Mohammed to visit Dubai, where they were received with overwhelming hospitality. They appreciated to what lengths the Maktoum family, father and sons, had gone in making Dubai a strategic port and financial and tourist centre of the Middle East. Although it has never been revealed what was discussed during this visit, Vincent did train several horses for Sheikh Mohammed and David produced the Sheikh's first Classic-winning colt, Authaal, a son of Shergar, who won the Irish St Leger in 1986. Subsequently, Sheikh Mohammed arranged for Jacqueline O'Brien to make a photographic trip into the Rub al-Khali (the Empty Quarter) of the Arabian Desert, which she describes as one of the greatest experiences of her life.

At Ballydoyle, 1984 had proved the peak of a long range of

successes. But that was the year of Vincent's last English Classic victory. El Gran Senor's defeat in the English Derby started the accelerating decline of Ballydoyle triumphs. In 1985, Ballydoyle had just one Classic winner, Law Society, who had been second in the Epsom Derby; he won the Irish Derby in the colours of Stavros Niarchos, his first classic winner. Irish winners for Ballydoyle over the next few years included the Irish 2,000 Guineas victor Prince of Birds in 1988, and, in the same year, the Irish St Leger was won by Dark Lomond. Then there were five winners of the National Stakes: Tate Gallery (1985), Caerwent (1987) and Classic Fame (1988), El Prado (1991) and Fatherland (1992).

1985 was a sombre year at Ballydoyle. A viral infection affected most of the horses, and consequently many of the expensive yearlings bought in Kentucky failed to come up to expectations. A few failed totally. Bloodstock is global, so when Kentucky sneezed, Europe wheezed. Big players in the syndicate elected to leave. Danny Schwartz bowed out; he was a bold gambler, but he was concerned about not knowing how much he would be called upon to provide for successive, expensive yearlings. Jack Mulcahy, Simon Fraser and Charles St George had all died. Niarchos, after the success of Law Society in the 1985 Irish Derby, had gone. From now on, he concentrated on building up his own efficient and highly successful breeding and racing business mainly in France.

Robert Sangster, who personified the syndicate with his colours on great horses such as The Minstrel, Golden Fleece, El Gran Senor and Sadler's Wells, was also feeling the pinch and reassessing Manton, his grand training stables and stud outside Marlborough. Manton's overheads proved untenable.

No expense had been spared under the unhappy regime of one of jumping's most brilliant young trainers, Michael Dickinson, who had produced the first five home in the Cheltenham Gold Cup of 1983 – an unmatchable feat of training. The well-known flat race trainer Barry Hills moved in from Lambourn as a tenant. He flourished, but still the upkeep of the estate crushed Robert. 'I need to sell at least a million pounds' worth of horses every year,' he said sadly, 'just to balance the books.'

All this, plus expensive delays in getting any insurance money paid out on Golden Fleece's early death, and El Gran Senor proving less than fully fertile (his fees were dropping rapidly), contributed to a severe lack of capital available to the syndicate. The three men vigorously discussed what next steps there could be. They resolved to go public, just as a private company with a few large private shareholders decided the time was ripe to float shares through a public offer for sale. The solution was discussed in detail with the very able and immensely successful Dublin stockbroker Dermot Desmond, later to become a close friend and partner of John Magnier in many business enterprises.

The syndicate would become the foundation investors in Classic Thoroughbreds. Their past record, at least until 1985, was excellent. The examples of The Minstrel, Sadler's Wells, Lomond, Glenstal, Storm Bird, Be My Guest and Caerleon were held up for admiration. However, shares are best offered to the public when trading is booming and profits are increasing. Unfortunately for Classic Thoroughbreds, business was moving in the opposite direction. Still, the partners believed that bloodstock was such an Irish passion and the skills of Vincent O'Brien were so highly regarded that the Irish public would be interested in taking part in the enterprise. Sangster, too, was a popular figure, owning successful horses in Ireland, England and Australia, and Magnier was a great power in the breeding world. The public would know that in his hands the disposal of the horses to the stallion sector of the bloodstock industry would be well handled. The enterprise seemed to have a great chance of success. With these three investing heavily themselves, the patriotism and pride of the Irish people, plus promised institutional support, would guarantee a very successful float and a happy outcome. At least, that was the hope.

Two prominent Irish figures joined the board of the new company. First, the redoubtable Dr (now Sir) Michael Smurfit, one of Ireland's richest men, head of an immense paper and packaging group, and chairman of the Irish Racing Board – a more than useful ally. Michael's father, Jefferson Smurfit, had been one of Vincent's first owners back in the 1940s. John Horgan, from Cork, one of Ireland's biggest cattle dealers and a famous figure among Ireland's still largely rural community, was the second person to join the board. These investors would come in as big shareholders in Classic Thoroughbreds, with Vincent as chairman.

The company was floated valued at IR£12 million, with the shares priced to open at 30p each. Vincent made the biggest personal investment – IR£1 million, over 12 per cent of the issue. Sangster and Magnier invested heavily too, with IR£600,000 each for 8.3 per cent each of the company. Smurfit, whose role in Classic Thoroughbreds was that of financial controller, matched this figure, and Horgan came in with IR£250,000 for a stake of just over 3 per cent.

Institutions, banks and insurance companies, including Citibank, were encouraged to invest by the shrewd and prosperous Dermot Desmond. They contributed a welcome IR£5 million. The public, in the shape of about 2,500 individuals, came in with around £IR2 million. The old days of buying yearlings with a minimum of interplay between the three partners were finally over. Much of the finance now belonged to the great Irish public. The burden on Vincent was severe. He was not just first of three equal decision-makers, he was chairman of a public company with thousands of share-holders risking their cash. It had always been vital for the Syndicate's own sake to find classically bred colts to be trained by Vincent to win Classics. He now had a large public responsibility to do just that.

In 1987, the company spent IR£7.6 million acquiring twenty-nine colts and nine fillies owned wholly or in partner-ship. Vincent combed the sales of America, France, England and Ireland to find suitable yearlings at the right prices. He had an awesome task. The following year he was due to return to the sales, but the previous year's purchases for Classic Thoroughbreds had not yet run and thereby established their worth. The company was like any business promising much, but without showing any profit. Indeed, it was as yet without any earnings at all. Non-racing investors were learning that the harvest in bloodstock can take years to come. Little in the top class was coming good at Ballydoyle that summer.

Michael Smurfit, with his shrewd businessman's eye, examined the figures. He calculated that the most Vincent could spend on yearlings in 1988 was IR£4 million. Constricted by this budget, but in a falling market, Vincent hoped he would find up to half a dozen yearlings, classically bred and capable of Classic performance, which might fit the bill. Elsewhere, the bearers of mighty gold bars from Dubai bought what they wanted. Here were the new rulers of Britain's Turf, who injected the much-needed lifeblood of zeal and money into the thoroughbred industry, not only through their purchases but through the redevelopment and the excellent restoration of many stud farms. Sheikh Mohammed spent nearly $19 million buying twenty yearlings at Keeneland in 1988; Sheikh Hamdan spent $6 million for another dozen. Against $25 million spent by just two Maktoum brothers, the average price of Keeneland yearlings that year was little more than $300,000, so far had the market fallen. It was half the sales average of only three years earlier.

The biggest names continued to scuttle out of bloodstock as if it was not a joy but a plague. Buyers were wounded. Breeders who had borrowed against their farms went broke as prices collapsed. Tom Gentry, a tremendous party-giver at sales times, went spectacularly bust, the banks seizing his mares and yearlings. All over Kentucky, 'For Sale' notices garlanded the posts and rails of even the most famous old farms.

In January 1988 Nelson Bunker Hunt, the oil man, industrialist and gambler in silver, in urgent need of money, auctioned off all 580 of his horses, including Empery, winner of the Epsom Derby. The sale fetched $46 million.

At Keeneland in July 1988 Vincent's companion and support was his nineteen-year-old son Charles, who was starting his six-year stint as pupil-assistant to his father before he too took out a licence to train, which he did on 1 January 1993. Vincent was still looking for that one outstanding individual for which he always searched. Sometimes you can look at dozens of horses without feeling that instant click of recognition of quality and worth. Charles remembers they had spent days looking at yearlings. Horses to fill their requirements did not seem to be there. Then, at last, in Barn 29, one of the furthest away, Vincent said quietly, 'Stop looking. We've found him.'

The *coup de foudre* for Vincent at that sale came when he spied a colt by his beloved Nijinsky out of Crimson Saint. He calculated he might have $2.5 million to spend on this exceptional-looking bay colt, but above that figure he reckoned he could not go. Sheikh Mohammed had bought the full brother, Laa Etaab, for $7 million, and he had been no good, so Vincent hoped this colt would come within budget. But his dam had already bred the outstanding Stakes winner Terlingua, dam of Storm Cat, trained by the rapid-talking, former quarter-horse trainer D. Wayne Lukas, a leading trainer of thoroughbreds in California and a regular habitué of Keeneland. He would be certain to be interested in the colt.

He was, so Wayne Lukas and Vincent joined battle. They bid and bid against each other until Vincent reached his maximum. Wayne Lukas stopped, thought, murmured something, then went on to $2.6 million. Now Vincent had to hesitate. This was a colt he dearly wanted; he felt he was a star in the making. But he hadn't the money. The auctioneer looked down at Vincent's famous dapper figure and begged him to go on. Vincent was looking down at his catalogue. Had he had Robert and John there he could have quickly consulted: would they come in with him as partners in the excess? But now he had to shoulder the decision himself.

Wayne Lukas and the auctioneer gave Vincent only seconds to come to a decision. But Vincent had been a calm, successful gambler on cards and horses. Tick-tock, tick-tock, the bidding continued to swing between the two trainers, Californian and Irishman. Vincent boldly bid $3.3 million; Wayne Lukas countered with $3.4 million. The auctioneer had his hammer hovering to knock the Nijinsky colt down to the American when Vincent, with cool courage, bid $3.5 million – getting on for the entire budget he had for these sales. He had far exceeded his own limit, but he loved this colt, and he got him. Would he come truly good, turn the tide and be a star to rescue Classic Thoroughbreds?

The colt's purchase proved to be the record price of that sale, the last Keeneland sale Vincent ever attended; his only other purchase was a filly by Kris. To ease the pressure on the company, Vincent and Robert each took 20 per cent of the $3.5 million colt, and John Magnier took 10 per cent, leaving Classic Thoroughbreds with the balance of 40 per cent. An American, Bruce McNall, a well-known coin collector, took 10 per cent. The second highest-priced colt, by Northern Dancer out of Detroit, was ironically not a purchase but a sale: the colt was bred at Swettenham Stud and sold by Sangster for $2,450,000.

Robert and Vincent left the sales together, and an era had ended. But the book was not quite closed. An astonishing chapter remained. The Nijinsky colt out of Crimson Saint who came to Ballydoyle was named Royal Academy.

* * *

While Vincent was fully occupied not only with chairing Classic Thoroughbreds but with running his stable, Robert

Sangster was quietly switching out of yearling colts to yearling fillies. His new plan was to concentrate and expand on breeding. Racing was proving economically unsound. He had sold Vernons Pools to Ladbrokes, the gambling giant which also owned Hilton Hotels. He had built up a large brood mare band in Australia and often remarked that people in Britain only knew of his horses with Vincent, and of his English-based horses now trained at Manton by the shrewd Barry Hills, his tenant, but that no-one seemed interested in his Australian activities. In 1986, in a record-breaking Australian deal, he had sold 70 per cent of his equine interests to a racing and breeding company for $17.5 million. The deal covered nearly a hundred brood mares and nearly fifty foals.

The third member of the syndicate, Vincent's son-in-law John Magnier, was busy extending the extraordinary Coolmore empire of stud farms, the property of the three partners. The performance of its stallions is never certain with any stud, for the popularity of stallions depends on their ability to sire winners. The superb Northern Dancer had been put down at the age of twenty-nine in 1990, after a bout of colic. In the same year, The Minstrel, forerunner and therefore standard bearer of all the syndicate's successes, had been put down at Windfields in Maryland, aged only sixteen. In an uncertain world, nothing is less certain than the future performance of well-bred horses on the course or at stud, or the length of their often fragile lives. But Coolmore would have a huge influence on the prosperity of the Triumvirate. Particular hopes rested on Sadler's Wells, Lomond and Caerleon. The last two finished top and runner-up on the first-season sires list in 1987. There were also Storm Bird and El Gran Senor.

Most had been bought and all had been trained by Vincent.

For a man like Vincent O'Brien, who declined publicity, detested crowds and darted away from social gatherings, chairing Classic Thoroughbreds should have proved an intolerable task. But the man could do all these dislikable things when duty called. So we had the extraordinary picture of this basically shy, quiet and undemonstrative man entertaining a large group of his share-holders, nearly all complete strangers to him, on escorted visits to Ballydoyle to see their assets. In the past, though close friends were always welcomed, strangers calling had always been dexterously avoided. Yet here, now, stood Vincent in front of a keen jostle of shareholders. Horses were pulled out, and like an experienced lecturer he would discuss them and the hopes he held for their futures, briskly answering any questions. It was a remarkable display. There was little he could not do if impelled by his career and duty.

Classic Thoroughbreds was not yet flourishing, although at the end of 1988 early indications had given encouragement. The shares in May 1989 went up to 41p from their 30p launch, valuing the company at £23.67 million. Expectations ran high. Classic Fame by Nijinsky had won all his three races as a two-year-old, including the Beresford Stakes and the National Stakes; Saratogan, a son of El Gran Senor, started well, beaten only half a length in the Dewhurst. These two featured in the top ten two-year-olds of Great Britain and Ireland, together with Puissance. Classic Thoroughbreds seemed to have hope for the future.

The company owned half of Saratogan, but alas, although heavily backed in the 2,000 Guineas, he failed, finishing only ninth of sixteen; Classic Fame also disappointed, and Puissance, a powerful sprinter, was injured. Classic

Thoroughbreds' shares never recovered from these blows. The company would find it very difficult to go back to the public for more money by issuing more shares. After half a year's trading in 1989, the books showed a substantial loss of IR£5.7 million. Serious discontent was voiced by individual shareholders at a public meeting.

* * *

So how was Vincent bearing up as a family man? His five children were all settled. Liz, the eldest daughter with one son, lives at Baltiboys, in County Wicklow, and was married to Kevin McClory, the film producer. Coolmore Stud in County Tipperary is the Irish base of Sue and John Magnier and their five children. David and Catherine also with five children moved from County Tipperary to Château Vignelaure, in Provence, France, to develop their award-winning vineyard. Baroda Stud in County Kildare is the home of Jane and Philip Myerscough and their four children. Philip is a director and auctioneer of horses at Tattersall's. Charles has two children and trains horses, including those of his father at his Baronrath Stables in County Kildare. Vincent's five children all have different memories of growing up with their famous father.

'One reason why my father was able to withstand the stress of training was his ability always to put setbacks and disappointments immediately behind him and to close the door on them,' David recalls affectionately. 'Not for him the anxious self-examination which strains your average businessman or trainer. Today was always over, done with. All thoughts were then switched forward to the morrow.'

Liz remembers how her father handled the bad times. 'Stress manifested itself in back and other health problems. He cut himself off effectively from people and things when he was focusing on a big event, and coped with the tension by retreating into himself. The tension was at its worst leading up to the big races. The moment the race was over, win or lose, he moved on without looking back.

'M.V. was capable of being very single-minded, tough, driven, capable and tetchy at times, very focused, incredibly resilient and self-contained. He was shy and industrious, paying great attention to detail. He was selectively deaf and would prefer to tune out of any conversation at family meals. Prime time for major mishaps was work mornings before big races, or when Lester came over to "test drive" the two-year-olds. Dad was able to express his anger without ever raising his voice. In fact, I don't believe I have ever heard him raise his voice. He was careful with money but incredibly generous to us all over the years.

. . . 'MV is always immaculately turned out and absolutely fastidious about his appearance', Liz says. 'He still has a great interest in good food and good wine. Meals are still always on time. Golf and fishing were his two hobbies, as he'd given up hunting after some bad falls in the 1950s, and shooting because he "didn't really want to kill things any more". He had a practice golf range at the back of stables and would hit a hundred golf balls in the afternoon. He'd make the lads pick them up and they'd count them so there was no possibility of a horse standing on one.

'One weekend he decided to go with me on a fishing break and we drove to Kerry. We met a herd of cows ambling in the same direction. Dad always treats herds of cows as a jockey treats a large field at Epsom, threading through them with minimum effort and amazing judgement. Unfortunately, one cow did not conform and he clipped her ear with the wing of the car.

'He loved fast cars and would test them out on the way home from the races,' continues Liz. 'It got to the stage where I refused to go racing, so great was the terror of these "adrenalin-fuelled" trips back to Tipperary.

'Dad enjoyed watching rugby, hurling and football. We went together to Lansdowne Road to watch Ireland win the Triple Crown in 1983 and he loved every moment of it. He watches soccer internationals with great interest, with the mute button pressed to avoid heart palpitations. Charles converted him into a keen Liverpool supporter and members of the team visited Ballydoyle in the 1980s.'

'Dad was passionate about trees,' Sue says. 'He must have planted hundreds of thousands of them. He loved to prune these and we would go out with him in the afternoons. The back of the Land Rover was always filled with a fearsome collection of saws, knives and pruning shears which we had to sit on if there wasn't enough room – a prickly ride. He loved the wildlife that could be found on the farm and planted shrubs to attract pheasants. These were always fed during the winter by Noel, who left messages in the morning of what he had seen on the farm in the way of animal life. We used to rush down after waking to see these notes.

'Dad was always very good with his grandchildren and now with his two great-grandsons – he always loved babies and animals. His "sweet" cupboard in the hall was always well-stocked and he used to do the handouts himself.'

David also remembers, 'Afternoons, between lunchtime and evening stables, were spent walking the gallops or pruning the young trees he planted all over Ballydoyle. All of our love of nature followed from his example. He taught me to fish as a small boy and I have loved fishing ever since. My earliest memory is of him coming into my room with a boxer pup in a box which he had driven to Drogheda to buy for my third birthday. We called the puppy Moss after Ballymoss. My father is a man who never hurries. He was never late, insisting on punctuality: tea at 4.30 exactly, and in the evening, a glass of champagne before dinner at 7.30. He was always a good listener, especially when someone was saying something which affected his horses, his family, or possible future improvements. He'd pick out what was important. He enjoyed discipline and exercise. Everything in moderation. He also loved making plans for new buildings, stables, barns – there was always a building project in the pipeline.'

Jane is fiercely emphatic, her passion matching the strength of her loyalty to her mother and father. 'What all we children would agree,' she asserts, 'is that Dad is absolutely straight and honest and could never do anything unjust or wrong to anyone. It would be against his religion as well as his moral character.

'We spent a lot of time with him when we were growing up. He liked us to go out to watch work in the mornings. We would leave with him in the jeep and bring the dogs, but if he got annoyed over the work or talked to the farm men for too long, we would run home.

'Dad was never frightened of any horse. I had a very

difficult pony that would charge you in the field and try to kick you. The only person that he never misbehaved with was Dad. The pony was like a lamb with him.'

'When I was very small,' Charles remembers, 'sadly I didn't realize the significance of watching work mornings. I appreciate their importance much more now. I wish I could go back and watch again. In those days two or three winners a day was pretty much the norm, and winning International Group races was no big deal! Dad was an excellent man manager and kept everyone on their toes. Looking back, I'm convinced he appeared in bad form some mornings, finding fault deliberately to achieve exactly that.'

* * *

In 1989, as in 1985 and 1986, Ballydoyle was again afflicted with 'the virus' that has become the scourge of the bloodstock industry. There are varieties of virus which, in global racing, can affect any stable, no matter how hygienically it is maintained, although modern medical advances have meant that vaccination programmes today are greatly improved.

Vincent's name vanished from the English Top Twelve trainers list, and Sangster's from the Top Twelve owners. But Royal Academy, the colt who had so taken Vincent's eye at Keeneland, was showing distinct promise. As a two-year-old he devastated a field of maidens at the Curragh, winning by six lengths, and he ran well in the Dewhurst at Newmarket, finishing sixth but only four lengths behind the winner. On this form he could well be on the fringe of top class. He was now the only horse of that calibre in Ballydoyle in which Classic Thoroughbreds had an interest.

In 1990, Royal Academy progressed to win the Tetrarch Stakes and was then only just beaten a neck in the Irish 2,000 Guineas by the very highly rated Tirol, who had beaten the top French three-year-old miler Machiavellian by two lengths in the Newmarket 2,000 Guineas. Ironically, Tirol was a son of Thatching who stood at Coolmore, having been trained by Vincent.

The courage, the will to win and the resolution shown here by Royal Academy were portents of what would be required that autumn on a strange course in a distant land. Those qualities now delighted Vincent, for nothing pleases a trainer more than seeing one of his horses proving brave under pressure. Vincent had a further reason for pleasure, of course: this was a good performance for his shareholders.

Conversely, however, nothing deflates a trainer more quickly than an unexpected failure. Royal Academy was sent to Royal Ascot for the St James's Palace Stakes, a race won by Vincent and Piggott with Thatch in 1973 and Jaazeiro in 1978. Royal Academy, for no known reason, adamantly refused to enter the stalls, stood rooted to the spot behind them, and was left there when the starter decided to wait no longer for him. The Ballydoyle team, severely disappointed by this surprising setback, still feel some fifteen years later that the Ascot stalls-handlers, normally so thorough, had not persevered with Royal Academy, nor had the starter waited sufficiently, even though their horse had been favourite.

Vincent next decided to go for shorter distances and aimed the horse boldly at Newmarket's six-furlong undulating July Cup. Royal Academy won a very testing race, tenderly ridden by John Reid, and went on to run a close second to the top sprinter Dayjur in the Ladbroke Sprint Cup.

However, the affairs of Classic Thoroughbreds were not, like Royal Academy, improving. The shares, once as high as 41p, had begun to dive when Saratogan disappointed. They tumbled down to 16p. The company sold nearly half of its three-year-olds at a loss. The small prize money then on offer in Ireland could not remotely cover the horses' costs.

The AGM of Classic Thoroughbreds was held on 10 June 1990. 'Vincent found walking into that crowded meeting as chairman,' members of his family agree, 'the hardest thing he had ever had to do. He felt desperately for the small investors who had displayed such faith in him by investing in Classic Thoroughbreds and would have given anything for the venture to have been a success. He was touched beyond words by the reception of the shareholders.' The Irish press declared, 'There can hardly be many occasions when the chairman of a company with accumulated losses of over seven million pounds arrives late at his company's Annual General Meeting to be greeted with a spontaneous round of applause. But that was the reception for Vincent O'Brien last Friday evening at the AGM of Classic Thoroughbreds. It became clear that many investors in Classic are not looking for share-price appreciation or large-scale profits. They would be happy to see one horse lift a Classic race, because they could then boast they are part owners of a champion horse. Many stressed their investment was an enjoyable gamble and the money didn't matter.' The chairmen of other companies must wish that their shareholders had the same attitude. The company's large institutional shareholders, wondering if they would ever see any return, did, however, complain powerfully.

During the rest of the summer of 1990, while Vincent was preparing Royal Academy for the last great race of his life, the shares of the company he chaired continued to dive, down to 4.5p. Classic Thoroughbreds was fatally ill. After a little flicker of life and hope in October they recovered a few pence, but by August 1991 the company had to announce that it had ceased to trade. Its shares had collapsed to 3p – one tenth of their issue price. The remaining funds, some £2 to £3 million, were returned to shareholders.

The concept had been bold, but timing was against it. The decline of the bloodstock market had naturally affected most of the industry, and the company did not own any of the successful, big earners, the Coolmore stallions. As everyone knew in the boom days of the syndicate, it required a Classic winner at least every other year to make a big profit. Vincent's last Classic winner in England had been El Gran Senor's 2,000 Guineas win in 1984. But for one last time, and in another part of the world, an altogether different race was awaiting the final champion from Ballydoyle.

CHAPTER 23

LESTER – AND ROYAL ACADEMY'S BREEDERS' CUP

'He was a genius with a great hunger'

As the autumn of 1990 came rustling in, Vincent, aged seventy-three – an age when most men have retired with some relief – was preparing for an astonishing long shot on the far side of the cold Atlantic. He had decided, with the inspiring spirit of a great gambler whose brave heart and cool head had brought off such triumphs over the previous fifty years, to have a crack at the richest prize he had ever attempted. He would send Royal Academy to America to contest the $1 million Breeders' Cup Mile.

In Vincent's crowded life, he had overcome many a difficult challenge, though this was undoubtedly one of the toughest. But once he had set his sights upon Belmont Park on New York's pleasant Long Island outskirts, Vincent was in no mood for failure. He had quite enough anxieties besetting the sinking ship of Classic Thoroughbreds. Then, just three weeks before the race, he lost his stable jockey, John Reid (who had taken over from Cash Asmussen in 1988), with a broken collarbone, suffered in France at the Prix de l'Arc de Triomphe meeting. Who could replace him?

Vincent seriously fancied his colt's chances: Royal Academy was improving steadily, as Vincent had predicted the previous autumn. His speed was proved. But Vincent considered he now needed a mile – certainly on a fast, tight track like Belmont. He knew the race might well be rough and jostling. He was unsure of having an American jockey at all, or if so, which one to ask.

When something gloriously unexpected occurs, many are the voices who subsequently declare how they helped it. It was Mike Dillon, however, the racecourse ambassador of Ladbrokes, who suggested Lester Piggott to Vincent and John Magnier at a Phoenix Park meeting. The three agreed that Lester would have been the ideal rider for Royal Academy, if only he had not retired. Moreover, Lester was now a grandfather; how fit could he possibly be? Was it possible that after five years out of the saddle the old champion might be coaxed back? If the notion sounded absurd, it was worth trying. After all, Vincent and Lester went back a long, long way.

'In my early days when I was training National Hunt horses,' Vincent says, 'I remember a pal of mine, Tony Murphy, a great Cork racing man, going to Haydock Park. He told me that he had seen there the successor to the great jockey Gordon Richards. It was Lester Piggott, aged twelve, riding his first winner. So he was in the limelight as early as that. I believe we first met at Cheltenham in the mid 1950s. It was really his reputation that led me to offer him the ride on Gladness in the Ascot Gold Cup, our first winner together in 1958. Valoris was the first Classic winner he rode for me in 1966, and this led to the much-publicized break-up with Noel Murless.'

Noel Murless, a man universally revered in racing, had a record of great success with Piggott: together they had won seven Classics. But in 1966 Murless cut the Piggott connection when, expecting him to ride his runner Varinia in the 1966 Oaks, he learned to his fury that his jockey had taken a ride for Vincent. The Jockey Club was also incensed, although at this stage the retainer was only a verbal agreement. A nimble Lester had snapped up the ride on Valoris owned by the property tycoon Charles Clore and trained by Vincent O'Brien. And Piggott had picked correctly: Varinia, beaten by five and a half lengths, was third to Valoris. This was Vincent's second successive Oaks victory. He had won his first Oaks the previous year with Long Look, ridden by his retained jockey the Australian Jack Purtell, owned by his great American supporter James Cox Brady, an eminent racing establishment figure in the USA. Vincent said about Lester's parting with Noel Murless, 'Well, it was the nature of the man. Lester was great at what he was doing; he had tremendous ambition and desire to succeed. He was a good judge at picking out what he figured was the best horse on the day and he did all he could to get on that horse.

'There's no doubt that he was a tremendous asset to us at Ballydoyle. I was very fortunate to have a claim on him for so many years. This was just a verbal arrangement. In fact, one night I had to make a speech at some event in London and I said to the other trainers present, "I can't understand how you people allow Lester to come over to Ireland to ride for me!"

'He studied individual horses. He might say nothing after a race, but a week or two later he would give me an opinion. It would be a hundred per cent accurate. His advice mattered because he really thought about the horses, their temperaments, their liking for different kinds of ground and their idiosyncrasies. His comments were to the point, quite profound in fact – and a tremendous help. It was also helpful in planning a horse's career to get his assessment of the opposition. He could figure out how best to beat them; he knew the strengths of the jockeys riding against him, every move they'd make. It was a tremendous advantage having him on board. It probably made a difference of five to seven pounds – and that counts for a lot.

'Lester was the absolute best at Epsom. It is a tricky course. He knew the track so well, but he gave so much thought as to how best to ride each horse that he rode in the Derby. For me, Lester was worth seven pounds at Epsom and more, as he wasn't riding against you! Also, he was at his best on the big day. It was his will and his thinking then that mattered.'

For many years, Lester and Vincent enjoyed a triumphant partnership. Piggott rode four English Derby winners for Vincent and nine English Classic winners between Valoris in the Oaks and The Minstrel in the Derby in 1977.

'Regarding instructions,' Vincent says, 'Lester was always prepared to talk about how a horse should be ridden and I never said overmuch. Neither of us will ever go down in history as talking our heads off, but we always had a word beforehand! I rarely left it until the parade ring as there would usually be too many people around to be able to concentrate.'

So what made Lester so special? 'Well, simply, first, he was a genius with a great hunger for success. After that it would be sheer application to what he was doing; he took the job seriously. He was cool, shrewd, a great judge of pace. He was capable of riding brilliant races, in particular the big ones. He revolutionized race-riding by being able to dictate the pace from in front, as he did on Alleged in the first Prix de l'Arc de Triomphe. He won many races that way, for example Teenoso in the Derby in 1983. He gave so much thought to how best to ride a horse. Many Ribot horses were notoriously difficult. Lester discovered they resented being asked to find early pace. He allowed them to lope along in the rear until he felt that they were beginning to take more interest. He could get them running from there and persuade them to put their heads in front before the winning post. He must be the greatest jockey of his generation, or indeed any generation.

'I used to get infuriated with Lester when he came to Ballydoyle and would sometimes test the two-year-olds to his own satisfaction. He would somehow manage to fix the work so that he was badly left and therefore could ask the horse to accelerate to catch up.' Vincent had brought his horses along so carefully he felt it was awful to work a young horse too hard against his clearly expressed orders. Lester would treat these episodes as slightly humorous, but Vincent would be very annoyed. When asked if he had found Vincent difficult, Lester replied, 'I didn't think he was – he just had his funny little ways.'

'In all the races Lester rode for me over a span of thirty-plus years,' Vincent continues, 'there were only three I did criticize. Nijinsky in the Prix de l'Arc de Triomphe, where I think Lester lay out of his ground; however, I don't think the horse was at his best. What Lester expected to find that day in the way of acceleration from a long way back, Nijinsky was not able to produce. Alleged in the St Leger, where he provided a second pacemaker for Dunfermline, and perhaps The Minstrel in the King George and Queen Elizabeth Diamond Stakes were the other two. When you consider the pressure under which a jockey rides and the split-second timing required, these are few indeed compared with the wonderful wins he achieved for the stable.'

At the end of 1980 Lester decided to cease riding for Vincent and had accepted a contract from Henry Cecil, who was on his doorstep at Newmarket. 'Much closer to home, and if he runs horses miles away, he'll get one of his good riders to go there!' said Lester. He had also had difficulties with Vincent, who 'would not decide until the last possible minute which horse would run'. Lester grumbles, 'That, as a freelance, could be awkward!'

When Piggott parted from Ballydoyle he was returning to the famous Warren Hill stables on the hilltop outside Newmarket. The previous arrangement between Noel Murless and Lester had not been a written contract but a verbal agreement only. It was Cecil's circular letter to his owners about Lester's special requirements for rewards, percentages and other bonuses that was leaked to the press by one disaffected owner. This led to the Inland Revenue's and Customs and Excise's pursuit of Piggott, his conviction and twelve months in prison.

When Vincent was given the 1994 Derby award for Outstanding Achievement, John Sexton, as president of the Horserace Writers Association, observed, 'For fourteen years, from 1966, Vincent harnessed the genius of Lester Piggott to his own in what was a partnership made in racing's heaven. The inter-relationship of these two men, each top of their own inter-locking crafts, has been intriguing for the racing public to observe, for neither is revealing. They are both so reticent, so introspective, so focused, and so unprone to show moments of joy.'

Following Lester's first retirement as a jockey in October 1985 at Nottingham, it had seemed impossible that the generally glittering, sometimes 'bloody awful' days (as Lester put it) shared with Vincent would ever appear again on any racecourse. But in 2005 Lester was able to declare, 'Vincent has been the most outstanding trainer of my time. Without doubt his record speaks for itself. In other words, he was special.' He added to Jacqueline, 'It was only Vincent who gave me my greatest thrill ever, at Belmont Park.'

* * *

Lester himself, in recounting his steps back to race-riding in 1990, relates how he received an invitation from Alan Lillingston, the renowned Limerick stud owner, who as a leading amateur had ridden the 1963 Champion Hurdle winner Winning Fair. Would Lester ride in a veterans' race at the Curragh the following year? Lester agreed to do so. He rode in another veterans' race at Tipperary, though, before his Curragh commitment. He finished second. Renewing his long friendship with Vincent on a spring trip to Ballydoyle, Lester asked, typically, if Vincent could produce 'a decent runner for him in the veterans' race at the Curragh'. Vincent obliged, and Lester finished third to Yves Saint-Martin and Willie Robinson.

Lester's success at the Curragh quickened Vincent's interest, and when the two next spoke on the telephone Vincent suggested, 'Why don't you make a real comeback?' A few weeks later, in September, Vincent, with all his old skilful zest, pursued the proposal by taking Lester to lunch in a private room at

Dublin's Berkeley Court Hotel. Vincent now put the proposition squarely. 'If you do return this season, I'll give you first choice of all rides for me in 1991.' He added, 'But you'd better get things moving.' Vincent knew the end of Classic Thoroughbreds was nigh and pointed out to Lester that he 'had in mind a much smaller string next year'. John Reid's contract expired that season, and anyway, Vincent had thought briefly of training only twenty to twenty-five horses for friends and family – a scheme he had to discard once he had weighed up the huge overheads of a great establishment like Ballydoyle.

Lester, with equal discretion, first approached Dr Allen, the Jockey Club's chief medical officer, to ask for a check-over. He feared the publicity if he were later rejected by the Jockey Club's Licensing Committee. He passed 100 per cent fit and applied forthwith for a licence. This was happily agreed to after a brief and friendly chat. It was greeted by public and press with a mixture of pleasure and amazement, that a grandfather of fifty-four could hope to have retained his skills and racing weight some five years since his last winner.

Lester made his return at Leicester on some unraced two-year-olds, trained by Henry Cecil. 'Three rides, no winners,' commented Lester, 'but wonderful to be back.' Next day at Chepstow he rode his first winner since October 1985 – and best of all, it was on a horse, Nicholas, trained by his wife Susan and himself.

Now the pace of the drama quickened again. Lester went to the Curragh to replace the injured John Reid on four runners for Vincent. This was an extra meeting put on by the Turf Club at the end of the season. It was a grey Monday evening, the boxes of racing's elite were empty, but racing fans had come from all parts of the country to see Lester and Vincent in action together again. Unbelievably, even for a racing thriller, all four horses won. The crowd were ecstatic, and the applause for both Lester and Vincent rang out movingly, loud and long.

Vincent was then prevented by flu from making the long flight to Belmont Park for what was going to be easily the most important race of his closing years. The doctor insisted that he should not fly; the journey could badly affect his ears. Vincent reluctantly agreed, and Jacqueline believes this was the only important overseas race that Vincent missed in his half-century of training. In his absence, Charles, his son and assistant trainer, and Jacqueline went to New York to represent him. Neither Robert, who like Vincent held 20 per cent of Royal Academy, nor John Magnier, who held 10 per cent, was able to go to Belmont.

There were even problems over the plans for the horse's journey. Vincent did not want the horse to fly as early as the other European contenders, who were flying from Paris, so he arranged an individual flight for Royal Academy with Air France. At the last moment, the airline went on strike and Vincent swiftly had to make new arrangements for a flight from Shannon to New York. Gerry Gallagher, Vincent's travelling head man, reported that Royal Academy travelled without any difficulty and arrived safely in the special quarantine yard at Belmont Park.

Vincent had not given Royal Academy any special work designed to give him the feel of Belmont's sharp left-handed track; indeed, it is a myth that Vincent ever used the extensive gallops at Ballydoyle in any special way to replicate the oddities of different tracks. There was no truth in the legend that he had ever built a copy of Tattenham Corner to give those Derby horses practice around the bends. The lie of the land at Ballydoyle dictated the placing of the gallops.

Lester Piggott rode at Newbury on the Thursday before the Breeders' Cup meeting on Saturday, 7 October. He dashed to Heathrow after the last race, caught Concorde to Kennedy, and checked into the Waldorf Astoria where rooms had also been booked for Jacqueline and Charles.

Further alarming problems arose out at Belmont, first with Lester's application for a licence to ride that day, and secondly as to whether Royal Academy, as the property of a limited company, was qualified to run in the race at all. Jacqueline and Lester went to the office at Belmont where both were finger-printed and had to complete detailed application forms to verify that they were authorized to be there. When they were looking at their forms they saw to their surprise that one question demanding an instant and honest answer was, 'Have you ever been to jail?' What was Lester to do? 'We both decided,' said Jacqueline, 'that this needed handling by some-one in higher authority, and mercifully this was sorted out quickly, even though Lester had left the difficult question blank.'

Meanwhile, Charles was wrestling with the problem of the ownership of the horse. Under New York Jockey Club rules owners must be fingerprinted; a horse cannot be owned by a company. But it would have been rather difficult to obtain fingerprints of all the thousands of small owners of Classic Thoroughbreds plc. It was agreed that the horse would run under the nomenclature of a Classic Thoroughbred partner-ship, which was happily suggested by the racecourse. Lester had to have his medical examination to get his licence, and Charles needed a temporary training licence.

Because of his delicate feet, caused by his habit of standing with his front feet too close together in the stables and pulling off his shoes, Royal Academy had been specially shod by the Ballydoyle blacksmith, Ken McLoughlin. He had discussed with Vincent using innovative shoes made of plastic-covered steel plates which could be glued to the hooves, which meant that no nails had to be driven into the brittle sides of the hooves. Lester, recalling the old racing dictum 'an ounce on the foot is like a pound on the back', thought these shoes were heavier than the usual aluminium or light steel racing plates. How would they perform at the racetrack? Would they slow Royal Academy down?

On the day before the race Lester, as had been arranged, went out to Belmont to get on Royal Academy and to canter him slowly and alone around the tiny two-furlong circuit by the quarantine stables. This was the first time Lester had sat on the horse. Vincent had made it quite clear to Lester, and Charles constantly reminded him, that the short canter was to be very slow indeed. All went well, and Lester was delighted with the feel the horse gave him.

Since the annual Breeders' Cup started in 1984, no Irish horse had even been placed in any race at any of the meetings. Jacqueline remembers that she had never seen Lester so anxious before any race in the thirty years she had watched him riding. Not just once but twice he walked the course to get the feel of it and to check out its idiosyncrasies. When Lester wasn't worrying about the course, he hovered around Royal Academy, quizzing Gerry about how the horse was feeling and feeding.

Jacqueline guessed 'that Lester felt this was the most important race of his entire life, and Charles and I definitely knew it was the most vital for Vincent, particularly as things were going so badly for Classic Thoroughbreds'.

Race day itself dawned bright and sunny, but it suffered two shocking deaths in the earlier races. The four-year-old horse Mr Nickerson collapsed in the Sprint and died a few minutes later of a heart attack. Then the American champion filly Go For Wand, who would almost certainly have been their Horse of the Year had she won, was battling out the finish of her race when her off-fore ankle shattered, and she had to be humanely destroyed.

Royal Academy had been an 8–1 chance on the Morning Line, but so great was the greeting given him and Lester on the course that sentimentality combined with informed betting from Britain resulted in him being sent off favourite at 7–2. Piggott, in the green, white and gold colours of the Classic Thoroughbred and the Irish national flag, and Royal Academy were not only applauded but absolutely mobbed in the small paddock behind the stands, and as they went out onto the course they were enthusiastically cheered. It was said that every Irishman in New York State, along with his wife and all their children, had turned out at Belmont that day.

Belmont Park has the urban feel of most American tracks, but the far side is wooded and attractive. It has typically immense American grandstands, with extensive Tote facilities. Bookies were booted out of American racing in the 1920s, ensuring a very high level of American prize money and a cheap day's racing for the public. Betting profits on the 'machine' are not taken away by bookmakers, but the chairmen of the New York Racing Association have to battle continually with the greedy government over the amount of their profits which are siphoned off by the state.

The October day sparkled in cold, clear sunlight. Jacqueline, Charles and Lester set off together in a large limousine and were in time to watch the first race, the Sprint. Here, Dayjur, who had just beaten Royal Academy in the Haydock Sprint, was only just beaten himself: he lost ground jumping the sharp shadow cast by the sinking sun onto the timekeeper's little trackside box.

The paddock behind the huge stands is small, but Royal Academy was reasonably calm until they got out onto the course. Here, as a demonstration of his *joie de vivre*, he let loose such a gigantic buck that the astonished Piggott was very nearly decanted during the parade in front of the stands. But Lester, knowing his sire Nijinsky's highly strung temperament, was on guard for trouble, especially as his horse, drawn one, had to be loaded first and so had a long wait before the off. Far from fretting, Royal Academy relaxed so much that Lester reported 'he seemed half asleep and came out all in a heap. Indeed, he came out last.'

With quite a long run by American standards to the first bend, there was plenty of time as the plan was to ride him off the pace. He had been sprinting, and his last run over a mile had been in the Irish 2,000 Guineas in the spring. Piggott had him fourth last, going easily. He began to improve his position on the turn into the straight, still on the bit and going wonderfully well. Then, near disaster! Royal Academy suddenly floundered, lost his action, lost his place and lost his acceleration. Lester said later, 'Probably put his foot in a hole. But no time to see what!'

He let the colt settle into his long, raking rhythm again. Then, still at least six lengths behind the flying leader and with only 400 yards to go, Piggott really got at him. They began to thunder down the centre of the track, gaining with every straining stride. Lester said simply afterwards, 'Just flew!' He caught the leader, the grey with the Shakespearian name Itsallgreektome, just before the post, but Royal Academy was going so well that Lester could be seen looking cheekily across at the defeated jockey.

'The American TV cameras were focused during the race on the various owners they anticipated might win,' remembers Jacqueline. 'We still enjoy the film of Charles almost lifting the horse home with shouts, gestures and some audible – and questionable – language.' There were a host of jubilant British and Irish visitors at Belmont to lead the lusty reception from the crowd as Jacqueline led Vincent's winner in. 'Just like old times,' Piggott murmured, thinking of the English Classics he had won for Vincent: Valoris, Sir Ivor, Nijinsky, Roberto, Boucher and The Minstrel in the eleven years from 1966 to 1977. He had ridden six Irish Classic winners for Vincent too.

'Old stone-face', as Lester was sometimes called, was, on the contrary, visibly moved when Brough Scott talked to him for television. He said, 'This was a very special moment. Felt ecstatic.' And afterwards he said, 'I give thanks to Vincent for encouraging me to come back. And for putting me up in such a hugely important race. But if MV thought I could still deliver the goods . . .' And M. V. O'Brien had, as so often, been absolutely right.

'Royal Academy was draped with a great floral wreath, which we struggled to bring back with us to show Vincent,' says Jacqueline. 'We hung it outside the door of the stable at Ballydoyle until all the chrysanthemums had withered and fallen to the ground.'

Royal Academy, described by Vincent, his purchaser and trainer, as 'one of the best yearlings I've seen', did not race again after his great triumph. He was initially syndicated at a value of IR£5 million to stand first at 30,000 Irish guineas at Coolmore, and then at Ashford Stud, Kentucky. He retired as European champion three-year-old miler. By 2004 he had joined the likes of his three-quarter brother Storm Cat, his sire Nijinsky and grand-sire Northern Dancer in the elite club of world-leading sires of a hundred-plus Stakes winners.

Thirty-five years to the day after Lester had had his first ride for Vincent, when Gladness won the 1958 Ascot Gold Cup, came their last Royal Ascot winner together, in the O'Brien red and white family colours that Vincent had inherited from his father fifty years earlier. In 1993, College Chapel – named after the beautiful fifteenth-century church at Eton built by King Henry VI – won 'quickening nicely', as Lester put it. He was one of only three three-year-olds left at Ballydoyle. Having only his third run, the colt won yet another Cork and Orrery for Vincent. Dressed in his usual Royal Ascot grey silk top hat, double-breasted grey waistcoat and tails with shining shoes, the trainer, normally so remarkably modest and reticent among crowds, broke his general rule and stepped out to greet his final Ascot winner and lead him in – something he had only done once, twenty-five years previously, with Nijinsky. The informed Ascot crowd round the winner's enclosure had grasped that retirement was imminent for both Vincent and Lester, and burst out into salvos of rapturous and fond applause.

'Every so often in the field of sporting endeavour, emotion and sentiment get the upper hand of a hard-bitten professionalism,' wrote Chris Hawkins of the *Guardian*, 'and there were more than a few misty eyes at Royal Ascot yesterday as Vincent O'Brien led in Lester Piggott after victory in the Cork and Orrery Stakes.' *The Times* enthused, 'Only rarely is the gallery fused in spontaneous joy. Both old masters gave a virtuoso performance: Vincent in producing an inexperienced horse to dismiss a field of richly seasoned sprinters, and Piggott in producing the colt with his customary late dash for his 116th victory at Royal Ascot.'

CHAPTER 24

RETIREMENT

'Racing has been good to me'

After Classic Thoroughbreds was dispersed, the number of Vincent's horses almost vanished. Only eleven remained. Still, from these few some big race winners kept coming. El Prado and Fatherland, ridden by Lester, were the winners of the National Stakes in 1991 and 1992 respectively. El Prado became champion sire in America in 2003.

But on a grey, cold day in October 1994, after leaving Goffs Sales, Vincent issued a brief notice. It was his decision to retire. His last winner had been Mysterious Ways at the Curragh in September, ridden by Christy Roche. It was exactly fifty years since the Drybob/Good Days, Irish Cambridgeshire/ Cesarewitch double. Vincent's short and simple announcement read:

> *Racing has been good to me and has enabled me to*
> *pursue a career which combined work with pleasure.*
> *When I started training, the bloodstock industry in*

*Ireland was still developing. Now we are one of the
major thoroughbred racing and breeding countries in
the world. I have had the good fortune to have had
many wonderful horses and owners and have been ably
assisted by friends and by a dedicated staff down the
years. To these and all my friends in racing I am most
grateful.*

Newspapers around the racing world carried the announce-
ment, not unexpected but still sad for all his admirers, under
headlines such as 'Greatest Trainer Retires', 'The Master Bows
Out', 'Simply the Best', 'O'Brien Closes a Glorious Career',
'Mover and Shaker Who Set the Trend', 'Genius Who Set the
Benchmark', 'Always a Step Ahead in Both Spheres', 'Master
Horseman' and, aptly, 'Thanks For Memories, and What
Memories!'

After Vincent's retirement the remaining horses at
Ballydoyle were sent up to Charles O'Brien at his new home
and training stables at Baronrath, Co. Kildare. Elder brother
David was now a thriving *vigneron* on his lovely estate Château
Vignelaure near Aix-en-Provence. It had become clear to the
whole family that Ballydoyle was not viable, unless there was a
large string of paying horses plus a great deal of liquid capital.

With the horses gone, the necessity of living at Ballydoyle
had vanished. But Vincent had originally intended staying on
there for the rest of his life. 'I've planted so many trees over
forty years,' he said, 'I want to see them growing.' Finally,
though, he decided it would be preferable to be nearer Dublin
and most of the family, where he could more easily attend
Curragh meetings and watch the family horses running.

On Vincent's retirement there had, of course, been busy but brief speculation about who would take over the immaculate training complex. Who might be able to afford the best and most successful place in Europe? While Vincent's stables had been swiftly declining in numbers, the great stud empire of his son-in-law John Magnier had been greatly burgeoning. First Robert Sangster and then Vincent decided to divest themselves of their interests in Coolmore. The Coolmore Bloodstock Empire spreads worldwide with its base at Coolmore and outer dominions in Kentucky and in Australia. Magnier, tycoon of the Turf, announced that he had bought the Ballydoyle estate, and Vincent was thrilled that Ballydoyle would continue. Later John installed Aidan O'Brien in the famous training stables. Racing people were asking, was this young fellow any relation at all of the Boss himself? No, he was no relation; as a trainer he had had great success in producing winners. So Aidan and his wife Anne-Marie, also a trainer, moved into Ballydoyle, and scores of the best, choicely bred yearlings which Coolmore could breed or buy began to fill the boxes around the yards. Great success has been achieved with a stream of beautifully bred horses.

Vincent O'Brien had brought great prestige and prosperity to a quiet corner of Tipperary. He was held in high esteem in the locality and greatly missed when he moved away. 'The Boss persuaded owners to make donations to the area from the great wins,' points out Peter McCarthy, accountant, adviser and friend who has been at Ballydoyle for thirty years. 'Charles and Jane Engelhard bought a sports field for Rosegreen and built a village hall. John McShain refurbished the church and helped with the building of the village school. Raymond Guest provided Larkspur Park for the people of Cashel where they can enjoy pitch and putt, tennis and squash. These gifts came when there were few community facilities available.'

Honours and awards flowed in for Vincent. He had already been awarded his honorary doctorates from the universities of Dublin and Ulster. At Cheltenham, scene of those mighty triumphs, they gave his name to that famous old race the County Hurdle, so long the last race of the March Festival. He received silverware, crystal, plaques and scrolls, and was genuinely astonished at the continual praise he received.

The root cause of Vincent's life's driving ambition had always been to achieve perfection – total, unblemished perfection. This unachievable desire – not wealth, not power – was the demon that constantly spurred him on. David O'Brien knows why his father so rarely said 'Well done' to anyone. 'Simple,' David declares, 'it's because he never said "well done" to himself.' In that sentence resides the essence of Vincent's character and the explanation of his discontent. It was this self-criticism that made him a stern critic of others too.

Vincent's legacy is put into perspective by John Magnier, who says, 'Going around the globe, you see the influence of the horses selected and trained by MV. In Europe, our own Sadler's Wells was jointly bred and trained by him. America's current wonder sire, Storm Cat, is a son of Storm Bird – selected as a yearling and trained by him. Also in the US, El Prado has ended the last three years either top or runner-up on the General Sires table. MV not only trained him but won Classics with his sire Sadler's Wells, his dam Lady Capulet, first time out, and her sire Sir Ivor. A vital element in

Coolmore's success was Vincent's early recognition of the merits of Northern Dancer back in 1968. At that stage Northern Dancer had yet to have a runner, but the colt MV wanted and got was Nijinsky, who landed the Triple Crown. Two years later and the Northern Dancer dynasty was well on its way.

'MV understood all aspects of racing. He understood the benefits of American-bred horses. He knew all about their breeding – he had no computer in those days to tell him what crosses had been tried. That's thirty years ago, or more. Today, people go round the sales with computers! He instilled in all of us the value of pedigree. And MV's knowledge of American pedigrees is quite extraordinary. He pointed out to me many years ago that the best mares will not make a good stallion and that a good stallion will be successful even if the mares are not top-class. I remember his words now, and from experience appreciate his wisdom.

'At Coolmore, as well as being a part-owner, he was our most valued adviser. He trained all three Coolmore champion sires to that date – Sadler's Wells, Caerleon and Be My Guest – and his contribution to the Coolmore success story has been immense. Many of the horses which were trained so brilliantly by Vincent played their part in making today's racing industry a thoroughly international affair.

'There's another example of his wonderful intuition when he bought The Minstrel at Keeneland. Due to his size we managed to get him for just $200,000. His syndication two years later for $9 million, along with that of MV's dual Prix de l'Arc de Triomphe winner Alleged for $16 million, raised the capital to allow Coolmore to expand and move forward. In anyone else's hands, neither of these colts might have realized their full potential, but MV's unrivalled patience and skill ensured that they did. He was a true master of his profession. Through his extraordinary success, first with his jumpers and later with his flat horses, MV was largely instrumental in putting Ireland in the first division of world racing – the position it enjoys today.'

Magnier remembers about his father-in-law, 'He had no interest at all in winning titles or championships,' by which he means the titles eagerly extolled by newspapers. And he praises Vincent's shrewdness: 'MV knew how to add value to a horse.' Equally, 'MV knew how to get out quick when a horse was no longer a good prospect for him. MV could be charming when he wanted to get his own way as I found occasionally!' he adds with a dry smile.

But by the mid-1990s training and breeding was a world Vincent had largely left behind. When he retired, Vincent discovered Perth in Western Australia, where both Jacqueline and David's wife Catherine had been born and brought up. In fifty years he had never found time for a visit, but he now joined Jacqueline for a short winter stay with her family. He fell in love with Perth and its famed climate. One day Vincent saw a house overlooking the lovely, broad sweep of the Swan River and, as he had formerly swooped to buy a yearling which filled his eye, he made an instant offer. 'I'll buy it now,' he told the owner, 'if I can have it as it stands and instantly.' The deal was struck. Nowadays, Vincent cannot bear the cold weather, so he and Jacqueline spend their winters there. Their children, and their seventeen grandchildren, whom Vincent truly loves, are in constant contact with them and frequently holiday in Perth.

To give Vincent and Jacqueline the base they wanted near

the rest of the family in Ireland, they built a charming house which they have filled with memories of his great horses. From Vincent's room he can walk out into the garden to prune the roses, pluck sweetpeas and stroll along the side of the lake watching the nesting swans or the hares nibbling grass.

In Vincent's study is the large television on which he eagerly follows racing. His special joy is watching the host of horses descended from those he selected and made, recognizing now as he did sixty years ago the family characteristics. He was so pleased to read in the summer of 2005 a tribute by Tony Morris, the foremost UK breeding expert: 'Proof that Vincent O'Brien's impact has been a global phenomenon came with the recent publication of a list of all-time leading sires of Pattern and Graded winners worldwide. No fewer than nine of the top 35 – Nijinsky, Sadler's Wells, Southern Halo, Caerleon, Alleged, Sir Ivor, Roberto, Royal Academy and Bluebird – were trained at Ballydoyle and have spread their influence over all five continents. Sons and grandsons of O'Brien-trained celebrities also feature, including Storm Cat (by Storm Bird), Green Dancer (by Nijinsky), and Sir Tristram (by Sir Ivor) with his son Zabeel. In addition Ballydoyle-trained El Prado, a son of Sadler's Wells bred at Vincent's own Lyonstown Stud, was North America's champion sire in 2003.' In the annals of sport-cum-industry only Federico Tesio has had a comparable impact in both racing and breeding world-wide.' Tony concluded with the words, 'That record indicates that the greatest of racing's greats in the twentieth century is just as surely the most important human contributor to the thoroughbred of the twenty-first.'

Vincent keeps his small string of horses in training with son

Charles close by at Baronrath, and the Boss keeps his eagle eyes on their progress. 'My father takes huge pride in any winner I train for him,' Charles remarks. 'He'd never tell me what to do.' But Vincent rings his son and says, 'I hope you won't run that filly again this week. Too soon, I think.'

The exceptional man who, all his long, triumphant life, has never said 'well done' to himself, gazes across his garden towards the setting sun. Must he not now, finally, give himself the smallest pat on the back? He smiles gently. And gives that little shrug.

Self.

MEETING	DATE	HORSE	Amt. On	Price	Tax	WIN	LOSE	CREDIT	DEBIT
		Brought forward						£15,576 . 15 . 7	
Navan	Jan 16	Churchtown	135.0.0				135.0.0	15,381 . 15 . 7	
Gowran	„ 21	Knave Lewis	66.0.0	7/2		165.0.0		15,546 . 15 . 7	
Leopardstown	„ 23	L.S. & Gal.	154.0.0				154.0.0	15,492 . 15 . 7	
„	„ „	Strathos	203.0.0	6/4	19.5.0	442.15.0		15,935 . 10 . 7	
Baldoyle	Feb. 15	Churchtown	25.0.0				25.0.0	15,910 . 10 . 7	
„	„ „	Gitchie	20.0.0				20.0.0	15,890 . 10 . 7	
Leopardstown	Feb. 6	Knave Lewis	48.12.6			83.18.0		15,973 . 8 . 7	
Baldoyle/Chelt.	Feb 20	Gal. & Prospect	98.3.1				98.3.1	15,875 . 5 . 6	
Cheltenham	Mar 3/5	Lovser	119.16.3			719.16.		15,155 . 9 . 3	
„	2	Ada Swan	87.5.0	3/6		65.8.9		15,220 . 18 . 0	
„	„	Strathos	218.2.6	2/1		436.5.0		15,657 . 3 . 0	
„ „	„ „	do	60.0.0	2/1		160.0.0		15,777 . 3 . 0	
„	„	Knave Lewis	241.15.0	5/2		654.7.6		16,431 . 10 . 6	
„	„	Early Brew	87.5.0			1090.12.6		17,522 . 3 . 0	
„	„ „	do	43.12.6	4/1		136.6.6		17,658 . 9 . 6	
Naas	Mar 6	Churchtown	65.8.9	9/2	13.2.6	157.17.4		17,816 . 6 . 10	
Limerick	„ 17	Port Egret	43.12.6				43.12.6	17,772 . 14 . 4	
Gowran	„ 18	Fair Factor	87.5.0				87.5.0	17,685 . 9 . 4	
„	„ „	do do	50.0.0				50.0.0	17,635 . 9 . 4	
Cheltenham	Mar 3/5	Knave Lewis	10.0.0	4/2		25.0.0		17,660 . 9 . 4	
„	„	Royal Tan/R. Thorn	29.0.0				29.0.0	17,631 . 9 . 4	
Leopardstown	Feb. 6	Knave Lewis							
Leopardstown	Mar 20	Athenian	130.17.6	3½/1		436.5.0		18,067 . 14 . 4	
Clonmel	„ 25	Oriental Way	110.17.6	5/4ea	5.17.9	98.16.3		18,166 . 10 . 7	
Liverpool	Mar 26/27	Other Horses	369.0.0	65/1		1570.10.0		19,737 . 0 . 7	
„	„ „	Galatian	10.0.0	7/1 aw		87.10.0		19,824 . 10 . 7	
„	„ 27	Royal Tan	187.0.0	ew 17/1		3959.15.6		23,784 . 6 . 1	
„	„ „	„ „	laid off			471.15.6		24,262 . 1 . 7	
„	„ „	Churchtown	100.0.0				100.0.0	24,162 . 1 . 7	
„	„ „	Royal Tan	laid place			225.7.11		24,387 . 9 . 6	

Vincent's betting book January to March 1954. This page is marked 'Self'. He ran separate accounts for staff and for owners and friends . . .

1. Check them in each morning. *Need them in yard ahead of them.*
   See that they are clean and properly dressed, ~~those~~ ~~but they want it held.~~
   They are to hay the horses they are doing. See they give them
   the right amount and horses going out first lot to get no hay.

2. Supervise the taking of hay and straw from the haybarn. See that
   right amount of hay is given and that it is in a neat bundle.
   (Use muck-sacks for this - Put enough hay in sack for two horses,
   first making a bundle of each?) Wires off the bales to be put in
   a drum and none left lying about.
   See that muck is neatly taken out in sacks and that it is not
   piled up in one place on manure heap.

   (2A) ──Muck out one or two. Show them how to muck out a box efficiently.
   Straw not to be wasted. Hay to be picked up and set aside before
   starting. Droppings to be picked out first, then all dry straw
   to be trussed against the walls. Then find the damp spot and work
   round it. Horse to be tied up before starting.
   Before lad starts to ~~muck~~ his horse he is to lay out his kit on
   the straw.
   See that bridle, saddle etc., are neatly and properly taken from
   saddle room to boxes and back.

3. Saddling Up. - See that it is done the right way. Advisable to
   tie up the horse after putting on bridle. See that he is properly
   straightened over and feet picked out. All straps on bridle to be
   in keepers. Pad under saddle. Check to see that there is no
   danger of horse getting sore back. Stable rubber (clean) properly
   placed under saddle. Mane and tail brushed out, quarters laid.
   Martingale correct length.

4. Horses are always jogged twenty or thirty yards when pulled out.
   Might be better to throw apprentices up before doing this. At all
   times colts must never be behind fillies. Never allow a lad to
   ride a horse a canter unless you are absolutely sure that they are
   well able to control the animal.
   Supply each lad with full kit, head collar and chain, fork, brush etc.,
   and check regularly for cleanliness etc.
   There must be a set place for these things to be kept.
   Horses to get a rub over after coming in and ensure that any horse
   sweating is dried off. On wet days important that horses be
   properly dried, particular care to be taken of head ears and loins.

5. Over the next few months concentrate on improving the inexperienced
   riders.
   While out at exercise keep your eye on all of them and do not
   hesitate to correct any fault.

   Assist Maurice and Danny at the working of the horses. Care at
   all times that no risks be taken. Watch for lads that may be going
   too fast or not keeping horses properly balanced, or not keeping
   hands or bodies or legs in proper position. Even while walking
   about they must be taught to sit properly.
   Until the inexperienced lads become capable they must not be allowed
   to work with horses fore and aft, better let them go on their own
   when the others have gone out of sight or behind horse if they are
   on something that does not take a hold.

[handwritten: Spend off time = hot Room. / No smoking = tack Room.]

6. Time allowed for cleaning of tack to be fixed, and when finished no loafing in saddle room. Arrange various jobs for them to do in the evenings such as cleaning up yard, windows (boxes and centre buildings) washing of feeding pots etc.,

7. Bell to be rung once for saddling up? IO ot I5 minutes before? Two rings – to pull out.

[handwritten: Kick long out but in straw]

8. Grooming.   Very important that apprentices be taught how to do this properly. Approximately half an hour to be spent at each horse. Make out a detailed description of how a horse should be groomed from tying him up to letting him down. *[handwritten: let in see it]*

    Include (I) Long strokes when grooming
           (2) Never hit a horse over the loins nor even use pressure
               on this part.
           (3) Never make a filly peevish by rubbing her with a
               brush underneath – if she does not like it just use
               a rubber.

                    KIT.

        Body Brush
        Dandy Brush
        Curry Comb
        Water Brush *[handwritten: ?]*
        Sponge
        Hoof Pick
    X   Wisp
        Neat's foot oil   *[handwritten: Regular inspection of Bits.]*
        Rubber.
                Kit for cleaning tack

        Saddle soap
        sand
        Sponge
        Cloth

    Show them how to clean tack.

    Regular check saddles They must not be allowed to get into bad
    repair.
    Regular check on bits and girths.

Vincent O'Brien's instructions to his assistant trainers in the 1960s.

PICTURE CREDITS

Unless otherwise credited, photos are supplied by courtesy of the author. Every effort has been made to trace copyright holders and any who have not been contacted are invited to get in touch with the publishers.

First section:
Page 1 – Mirropix
Page 5 – bottom: Empics
Page 6 – bottom: Baron
Page 7 – Irish Press
Page 8 – top: Associated Press

Second section:
Page 1 – top: Empics, bottom: Sport & General
Page 2 – bottom: Sport & General
Page 4 – Central Press
Page 5 – top: Chris Smith, bottom: Jacqueline O'Brien
Pages 6–7 – Jacqueline O'Brien
Page 8 – Empics

Third section:
Page 1 – bottom: Leonard Trievano
Page 2 – top: Maymes Ansell
Page 3 – bottom: Jacqueline O'Brien
Page 4 – top: Wallis Photographers of Doncaster
Page 4 – bottom: Gerry Cranham
Page 5 – Wallis Photographers of Doncaster
Page 6 – Sporting Life
Page 7 – David Hastings
Page 8 – top: Reportage Photographique A. Well
Page 8 – middle: Bernard Gourier
Page 8 – bottom: Jacqueline O'Brien

Fourth section:
Page 1 – top: Jacqueline O'Brien
Page 1 – bottom: Jacqueline O'Brien
Page 2 – top: Gerry Cranham
Page 2 – middle: Jacqueline O'Brien, bottom: Jacqueline O'Brien
Page 3 – bottom right: Jacqueline O'Brien
Page 3 – bottom left: Empics
Page 4 – Jacqueline O'Brien
Page 5 – Jacqueline O'Brien
Page 6 – Jacqueline O'Brien
Page 8 – Gerry Cranham
Front cover image of Vincent O'Brien with The Minstrel by Jacqueline O'Brien
Back cover image by Jacqueline O'Brien.

VINCENT O'BRIEN'S RACING RECORD

Compiled by Dr Tony and Annie Sweeney

First winner: 20 May 1943. Oversway. Elton Plate, Limerick Junction

Final winner: 17 September 1994. Mysterious Ways. Macdonagh & Boland Stakes, The Curragh

Career total: Irish Flat and National Hunt Races: 1529
In Britain he won twenty-five races at Royal Ascot and twenty-three at Cheltenham's National Hunt Festival, including ten Gloucestershire Hurdles.

Irish Champion Two-Year-Olds: Between 1967 and 1991 he provided 18 top rated.

Irish Trainer Championship Titles: 1959; 1969; 1970; 1972; 1977; 1978; 1979; 1980; 1981; 1982; 1984; 1988; and 1989

English National Hunt Trainer Championships: 1952/53 and 1953/54

English Flat Trainer Championships: 1966 and 1977

Flat race triumphs at home and abroad

IN ENGLAND

2,000 GUINEAS
1968: Sir Ivor
1970: Nijinsky
1983: Lomond
1984: El Gran Senor

1,000 GUINEAS
1966: Glad Rags

THE DERBY
1962: Larkspur
1968: Sir Ivor
1970: Nijinsky
1972: Roberto
1977: The Minstrel
1982: Golden Fleece

THE OAKS
1965: Long Look
1966: Valoris

THE ST LEGER
1957: Ballymoss
1970: Nijinsky
1972: Boucher

CRAVEN STAKES
1976: Malinowski

CHESTER VASE
1985: Law Society

ORMONDE STAKES
1950: Olein's Grace

MUSIDORA STAKES
1973: Where You Lead

CORONATION CUP
1958: Ballymoss
1973: Roberto

QUEEN ANNE STAKES
1975: Imperial March

COVENTRY STAKES
1977: Solinus

QUEEN'S VASE
1958: Even Money
1975: Blood Royal

ST JAMES'S PALACE STAKES
1973: Thatch
1978: Jaazeiro

JERSEY STAKES
1956: Adare
1975: Gay Fandango

QUEEN MARY STAKES
1964: Brassia

NORFOLK STAKES
1984: Magic Mirror

ASCOT GOLD CUP
1958: Gladness

CORONATION STAKES
1974: Lisadell

RIBBLESDALE STAKES
1975: Gallina

WOKINGHAM HANDICAP
1975: Boone's Cabin

CORK AND ORRERY STAKES
1970: Welsh Saint
1974: Saritamer
1975: Swingtime
1979: Thatching
1993: College Chapel

HARDWICKE STAKES
1977: Meneval

KINGS STAND STAKES
1962: Cassarate
1973: Abergwaun
1977: Godswalk
1978: Solinus
1987: Bluebird

ECLIPSE STAKES
1958: Ballymoss
1966: Pieces Of Eight
1977: Artaius
1983: Solford
1984: Sadler's Wells

CHERRY HINTON STAKES
1977: Turkish Treasure

JULY CUP
1973: Thatch
1974: Saritamer
1978: Solinus
1979: Thatching
1990: Royal Academy

KING GEORGE VI AND
QUEEN ELIZABETH STAKES
1958: Ballymoss
1970: Nijinsky
1977: The Minstrel

GORDON STAKES
1975: Guillaume Tell

SUSSEX STAKES
1973: Thatch
1977: Artaius
1978: Jaazeiro
1981: King's Lake

GOODWOOD CUP
1958: Gladness

BENSON & HEDGES
GOLD CUP
1972: Roberto
1983: Caerleon

GREAT VOLTIGEUR STAKES
1977: Alleged

EBOR HANDICAP
1958: Gladness
1961: Die Hard

WILLIAM HILL SPRINT
CHAMPIONSHIP
1978: Solinus

GEOFFREY FREER STAKES
1964: Sunseeker
1977: Valinsky

WATERFORD CRYSTAL MILE
1975: Gay Fandango
1977: Be My Guest

VERNONS SPRINT CUP
1972: Abergwaun

CHAMPAGNE STAKES
1981: Achieved

FLYING CHILDERS STAKES
1981: Peterhof

DIADEM STAKES
1971: Abergwaun
1972: Home Guard
1974: Saritamer
1975: Swingtime

ROYAL LODGE STAKES
1975: Sir Wimborne

MIDDLE PARK STAKES
1978: Junius

CHEVELEY PARK
STAKES
1967: Lalibela
1981: Woodstream
1990: Capricciosa

DEWHURST STAKES
1969: Nijinsky
1973: Cellini
1976: The Minstrel
1977: Try My Best
1979: Monteverdi
1980: Storm Bird
1983: El Gran Senor

CHAMPION STAKES
1966: Pieces Of Eight
1968: Sir Ivor

JOCKEY CLUB CUP
1975: Blood Royal

OBSERVER GOLD CUP
1973: Apalachee

IN IRELAND

IRISH 2,000 GUINEAS
1959: El Toro
1978: Jaazeiro
1981: King's Lake
1984: Sadler's Wells
1988: Prince of Birds

IRISH 1,000 GUINEAS
1966: Valoris
1977: Lady Capulet
1979: Godetia

IRISH DERBY
1953: Chamier
1957: Ballymoss
1970: Nijinsky
1977: The Minstrel
1984: El Gran Senor
1985: Law Society

IRISH OAKS
1964: Ancasta
1965: Aurabella
1969: Gaia
1979: Godetia

IRISH ST LEGER
1959: Barclay
1966: White Gloves
1969: Reindeer
1975: Caucasus
1976: Meneval
1977: Transworld
1980: Gonzales
1985: Leading Counsel
1988: Dark Lomond

IRISH LINCOLNSHIRE
1949: Hatton's Grace
1950: Knock Hard

GLADNESS STAKES
1970: Nijinsky
1971: Minsky
1973: Dapper
1974: Apalachee
1980: Night Alert
1983: Lomond
1984: El Gran Senor
1990: Great Lakes

ATHASI STAKES
1962: Lovely Gale
1968: Rimark
1972: Arkadina
1974: Lisadell
1979: Godetia
1990: Wedding Bouquet

TETRARCH STAKES
1968: Harry
1969: Sahib
1971: Minsky
1972: Homeguard
1973: Dapper
1974: Cellini
1982: Achieved
1983: Salmon Leap
1985: Northern Plain
1988: Prince Of Birds
1989: Saratogan
1990: Royal Academy
1993: College Chapel

ROYAL WHIP
1959: Ross Sea
1965: Ballyjoy
1970: Reindeer
1971: Tantoul
1972: Manitoulin
1973: Cavo Doro
1977: Alleged
1978: Alleged
1981: Last Light
1982: Lords

1984: Empire Glory
1987: Baba Karam
1990: Splash Of Colour

TRIGO STAKES
1957: Ballymoss
1960: Die Hard
1962: Larkspur
1965: Donato
1966: Beau Chapeau

BALLYMOSS STAKES
1963: Nardoo
1967: White Gloves
1969: Selko
1973: Cavo Doro
1982: Golden Fleece

DERRINSTOWN STUD
DERBY TRIAL STAKES
Started as the Trigo Stakes,
became the Nijinsky Stakes
1972: Boucher
1974: Hail The Pirates
1976: Meneval
1982: Golden Fleece
1983: Salmon Leap
1984: Sadler's Wells
1987: Seattle Dancer
1988: Kris Kringle

GALLINULE STAKES
1953: Chamier
1965: Baljour
1969: Onandaga
1970: Saracen Sword
1971: Grenfall
1973: Hail The Pirates
1974: Sir Penfro
1975: King Pellinore
1976: Meneval
1977: Alleged
1978: Inkerman
1980: Gonzales
1984: Montelimar

1987: Seattle Dancer
1991: Sportsworld

PRETTY POLLY STAKES
1959: Little Mo
1964: Ancasta
1967: Iskereen
1969: Rimark
1979: Godetia
1980: Calandra
1988: Dark Lomond

RAILWAY STAKES
1962: Turbo Jet
1965: Glad Rags
1968: Sahib
1969: Nijinsky
1970: Minsky
1971: Open Season
1975: Niebo
1976: Brahms
1978: Solar
1980: Lawmaker
1982: Ancestral
1983: El Gran Senor
1984: Moscow Ballet
1991: El Prado

ANGLESEY STAKES
1959: Arctic Sea
1962: Philemon
1965: Bravery
1969: Nijinsky
1970: Headlamp
1971: Roberto
1973: Saritamer
1975: Niebo
1977: Solinus
1980: Storm Bird
1982: Caerleon
1984: Law Society
1985: Woodman
1987: Lake Como

PHOENIX STAKES
1976: Cloonlara
1981: Achieved

DESMOND STAKES
1964: Restless Knight
1966: White Gloves
1967: White Gloves
1969: Reindeer
1972: Boucher
1973: Hail The Pirates
1974: Sir Penfro
1976: Niebo
1977: Be My Guest
1981: Belted Earl
1985: Sunstart
1986: Wise Counsellor
1987: Entitled
1992: Villa Borghese.

MOYGLARE STUD STAKES
1981: Woodstream
1990: Capricciosa

**JOE MCGRATH
MEMORIAL STAKES**
1978: Inkerman
1979: Fordham
1980: Gregorian
1981: King's Lake

PHOENIX CHAMPION STAKES
1984: Sadler's Wells

NATIONAL STAKES
1967: Sir Ivor
1971: Roberto
1972: Chamozzle
1973: Cellini
1975: Sir Wimborne
1979: Monteverdi
1980: Storm Bird
1982: Glenstal
1983: El Gran Senor
1984: Law Society

1985: Tate Gallery
1987: Caerwent
1988: Classic Fame
1991: El Prado
1992: Fatherland

BLANDFORD STAKES
1959: Little Mo
1961: Silver Moon
1965: Donato
1968: Wenona
1970: Riboprince
1971: Wenceslas
1972: Manitoulin
1974: Richard Grenville
1975: King Pellinore
1980: Gonzales
1981: Magesterial
1982: Lords
1983: South Atlantic
1988: Kris Kringle
1992: Andros Bay

BERESFORD STAKES
1947: Barfelt
1962: Pontifex
1967: Hibernian
1969: Nijinsky
1970: Minsky
1971: Boucher
1972: Chamozzle
1973: Saritamer
1979: Huguenot
1980: Euclid
1982: Danzatore
1983: Sadler's Wells
1984: Gold Crest
1988: Classic Fame
1991: El Prado

**BIRDCATCHER
NURSERY STAKES**
1962: Turbo Jet
1966: Theo
1977: Pull The Latch

1981: Afghan
1982: Treasure Trove
1983: Western Symphony
1988: Kyra

IRISH
CAMBRIDGESHIRE
1944: Dry Bob
1957: Courts Appeal
1961: Travel Light
1968: Hibernian
1979: Habituate

IRISH CESAREWITCH
1944: Good Days
1947: Cottage Rake
1948: Hot Spring
1949: Hatton's Grace
1950: Hatton's Grace

NAAS NOVEMBER
HANDICAP
1946: Cottage Rake
1949: Wye Fly

LEOPARDSTOWN NOVEMBER
HANDICAP
1959: Coologan

IN FRANCE

PRIX DU JOCKEY CLUB
1983: Caerleon

PRIX DE L'ARC
DE TRIOMPHE
1958: Ballymoss
1977: Alleged
1978: Alleged

PRIX MAURICE DE GHEEST
1993: College Chapel

GRAND CRITERIUM
1967: Sir Ivor

IN THE UNITED STATES

WASHINGTON DC
INTERNATIONAL
1968: Sir Ivor

BREEDERS' CUP MILE
1990: Royal Academy

Under Irish National Hunt Rules

IRISH GRAND NATIONAL
1952: Alberoni

THYESTES CHASE
1956: Sam Brownthorn

LEOPARDSTOWN
CHASE
1953: Lucky Dome

GALWAY PLATE
1952: Alberoni

GALWAY HURDLE
1951: Wye Fly

Under English National Hunt Rules

GRAND NATIONAL
1953: Early Mist
1954: Royal Tan
1955: Quare Times

KING GEORGE VI CHASE
1948: Cottage Rake

CHELTENHAM GOLD CUP
1948: Cottage Rake
1949: Cottage Rake
1950: Cottage Rake
1953: Knock Hard

NATIONAL HUNT CHASE
1949: Castledermot
1954: Quare Times

NATIONAL HUNT HANDICAP
CHASE
1952: Royal Tan

CHAMPION HURDLE
1949: Hatton's Grace
1950: Hatton's Grace
1951: Hatton's Grace

SPA HURDLE
1954: Lucky Dome

BIRDLIP HURDLE
1955: Ahaburn

INDEX